Recognizing Beauty

A Memoir

Cyndi Burrough

This book is dedicated to those in pain
Those who were in pain
And those who love us up and out of our pain

"Only in suffering do we recognize beauty."
MARCEL PROUST

Contents

Introduction

This Is the Best Place to Start

I've done a number of jobs to increase my income. I've cleaned business office buildings, mowed, and groomed office grounds too. I've pulled weeds for people and done whatever the heck they want me to do, such as pruning trees and watering and planting plants. I've worked in the electronic environment doing all manner of assembly jobs. I've also cleaned some houses and painted others. And this is what inspired me to write.

I've a lifetime of doing trivial jobs. I excel in art, and this turned out to be my chosen profession. One day I asked myself, *Why have I spent so much of my time doing work that was repetitive, boring, and well below the jobs I've held as an artist?*

Low self-esteem was the answer.

All along the way I've wanted to write a book. On one hand, I knew that the project would succeed, but in the same breath, I had extreme doubts about my ability. Once I faced this, I knew I would one way or another write and follow it through to release. I had time to try, and who else is there to talk to at three in the morning, which is normally when I get up?

So I screamed at myself, "Just do it!"

I was hired to clean a huge two-story, two-bathroom house every other week for fifty dollars a week. I've cleaned houses and college dorm bathrooms, as well as campus buildings, for most of my life. I was taught how to clean both by my fanatical mother and later by a college maintenance manager. I was good at it. Hated it. One reason that I didn't like to clean was that I was always in extreme physical pain. But I needed the money to live, so I cleaned.

The previous housekeeper, whose job I took, could finish the cleaning in one and a half hours. To do an exceptional job took me much longer. The only time I cleaned the house within an hour and a half was when the owner and her husband were gone. In any task, I do my best work when no one is around. On this occasion I thought that I had done a piss-poor job and felt guilty as I left the house. I assumed that the previous house-keeper did a complete cleaning job within an hour and a half or wore roller skates to meet the goal. I would fall on my butt if I wore roller skates, so that was not an option. I can barely walk without falling.

The lady I cleaned for is my landlady and money mentor. She has kept me employed with odd jobs and job referrals for years. She has been aware of how moneyless I am. Poor. She's also been my spiritual life example. I look up to her, respect her, and try to emulate her. I have learned so much from her. In a way, she has treated me as a mother and father should treat their grown child.

I walked into her house deciding that I would aim for the hour-and-a-half mark one more time. The house had obviously been visited by children. Inwardly I groaned, but I plowed my way through the crumbs, globs of food, dust, and dirt. Do you know that dust is partly bits of dead, shredded skin? Dander. Let us just add to that the dead microscopic insects that crawl on our bodies too. (Gosh, I never looked at housecleaning as a spiritual thing before I began writing this morning. We breathe in the gunk and "all become as one." Amen.)

The work that I do is also difficult because I carry a demon on my back. I have always had this demon, who is relentless and sneaky. It screams at me, saying that I am not good enough, smart enough, or talented enough to measure up to most people. A lot of times I hear my mother in my mind repeating the same old phrases that I was told during childhood. Self-talk takes on a whole new meaning when my demon talks to me, which is nearly all the time. It's sometimes inactive when I sleep, so sleep is my sanctuary.

I've worked hard maintaining my usual standard of cleaning. Oh, did I say *my* work standard? Excuse me. My demon's work standard. As I cleaned the house, I thought that I still had not done as good a job after having worked for three and a half hours. I finally finished cleaning the main house as well as the owner's man cave downstairs, but the job was not complete.

As I moved to go outside for the final phase of leaf blowing, I heard my landlady say to someone on the phone, "She just doesn't manage her time well," referring to how I had been cleaning her house. "She does the important things, then continues on with those things that aren't that important."

I was crushed, and I wondered why she was talking about me to someone else. I know what a therapist would say: "But you really didn't *know* it was *you* she was talking about, did you?"

No, but it felt like it. I didn't get it. I had been working so hard each time I cleaned for her.

What was wrong? I asked myself. *I did a good job and worked fairly quickly.* I wanted to please her. Even more, I didn't want to displease her. Was it because she just didn't want me to be in her house that long? Was she, in a funny way, trying to give me a square deal knowing that I had committed to the one and a half hours and not three or four hours? I did not have a clue. I got into my car and pulled away without saying goodbye to my friend and landlady, which was a first for me.

I felt humiliated. What had I done to cause her to express her dissatisfaction? And I was angry. Oh yes, and there was anger. I didn't mention anger? Ah, poop. Yeah, anger.

This gives you an idea of the emotions and unrelenting chatter I struggle with that motivated the writing of this book. I have carried into adulthood the abuse that as a child and adult I received from others. Part of my thought process is flawed, which I developed as a result of abuse. My brain is wired differently than what might be considered the norm. The example above shows how hypersensitive I am when criticized. I've struggled with depression, and socially I've felt inept. Trust me. I'm not being humble. Old patterns are still present, and it is difficult to navigate away from a number of ill-gotten lessons.

I've written this book primarily for the walking wounded. This is one way I can help the abused and depressed and those who wish to help themselves. I show the progression from childhood to teen years so that you may see what goes on in the mind of someone who has been abused physically, mentally, emotionally, psychologically, and sexually.

The mind and spirit are broken as abuses progress. As a young child I was confident and humorous. The humor dwindles as my story continues. My self-confidence slipped away quickly, even though it may appear that I had a huge ego.

When you are abused over and over again, reasoning power is greatly diminished; thinking is confused, and the concept of rules and demands is turned into entrapment.

The abused brain navigates life in self-blaming circles, thinking, *If this thing is true, then the other thing is not true, and I don't seem to be choosing the correct behavior.* The nerves in my brain misfire as I grapple with life. My self-confidence is further diminished and self-awareness is heightened when I misinterpret directives. Navigating life is difficult. An internal dialogue sets out to make sense of social mandates, falling short due to faulty intake of information. Correct reasoning is not possible. Social abuse or bullying is added to the confusion, and gradually physical withdrawal ensues.

However, significant adults outside the family helped begin my healing process even before professionals detected the abuses. In our family, all was "normal," but we were not allowed to tell anyone about what went on within the family. Before therapy, I had no idea that I had been abused, and it took great courage to reveal what had taken place.

I debated bringing my teen sexual issues to the table because writing about them made me feel extremely uncomfortable and vulnerable. But the truth had to be told. I decided that my confusion about sex played an integral part in my development, so it was included. I show how naive an individual can be when they come from a background such as mine. Even though I scoured the high school library, I didn't learn much about sex until I was in college.

I have had difficulty sharing the blatant physical abuses as well because I still do not wish to hurt or embarrass my immediate family. Of course there would not have been much of a story if I left this out. But just the debate within myself regarding the abusers shows a degree of unhealthiness and general lack of emotional rationality.

I've no doubt anymore that true mental illness is hiding in the family genes.

I can speak only to what I remember, not to the accuracy of what I recall. My memory is tainted with emotion, and rarely do I pretend to know all the details. But all that I tell you truly happened. Dad is dead now, and Mom is hitchhiking her way toward the other side, so there is very little that I can hold up to the light. This is my story, and as a dear friend suggested, I write it for myself. Hopefully it will touch the lives of many, such as doctors, students, social workers, therapists, and those who have experienced a similar life.

If this happens, I will have done my job well.

There is a reason I use lowercase instead of capital letters for some of the adults throughout the book. An adult hurt me, and my trust in them diminishes.

Chapter 1: The Iniquity of the Fathers

1939

About once a month Daddy and Grandpa Burrough would walk down a dusty road toward town. The road had deep indents on either side that had been carved with wagon wheels and a car or two when the road was muddy. It had since dried in the hot sun of summer. It seemed like years since the last rain. Now the road was dusty, lined with wheat fields on one side and cows lazily chewing dry grass in a pasture, seemingly unbothered by the heat, on the other side. The walk was hard and long for young Billy (my father), but those two were used to it.

Well sort of used to it. They didn't go to town that often because of the heat.

Grandpa pulled out a dirty handkerchief, took his hat off, wiped his forehead for the third time while they walked. He rarely talked on the way to town, but after mopping his sweaty brow, he looked at my dad and said, "It's hot today, son."

The boy only nodded, not sure if his father saw him answer.

There was a buzzard in the distance circling its dying prey. The out-of-sync crickets rubbed their legs together, hoping to find romance, while a fly pestered my dad, darting near his face and head. All he thought about as he continuously batted at the fly was the new moving picture show he'd heard about.

Once in town, Grandpa walked my dad to the movie house. Then he went to the five-and-dime store and set about buying necessities for the family and doing manly things, like chewing the cud with the other men who were in town. After that, Grandpa hit the whorehouse for his special gratification. It makes sense that he would do this since he never saw Grandma in the raw to his dying day. I suppose he had to work out his frustration in the only way he knew. After all, it was right there available to him.

Grandpa had quite the temper, and on this return trip my dad was kicking a can over and over again. Grandpa hardly noticed at first, as he was thinking about the whore he had just been with. But after a while he realized what his son was doing. Grandpa became more and more angry but said nothing. He'd told the boy time and again that kicking cans made a wreck of his shoes.

On the way home my dad reached into his overalls pocket, took out a piece of candy, and popped it into his mouth. Grandpa had given him only enough money to buy a ticket to the movie house, He knew full well that the boy didn't have one cent more than that. It was obvious that he'd stolen the candy.

Grandpa's anger grew. "Spit it out!" he said.

My dad asked, "Why?" thinking that he surely could fool his father. "Someone give it to me," he said while grinning.

There was a two-by-four piece of wood lying on the edge of the road. It probably had slipped off someone's wagon. Grandpa walked over to the piece of wood and picked it up.

Pow!

My dad didn't know what hit him. And he wasn't hit just once or twice. Grandpa continued to hit him the rest of the way home. The whole incident seemed uncalled for because Grandpa had just spent money on a whore, and splitting hairs over a moral issue could give anyone pause regarding the double standard put forth.

∞∞∞

My father's parents were said to be Dutch, Irish, and possibly Choctaw Indian, though his family were so bigoted that they denied their Indian heritage. Great-Aunt RD (yep, RD was her given name) for all the world looked like a pure-blooded American Indian, and everyone said so. However, in the same breath they said that it just couldn't be true. She was the one who told us that we had Choctaw blood in us. All I know is that her skin was very dark, very wrinkled, and leathery, and for all the world, with her high cheekbones, she looked like an Indian to me. I figured someone that old knew what they were talking about.

I don't know much about Grandpa Burrough's parents. He never talked about his upbringing, or maybe I just didn't listen to him when he spoke. Actually, many times I couldn't hear what he said because he spoke softly, and if I did listen I couldn't understand a word he said because he slurred and mumbled. He must have had some speech impairment because he could not pronounce my name, Cynthia, or my nickname, Cyndi. He called me Cympi. Many times I'd ask Grandma, "What did he say?" She would translate without being at all irritated.

Grandpa was average in height and wore a fedora much like the one Humphrey Bogart sported in some of his movies. He wore a T-shirt covered by his gray work clothes. Sometimes he would wear a plaid shirt when he was dressing up. His hair was thin and a light brown, and later in life he dyed it with a red henna. He smoked a pipe later on, past the chew and cigarette stages. Grandma said that the chewing tobacco was nasty, and I agree with her because he spat into coffee cans and the house held the odor of the liquidy chew. But I loved the smell of the pipe, asking over and over again if I could smoke it. But he never gave in.

Grandpa had a very serious side to him except for when I was doing something to gain attention, then he chuckled and smiled at my antics. I know he had a temper but rarely did I see it. He had a regular gait but walked around with his head down as if he was thinking hard about something. He probably was trying to walk normal so that no one knew he had been drinking. I was told that he was an alcoholic and hit Grandma, but I'm not one hundred percent sure of that. I never saw him drink unless other menfolk were around watching a boxing match on the little black-and-white TV set.

Note that there isn't an *s* at the end of Burrough. You will find very few Burrough folk in a phone book (when there is such a thing), whereas there are several Burroughs listed. I joke about there being a feud within the family, much like the Hatfields and McCoys. In an argument, someone in my family huffed away, taking the *s* off the name so that they would never again be associated with those they fought with. I wouldn't put it past the Burrough family. They can be a highly emotional and argumentative bunch of people. You've never seen real stubbornness until you've seen their bullheadedness. They are miles and miles away from diplomacy. I don't think they have even heard the word much less understood it.

I suspect that my kin migrated from Holland to England and on to Ireland, then floated over to America, where they settled for a while in the backwoods of Appalachia. From there I think Grandma and Grandpa moved to Oklahoma, then on to Turkey, Texas. Once, Beefeater Gin of England contacted Grandpa trying to locate the closest relative of Thomas Burrough, the company's founder. There seems to be quite a few men named Thomas in the Burrough family—my younger brother being one of them. Due to ignorance, simplemindedness, the poverty-soaked background, and their lack of education, Grandma and Grandpa decided not to do much about the inquiry, thinking that no one of worth in our family was related to the Beefeater Gin family.

Damn it! An opportunity for wealth slipped right through their fingers, but they could have been right.

Dad said that, prior to the family crossing the country, his great-grandfather built a covered wagon using only one tool, which was a handheld push-pull instrument that looked like an old-fashioned logger's saw. It was about twenty inches long. There were two handles on it, and it was pulled backward to shave off pieces of wood. I can't begin to imagine how my dad's great-granddaddy used this one tool to make an entire wagon, let alone how long it took him to complete the project.

I remember another thing about Aunt RD's visits. She chewed tobacco and rolled her own cigarettes, as did my grandpa. When they hankered for a cigarette, they rolled their own, and the making of this kind of cigarette was a ritual that fascinated me. The tobacco came out of a light-brown muslin bag tied with a red string. It was about half the size of a deck of cards and as thick as one. In unison, Grandpa and Aunt RD would loosen the red string at the top of the little bag and carefully place the bag on top of an end table. They then would take small reddish-brownish pieces of paper out of their wallets and place them on the table beside the bag. This cigarette paper was almost as thin as a page in a Bible. Taking the paper from the table, they would hold it between their thumb and index finger, thereby making a slightly indented curve in the paper. They picked up the sack with the other hand, tapped the bag gently with the first finger, and sprinkled just the right amount of tobacco in a straight line where the indent was. They closed the bag by pulling the string with their teeth.

With a twinkle of anticipation in their eyes, they rolled up the paper using both thumbs and first fingers, barely to the top of the roll, where a thin line of shiny glue was. The tip of their tongues moistened the glue. Then, finishing the final roll, they smoothed the area where the glue was, going back and forth with the first finger and thumb to make sure the glue took. They lightly tapped the cigarette on the table before they lit the other end of it. The tip glowed like embers in a fireplace. I loved the smell of the smoke. It was unlike any cigarette aroma that I've smelled up to the present time.

Grandma Burrough came from a family of fifteen. Twelve of the thirteen children were born in the order of boy, girl, boy, girl. Because of that order, Grandma was supposed to have been a boy. It didn't turn out that way, but she did end up as the baby in the family.

She was tall compared to my other grandma. Most of the time she wore handmade, short-sleeve dresses that had small floral print on the fabric. When we went shopping, she mostly shopped for material even though she had a big stack of it at home. She wasn't a "looker," but she was pleasant enough to look at. She wore lipstick and rouge—*blush,* as it's called now—when she joined our family at church. She was slightly overweight, probably from all the fatty food she made, but boy, could she cook. Her hair was dark brown and wavy. She held herself up tall but fluttered around worriedly, always saying, "Blah beddy blah blah … your old grandma … I wish Virgil didn't drink." Virgil was my grandpa's name, though most of his friends called him Joe. Despite all her worrying, Grandma couldn't stop Grandpa from drinking.

I don't know anything about Grandma's father, but her mother was supposed to have been a very kind and loving individual. There was a large, colorized photograph of Grandma's mother in an oval frame that hung in the front room of Grandma and Grandpa's house. In those days, black-and-white photos were painted with Dr. Martin's watercolors to give them a "life-like" appearance. Great-Grandma looked very serious, stern, and a bit frightening to me when I was a child.

My father was born in Turkey, Texas, and raised with his younger brother on a farm in Oklahoma. At any rate, they were "Okies." His mother's maiden name was Bardwell. I don't get it, but there were several names that were initials in the family, such as Uncle CM, Aunt RD, and the like. These were not short for other names. These were their given names. Strange, I know. And there were just plain old weird names, such as Colleen, or Ora, which was my grandmother's name.

To earn money for his family, Grandpa rode the rails in a push-pull cart, which rested on the train track. He and another man, facing each other, would pump the handles up and down, moving the cart to the rails and ties that needed repairs. It must have been a very hard job, with all the heavy lifting and the horrible three-digit Texas heat.

One day a train was headed their way. The switch man had been drinking heavily the night before and was sporting a heck of a headache. He was supposed to trip the track, but he stumbled, fell, and passed out, hitting his noggin on a large rock. The oncoming train was speeding right toward Grandpa and his co-worker. Grandpa wondered if there was enough time to pick up the tools that were loose on the wooden ties. The vibration from the train became pronounced.

The engineer spotted Grandpa and his coworker, and he bore down on the brake handle, blowing the horn at the same time. He knew he would never be able to stop the train in time. Grandpa wondered if the half-done repairs would hold.

"The tools! The tools! Joe, get those tools!" Grandpa's coworker yelled. These were the tools that they had bought on loan with hard-earned money. Money that they were still paying back. Chunks of money that were taken out of their paychecks every week. These tools were their livelihood. They panicked! As Grandpa tried to pick up the tools, two fell out of the toolbox and onto the rail tie. His fumbling, sweat-soaked hand just wouldn't hold the tools. The engineer blew his horn again. Finally, finally the tools were back in the toolbox, but Grandpa had to jump and roll to safety.

The two men just barely got off the track in time. If Grandpa had been hit, his family certainly wouldn't have survived without the income. It sounds pretty scary to me.

Life on Grandma and Grandpa's farm wasn't easy. With Grandpa out on the railroad, many of the farming tasks landed on my father's small shoulders. With Grandpa not around, my dad had to feed and milk the cows, turn them out to pasture, clean the barn, put the cows back into the barn in the evening, and do all the things that needed to be done before he headed into the house morning and night. Dad had named each of the cows and called them into the barn by their names, and they came to him as called.

Have you ever stood next to a cow? They are huge!

I don't know what age he was when he had to do all of these chores, but Dad had to have had some gumption. During the day he would attend a one-room schoolhouse if and when all the chores were done. Once school let out, he went home to do more chores. I don't know how he fit homework into all of this, but I'm sure Grandpa made him toe the line.

Later on in his life, my dad had to pick cotton to help the

family out financially when times were tougher. He would come home with bloody fingers because of the thorns on the bushes. The next day Grandma would send him to work with bits of rag wound around his fingers. But after only a bale or two, his bandages were too wet with blood. So he'd remove the bandages and continue to work, wincing every time his hand connected with the mean end of the cotton bush.

Meanwhile, Grandma raised a garden to help stretch the family income. She took care of the smaller animals. Yet, even with all this industry, the family was still poor.

I don't know how my dad ever had time to play, though he somehow worked that in. He once related to me a story that happened between him and a schoolmate. Dad had a big cat, and he and another little boy, who owned a dog that was kept behind a fence, began to play a "Mine's Better Than Your'n" game. The subject of most serious debate was whether or not the dog or the cat would win a fight with each other. Well, it turned out that Dad was a sneaky little cuss. When the dog came over to the fence barking its head off, Dad dropped his cat on the dog's back. The cat won the fight.

Daddy loved to tell that story.

Dad was the apple of Grandma and Grandpa's eye until his brother (Uncle Jenny) came along. Then Dad was ignored. Thrust aside. This hurt him deeply, but unfortunately his pain and anger were directed at Uncle Jenny, who had nothing to do with it, and the two became estranged from each other emotionally in their adult life. Dad, not receiving the attention he should have had from his parents, took off into the woods, where he spent hours by himself.

Suffering from the hardships of the Dust Bowl, the family of four decided to move to California. The crops had failed and there was barely any water in the well. They sold the livestock to raise money for the move, then the farming folk who moved in mass for the most part to the West. In my dad's case, the family moved to San Pablo, California, across from the San Francisco East Bay area.

World War II broke out, so both Grandma and Grandpa became welders and riveters for the ships that came to dock in the East San Francisco Bay area in need of repair and construction. Grandpa taught Grandma how to weld. Grandma was very proud of being a welder, and she stood noticeably taller when she referred to that time. As far as I know, that was the only time Grandma was employed outside the home.

Grandma Burrough was a talented woman. She bought a guitar from the Sears and Roebuck mail-order catalog when Dad was young and taught herself how to play it. This was the guitar I learned to play on, and I still have it. Sometimes she would dance a Texas jig as she played harmonica and Jew's harp. It was fun to watch because she would pound her foot on the floor while tipping side to side. She played both guitar and harmonica by ear. The song she would sing and play on the guitar that I most loved as a child was the old church song:

I Come to the Garden to Pray
Verse: I come to the garden alone
While the dew is still on the roses
And the voice I hear falling on my ear ...
Chorus: And He walks with me, and He talks with me,
And He tells me I am His own;
And the joy we share as we tarry there,
None other has ever known ...
C. Austin Miles
March 1912

Grandma sang alto in the church choir, and when others began to sing the melody on a chorus, she would slip into harmony.

She also had a little self-taught artistic talent. She was a wonderful seamstress and made Dad's and Uncle Jenny's pants and shirts as they grew. The boys didn't have many clothes to wear, but Grandma made sure that their clothes were always clean, starched stiff, and ironed.

My dad was a dark-haired, handsome young man—lean,

14

tough, and strong. Definitely an Okie. In high school he was known for fighting anyone who picked on him, be it (in his language) a "nigger, chink, kike, dago, redskin," or any person different from his "pure" ivory skin tone. I'm sure he started a few fights too if he took offense to anyone. He had been taught at home to hate the "niggers" especially. To him they were the scum of the Earth. He made it known that he could not stand the likes of one, and they in turn could not tolerate the likes of Billy Burrah (as he pronounced his last name). Most thought he was easy prey because he was so delicate looking.

Unbeknownst to many, he carried brass knuckles in his pocket. He used these as a weapon to defend himself and attack his opponent. These brass knuckles could cause a great deal of damage, and that's just what he intended to do. There was joy in his heart when he broke skin or bone as he landed a blow with these on.

On one particular day my dad arrived late to school, which was rare because Ora made certain that her boys left with plenty of time to get to their lessons. A group of Black boys decided to gang up on him. They planned this attack well in advance and merely needed my dad to be alone outside and away from his best friend, Jesse. They were angry and tired of his slurs about them in particular and their race in general. On this day, they lay in wait for the scrawny whitey as he walked outside. He saw those young boys at the last minute heading his way. He took off running, and though he ran pretty good "for a White boy," he wasn't fast enough. As planned, one of the fastest boys ran ahead of his pals and tackled my dad on the school lawn. Dad got up and began to beat the poor fellow with his bare fist. As the boy fell to the ground, the others had nearly caught up. Dad ran again, heading toward the school wall. He whipped out his brass knuckles and nailed one of the boys in the jaw. Another boy crumpled to his knees after my dad landed a blow to his stomach. He had "whooped them all." At least that's what he thought.

He walked slowly to the classroom, chuckling as he went. He told the story of how a group of Black guys had ganged up on him and he'd won the fight because his back was to the wall. Since we children were strictly forbidden to fight, it was a moot point. I'm guessing that the incident underscored his prejudice toward Black people.

In my family, Black people were not referred to as *negros*, but as *niggers.* Even as a child I knew by the way it was said that it meant niggers were bad. I hated that word, but I didn't know why I did. It just sounded ugly to me. Plus, Mom always used the words *colored people*, which was thought to be more polite. Sometimes I wondered why a word shouldn't be used. But in the case of that word, there was no doubt that it was bad because it was said with anger, superiority, and disdain that cut the air.

This made me a little bit more than uncomfortable. But I wonder now what could have been a different name, given the meaning in the hearts of those who used it so hatefully. Could an alternative word have been said with any less bitterness in their voices? They hated Black people, but I now understand that they were mostly afraid of them.

On the occasion when Grandma would have to pick up Grandpa from work, we had to ride through "Colored Town." My sister and I were told in hushed tones filled with fear, "Hurry! Lock all the doors and roll up the windows." When menfolk were in the car, this command was never spoken. So I assumed that the men made it safe to be around Black people. This also underscored the concept that women were weak.

The light-blue Chevy Bel Air would be loaded to the gills with Grandma and Grandpa Burrough, Aunt Gracy (Grandma Burrough's sister), Uncle Clod (Grandpa's brother), my parents, my sister, and me. Gracy and Uncle Clod were married to each other, just like Grandma and Grandpa were. I would be told to sit on Grandpa's lap, which made me feel edgy and uncomfortable inside. I wondered about these feelings and why they happened only when I had to sit on his or my father's lap. I was small and was always being told to sit on this one's or that one's lap when the car was full. I was the smallest at about three years old.

"I don't wanna," I'd say. I hated their sharp, bumpy knees, and they always had sharp, bumpy knees. I'd skooch forward away from their lap to sit on their knees. "So I can see better," was the reason I gave, but with Grandpa it was something else that bothered me.

On one occasion we drove through Colored Town, which smelled awful, and I thought this was how colored people smelled and that was why nobody liked them. I found out later in my young life that the town smelled that way due to an oil refinery that had been built near their homes.

We were going to the whaling docks, trying to find some breeze cooled by the water to give us some relief from the heat of the day.

These docks were where they cut up whales, leaving bits and pieces to rot, and the stench was awful. My sister and I crawled around on the jagged boulders while the adults sat on or stood near the car.

I was told, "Don't git too close to the water or you're going to git a spankin'." I was told this more than once. My sister always obeyed, while I wanted to explore without limits.

Once we cooled down a bit we drove back through Colored Town with all the car windows down. We moved slowly because it was Sunday. Everyone seemed to move slower while riding or walking on a hot Sunday afternoon. Since all the car windows were down, I figured that that side of town was safe. I liked seeing all the Black people we rode past because of how different from us they were. What they wore and how they spoke was so very unusual to me.

We stopped at a red light, and as we pulled away I saw this very old and very dark-skinned man sitting on a crate on the sidewalk corner.

I was surprised by the man's dark complexion and said to Grandpa, "Granpa, that man suuuuuure is black." The man heard me and smiled real big. Inside the car I got a bunch of shushes.

Grandpa chuckled and said, "Did you hear what Cympi said? She said 'That man suuuuuuure is black!'" Out of a chorus of shushes came, "Yes we did. Now hush up! They might hear you!"

Evidently, having men in the car was not enough, just better. 'Nuf said?

Chapter 2: Running ... in the Family

My mother's linage is quite different. Starkly so. And I'm not sure about the connections. It's all rather confusing.

My Great-Great-Grandfather Vielleux originated from Nice, France, and relocated to Quebec, Canada. Then he moved to Waterville, Maine. Grandma's grandfather was a real work of art. He married his first wife and had twelve children (one of them my grandmother), whom he adopted out to family members and other people in the community. When my grandmother, Rosemarie, was given up for adoption, she was sent to Catholic school, then on to a convent. After sending all his children along their way, my great-grandfather remarried and had another twelve children, whom he kept.

My mother, Jeannine, didn't know this part of her history until she was in her late seventies and a Canadian relative sent her a big book that told the whole story. Up until that time, my mother thought she was the Lone Ranger in her family.

My Grandma Rosemarie was a novice (almost a nun) in the convent when she met and fell in love with my Grandfather Vigue. How they met and developed a relationship is not clear, for she was cloistered away in the convent. That seemed romantic to me as a child. It wasn't until I became an adult that I found out that they were first cousins. (His last name, Vigue, is the English version of Vielleux.) That can certainly wreak havoc in the ol' family genes. As my grandma would say, *mon dieu*, meaning "my God." My grandmother had been schooled by Catholic nuns and retained her education. She had impeccable grammar and beautiful handwriting. She never lost her French accent, which I adored.

Grandfather Vigue was talented and played the fiddle by ear. If challenged to a musical duel, Mom said he "could sure give them a run for their money, and would always win." He was also very wealthy when he married my grandmother. He had planned to increase his wealth via the US stock market. But he lost it all in the 1929 crash.

I, for one, am glad he didn't toss himself out a window, which was what some of the men did. Instead, he started drinking. Eventually my grandmother divorced him because of this. He died destitute and impoverished.

In addition to all of this, he had some sort of psychic ability. Evidently, he could place his hands on an outside wall of a house and raise a table inside the house. I was fearful and stunned when I first heard about this when I was a child. I've inherited psychic abilities: I am clairaudient, which means I can hear psychically.

After her divorce, Grandma fell deeply in love with another man. But his family would not allow them to marry because they were fanatical Catholics and divorce was strictly forbidden by the Church.

After that my grandmother "ran around partying," as my mother bitterly put it. So Mammay and Pappay, my grandma's adoptive parents, raised Mom until she turned fourteen. My mother swears that their daughter, my Aunt Cecile, who was much older than my mother, was her best friend and sister. My own sister Cecilia was named in honor of Aunt Cecile. And they were both named after Saint Cecilia, the patron saint of music.

Well hell, my sister was given Teresa as a middle name after my grandmother's and mom's middle name. I don't know how well my sister sits with this, since our mother loved Aunt Cecile and despised our grandmother. Well, *despised* is a rather harsh word. Perhaps tolerated? She didn't like her mother all that much. How's that?

Mom recalled to me that when World War II was on its way, there was a curfew and rationing, and they had to place black material for curtains on windows at night. The black curtains were there to block out all light in case the enemy tried to find towns and bomb them.

For some reason, Grandmother Vielleux decided to move from Maine to the San Francisco East Bay area in California. Just like Grandma and Grandpa Burrough, she became a welder on the ships that were made or repaired at the Richmond docks.

"There I was," my mother said about the move, "yanked away from my friends and family, not knowing a word of English." Mom was duly upset with her mother and with a French priest who had promised her a box of chocolates as a farewell gift and didn't honor his promise. My mom was kind of bitter about a lot of things and kept a list of these things while traveling through life.

My mother had a tough time in school because she could speak only a few words of English and mostly knew French— and it was broken French to boot—so her grades were very low. I can't even imagine how she navigated life during that time. She told us that her grades were so low that she decided to take French in school. "I thought I would at least do well in that subject," she said. Unfortunately, she bombed out in that course too because she didn't speak classic French. As luck would have it, a colored girl became her best friend and helped her navigate the world. What a loving and awesome task this young lady must have taken on with Mom. My mother stayed friends with this young girl into adulthood.

In her new town, Grandma fell in love with and married another man. His last name was Cameron, though in my family he was known as "that Cameron." Well, actually I'm just guessing at the "love" part because Grandma became pregnant by Cameron right before she divorced him and married yet another man.

That Cameron turned out to be an abusive alcoholic. After work one night, he went to the local, dimly lit bar. "Set 'em up, Bob,' he said to the bartender. "It's been a tough day at work, and

21

Rosemarie won't git rid of that brat Jeannine."

The bartender said, "Jeannine. Pretty name. Who is she?"

Cameron shot back, "Rose's daughter from her first marriage."

Bob asked, "Rose was married before you?"

"Yeah." Cameron downed his whisky and moved on to two more. "Yeah, that bitch Rosemarie was supposed to dump Jeannine when we first married. Hey, Bob. Don't be stingy. 'Nother one over here, buddy." Cameron was beginning to slur his words. "I gotta take a piss. Keep 'em comin', Bob."

"You got it, friend."

Cameron drank late into the night. He said to anyone who would listen, "Do ya know I have to share a bed with that brat Jeannine? I shoulda never married Rosemarie. All she does is moan, groan, and complain. I earn the money 'round here, and I'm the man of the house, goddamn it! I should git to spend *my* money any which way I wanna, right? Bob, how 'bout 'nother for the road?"

"Sure, pal." But Bob looked a little more concerned than usual regarding Cameron, as the drunk was becoming belligerent. It seemed that the more he drank, the angrier he became.

"Yeah, that bitch shares the bed with me and that Jeannine. Jeannine says she's always hungry, and Rosemarie begs for my money. It's my money, goddamn it!"

Finally, after a few more drinks, Bob told Cameron, "Look, guy. I think you should pick up your hat and head on home."

"Yeah, you're right. Got to be the man of the house and show Rosemarie who's boss. Yeah, I'm goin' home. You're goddamn right, Bob."

That Cameron left the bar and could barely hit the keyhole on the car door with his key. He mumbled to himself, "That bitch Rosemarie is gonna hear from me, all right. I'll show her who's boss."

The ashtray in the car seemed to be moving around, so Cameron tossed his live cigarette butt out the car window. He did drive home, but not straight. Once home, he staggered out of the car, having to swing at the car door twice before he closed it. As he neared the house, he cleared his throat and landed a large one on the front porch.

Grabbing the porch rail, he climbed the stairs, swinging from side to side. "Yeah! I'll show them!" he shouted. He turned the doorknob and stumbled over the threshold.

"Shush!" he quietly mouthed, putting his index finger to his lips. "I got a surprise for you, Rose!" he whispered as he staggered toward the bedroom.

My grandmother and mom were sharing the bed in the back room and were sound asleep. It was a Friday night, and there was no doubt in their minds that Cameron was going to come home, if he came home at all, drunk and angry. While they were dead asleep, he came into the bedroom and flipped the mattress as hard as he could up against the wall.

I do know that the man drank up the family paycheck over the weekends. The night of the tossed mattress was one of many last chances that Rosemarie gave Cameron.

Around the time of that incident, my mom decided it was time for the chick to leave the nest, so fourteen-year-old Mom dated skinny sixteen-year-old Daddy just to get out of her bad home life. Mom and Dad got married, and Grandma and Cameron stood up for them in a courthouse because Mom was underage.

When my dad first spotted my mother, he told himself, *She's the one for me.*

How in the heck does someone figure that out after just seeing someone? Dad said that when he took her out on dates, he'd never seen anyone eat as much as she did. I'm sure that she didn't tell him that she was starving most of the time. Mom loved to dance, so many of their dates were at the dance halls where Mom would "clear the floor" dancing her jitterbug and other popular styles with Dad while the other dancers watched appreciatively.

My parents always looked funny to me when they danced at home because Dad was six foot three and Mom was a mere five foot two. And, as I said before, Dad was lanky. He often sang the song, "Five Foot Two, Eyes of Blue," which actually described Mom, right down to the blue eyes.

Dad promised that if Mom married him, she could complete her education and graduate high school.

He didn't keep his promise. He dropped out of school in his senior year. Mom is still offended that not only did Grandma not stop the marriage, but she in fact stood up with that Cameron as witnesses in Las Vegas. Within the same breath, Mom would say she was glad to have married because it took her out of an abusive home life with that Cameron. (From here on forward, if anyone is called "that so and so," it means that they were on Mom's S list for one reason or another.)

Grandma became pregnant with my Uncle Billy while still married to that Cameron, and a year later Mom gave birth to my older sister Cecilia.

It wasn't until recently that I pondered the difficulty of having a child at sixteen, as well as how hard it would be for that child to be raised by naive seventeen- and twenty-year-old parents who didn't know how to go about parenting when they were that young themselves.

Cecilia, my sister, was all-around healthy, while I came out a shrimp and was known as such for what seemed like forever (in child years). I came on the scene about two and a half years after my sister. I've repeatedly told her that she was a hard act to follow because she was a "good child who hardly caused much trouble at all."

I, on the other hand, was not.

Grandma divorced that Cameron shortly after Uncle Billy was born and married George Rasmussen. That was three for her. Marriages, I mean.

Wowee! The lady had balls. At that time in society, one divorce made you a slut. So I guess that divorcing and marrying as many times as Grandma did made her a whore? At any rate, it was taboo. This would have given social elites something to gossip about if they had known Grandma.

∞ ∞ ∞

There couldn't have been much time in between Grandma's two husbands because Uncle Billy, or Little Bill as he was called in our family, was born shortly after George Rasmussen came along. That was cutting it pretty close for any society at the time. Good God, Grandma could have waited at least a little while longer before marrying George. Fear does funny things to people and makes them act in funny ways.

I'd always wondered why Grandpa George and Grandma Rasmussen slept in separate beds. It was just odd to me. Well, it turns out that Grandpa George fought in World War II and had an injury that prohibited him from having traditional sex. I'm guessing that he didn't know that making love didn't always have be "bongo bongo sex," per se. He should have been married to Grandma Burrough, considering all things as semi equal.

Chapter 3: Jesus, Me, and the Glory Daze

1950

Jeannine and Billy were leaving Ora and Virgil's house with their little bundle of joy, Cecilia. The baby was sound asleep. Billy was irritated about something long before he left his parents' place. Billy took Cecilia from Jeannine. Billy always carried the baby when going outside.

As Jeannine and Billy walked away from the front porch, they heard Billy's mother's usual send-off: "Ya'll come back now, you hear?"

"Billy?" Jeannine asked.

"Yes?"

"You *got* to fix that hole in back of the car. We can't have Cecilia there with that big old hole in the floorboard. It's not safe," Jeannine said.

Billy put their baby daughter on the back seat and said, "Never you mind. I'll fix that when I'm dadgum good and ready to."

He was beginning to notice how much Jeannine pestered him. She noticed how stubborn he was.

Billy slammed the back door, sat in the front seat, bent his long, spidery legs, then slowly and carefully placed them inside the car. He was forever hitting his knee on the steering column.

Jeannine jumped into the passenger seat, pivoted, grabbed the door handle, and closed her door in one fell swoop, looking over her shoulder to check on Cecilia.

Billy hit the accelerator hard, causing the car to jerk forward.

"Billy, slow down," Jeannine said.

"I *am* going slow. This old car has guts. I've told you that before! How many times do I have to tell you?" Billy mumbled, "How many times ..." He said that to Jeannine a lot.

Ora stepped out into the street and waved furiously at the couple as they rolled down the potholed road.

Jeannine looked in the mirror. "What in the world? Billy, pull over, pull over. Ora is trying to say something. She's running toward the car. Pull over!"

Billy moved to the side of the road, slowing the car to a near stop as Jeannine looked again at the mirror outside her window. She turned white and her jaw dropped. She jumped out of the still-moving car.

Billy slid to a soft stop and said, "What's all the commotion about? What now?" He looked at Jeannine and said, "That crazy French woman!" He jumped out of the car after throwing it into park and pulling the emergency hand brake up.

"Billy! Billy!" Jeannine screamed. "Billy, she fell out! Oh, dear God! Cecilia fell out of the car!" She ran toward Ora, who was already kneeling beside the baby. "Ora, is she hurt? Oh my God! Oh my God!" She rushed to the baby's side, knelt, then slowly opened the covers on the papoose-wrapped baby.

Billy ran up, picked up the baby, then ran back to the car. He gently laid the screaming infant on the back seat.

Jeannine followed him, running to the car. "Billy, get away! Get away!" She roughly elbowed him out of the way.

By this time, Virgil had caught up to where Ora was and said to her, "I don't know how many times I told that boy to fix that floorboard." Guilt always snaps a person into saying the right thing just at the right time.

Ora and Virgil ran to the car. "Is she all right?" Ora asked Jeannine. "Good Jesus! Oh, dear Lord," she said.

Jeannine was rolling the child slowly right to left. She lifted and turned Cecilia on her stomach, checking for injuries. The baby was just fine, except for a small, deep cut on her forehead.

∞∞∞

Grandma Rasmussen subsidized Mom's diet with steaks and other healthy food when she was pregnant with Cecilia, so she was born healthy a year after Grandma's son, Uncle Bill. I believe my little brother Thomas's nutrition was up to snuff too. I, on the other hand, was plunked right dab in the middle between Cecilia and Thomas. Mom and Dad were very poor. I didn't mention that? We were very poor.

Well, Grandma Rasmussen decided that I should not have been conceived, so she withheld food. Mom would eat chocolate cake to ease her hunger pains and satisfy her cravings, which were frequent. However, amazingly, she didn't gain weight. That may be why I ended up the runt in the family. Compared to children my age, I was always the shortest, puniest, and scrawniest one.

As luck would have it, my father had been too young to serve in World War II. Then he had a family, so he didn't serve during the Korean War either. Nonetheless, he had to go into the merchant marines. He kept a peacoat of navy blue when he was discharged, along with an ugly, brown, scratchy wool blanket that had holes in it. I felt my dad looked real snazzy when he wore the coat. I liked it mostly because he didn't look so thin. Dad was tall, lanky, and skinny. He was extremely handsome, but his body wasn't at all masculine or attractive. He had a hunched back, and Mom was constantly saying to him, "Billy, stand up straight!" But he couldn't because he had scoliosis and stood on his feet all day long at his job, stooped over a tool-and-dye press. Neither of them knew these things contributed to his bad posture.

1952

My cloth diapers dry. I go potty. I cold. I cry so one come make me warm. One no come. I cry loud and louds for Lady come. Lady come. I like Lady. Lady come and take off cold diaper. Yucky stuff in it. Lady make warm. Lady powders on me. Lady rubs my toes lotion. I giggle. Lady talk and sing to me. I giggle lots. She makes me happy. Lady "gibber gabber." Lady gots lotion when rain. My tummy feels happy.

[The *rain* refers to a baby's shower. I couldn't speak at that point, but I was beginning to try out words in my head. The above is one of my first memories about body feelings. Wet, dry, warm.

Many years later, as I wandered down my spiritual path and learned how to meditate, I could see, during three of those meditations, my father molesting me when I was an infant. It was as clear as if it were happening all over again.

Only this time I was an onlooker.

The subconscious eventually reveals what an adult can handle. I was shaken upon seeing the particulars of the molestation. Before I found that memory, I had no idea how an infant could be molested. I'm not saying that it was easy or less painful when the memory came to me as an adult, but that was when my mind revealed all to me.

When I was an infant, Dad had me suck his private part.]

∞∞∞

The bottom barrel for food in our family is tomato soup. Watered down. Lady Mommy is sad I ever knowed. Times soup watered down so much, is yucky. Lady Mommy gits ketchup in it iffin' we have it to the soup, for so it don't taste bad. Soup is little teeny tiny money. After that, only crackers. Lady Mommy puts crackers in the soup too.

I heared sad Lady Mommy and the Big daddy Mans talk real loud in kitchen. Sad Lady Mommy come git me "to keep an eye on" me all times. Sad Lady Mommy carries me to the kitchen. I see crackers on table. She puts me on the floor. Table high up so I don't reach crackers. The table and chairs used to be Lady Grandma's, and she give it to Sad Lady Mommy and Big daddy Mans 'cause they have ones not. When there are only crackers, Sad Lady Mommy puts yellow stuffs on the top if any in the house. Make cracker taste gooder. This time, no yellow stuffs.

I hungry, so I reach up on my tippy-toes for the crackers I see. Me oh, my tummy hurt.

The Big daddy Mans say, "No." I like Big daddy Mans. My tummy hurts lots. I wait as long I can. I reached up, git cracker.

The Big daddy Mans says, "No! Supper will be on in a little bit." He looks at Sad Lady Mommy, and her head goes up and down not big. Big daddy Mans and Sad Lady Mommy talk 'n' talk. I reached for cracker.

The Big daddy Mans talk loud. He say, "Doggone it. I told you NO!" He grabs me hard. Afore I knowed, I slide fast 'cross room. I see gray shiny wall in face. I 'fraid. I don't like Big daddy Mans no more. He makes me 'fraid. He makes me 'fraid lots. I hurt. I hurt. Sad Lady Mommy lift me up, give Big daddy Mans what for. Sad Lady Mommy carries me to my crib. I dreamed this lots.

[You see, I couldn't believe my "Big daddy Mans" would hurt me physically and emotionally, and my complete trust in him diminished.

I'm not clear if he kicked me across the room or just flung me, but the damage had been done. I didn't think I was doing anything wrong, and my total focus was on the food. So I couldn't understand why he was so angry with me. I certainly cried for a long time. Mom went back and forth from my room to the kitchen several times and yelled at Dad about what he'd done. After a few minutes, she checked in on me, and I finally stopped crying because I was exhausted. As I fell asleep, my back hurt badly. Who knows the extent of the damage. I was still in pain when

30

I woke up. I do know that when I did something "wrong" after that incident, my father would lightly pop me on the butt but never hurt anything but my pride until I grew older. I guess for the moment, he'd learned his lesson.

I was beginning to say words aloud, but they were simple and mostly nouns.

I had two stuffed animals. One was a little lamb that looked happily asleep, and the other was a small teddy bear that played "Rock-a-Bye Baby" when wound up. Mom sang along with the bear's music box. I'm glad I didn't understand too many words at that point. From the time of the cracker incident forward, my teddy bear was my closest friend. I clung to it and the white lamb for dear life. I began to talk to the bear, and this calmed me after punishments, before I took naps, and before regular sleeping times. Some children have imaginary friends. I had a bear to talk to who always comforted me. He always thought I was a good child too.]

Big daddy Mans smiles and plays with me by tossing me up in the air and holding me in the palm of his hand as I stand there or sit there.

[Dad was trying to show just how tiny I was for my age, but I didn't like this. I was afraid, so the trust was diluted . Eventually Mom made him put me down because it was so dangerous.]

∞∞∞∞

1954

Mommy play with me. I giggle. I on Mommy lap. Mommy point and tap my top head face and say, "A chicken lives here." She smile. She touch my nose and say, "A pullet lives here." She touch my chin and say with smile, "A hen lives here. What did I say lives here?" She touch my nose. I say, "Pullet" and she say, "Pullet?" I say, "Pullet." She smile real big and say, "Pullet," then she pull my nose. I laugh and say, "'Gin." We do this over and over.

Times she sing to me in French. Daddy try French but he don't know much. I do.

[My verbal skills had some limited structure that began at this stage in my development. Repetition by adults allowed me to speak more words out loud, but my internal speech was developing at a much faster rate.]

∞∞∞

1955

Mommy talk to Aunt Carol on phone all the times! If I want somthin', shouldn't Mommy git it for me right then? Mommy is for me and me alone. I tug on her dress. She don't pay 'tention to me.

"You not pay 'tention to me!" I say. I tugs and tugs on her dress. But she keep talkin'.

I 'cide I leave home. I go to water. I show her.

"I go to backyard.

My trike is littler than my big sister's. I stand on the peddles. I go fast. I see the ocean. I not that far way. I go fast. I can fly to water. I plan the whole thing out before I take off. I do this and that to fly.

I push trike back to wall and take off.

I too slow. I back trike to the wall and start peddlin' as fast as I can on tippy-toes.

"I flying! Uh oh!"

I fly off the ground onto the big boulders below. Everything is turning white. "It's Jesus!" I say. "Look at all the children around Him. They don't have no mommy and daddy."

Love? This is like what my mommy and daddy tell me they do to me. I feel bunches.

I never feel before. It feels soooooooooo good.

Jesus says in my head, "You must leave."

I says back to Him, "I don't wanna." I want to know why the other children get to stay with Him and I can't. This hurts my feelings.

He says in head, "You cannot stay here."

I angry. I say, "I don't wanna go."

He says out loud, "Go!"

Bang! I back in my body.

Mommy holds me. She screeching as loud as loud can. "Help me! Help me! Somebody help me!"

Mommy never screech. I 'fraid.

Someone calls the doctor. He says, "All children fall. Don't worry too much. Just keep an eye on her."

My head hurts bad.

[When I became an adult, Mom told me that I fell two stories that day I rode my bike off that cliff in Arlington Hills. My eyes rolled back in my head, and I was convulsing.

When I've told the story to others as an adult, they can't believe that my mother didn't take me to the hospital. We couldn't afford that. They are also appalled by the doctor's reaction.

Being poor is an awful way to live. Later, as an older child, I would frequently pass out and convulse. This happened until I went to college. Knowing the feeling well, I developed enough sense to slide down a wall or sit on the floor when I felt it coming on. Also, from childhood until now, my back hurts constantly.

Dad hid my tricycle and, at some point deeming that I was old enough to ride it again, repainted it. But it was my old, ill-fated trike. I knew it was the old one, but because everyone made such a big deal about it, I acted like it was new.

After that little incident, my mom insisted we move from "that" place to San Pablo, California. It was just a short flight, I mean jump, I mean car ride away. I think the house we moved into belonged to Grandma Rasmussen. It was a short distance from where Grandma and Grandpa Burrough lived. Across the road was a vacant lot that belonged to Grandma Rasmussen. The house we moved into was extremely tiny.]

Chapter 4: Wam Bam, Thank You

1955

There is a rickety chicken coop in the backyard. When it's hot, me and Celya climb up to its roof to watch cartoons on the drive-in movie screen. Celya can climb up to the roof, but daddy has to put me up there. It's a treat to watch cartoons on the movie screen. We don't have no TV like Granma and Granpa Burrough have. Sometime it's so hot Celya has to climb to the ground and ask Mommy for a blanket to sit on so our bottoms won't boil off us.

On the roof I say to Celya, "I hope the peoples down there turn up their speaker loud." If them people in their parked cars don't play their speakers loud, we still can see the cartoons but not hear the sound. We like the colors anyway. My stomach make gurgle noises when I smell the hot dogs and popcorn.

∞∞∞

Big people say that I "can't sit still for a minute" and that I'm "an impatient child." I don't know what that means. I think Mommy "can't sit still for a minute." Mommy's in a hurry and tries to git ready for a church women's meeting. In the middle of this she is runnin' water in the kitchen sink to handwash some clothes. Mostly underwears. Most times we go to Granma Burrough's, and she washes her clothes in a big tub, then the clothes git squeezed out between two rollers and into a laundry basket. I'm not suppost to go anywheres near them rollers.

∞ ∞ ∞

Mommy does bunches of stuff at same time. Mommy says, "I don't have any time for you right now." That means she don't love me right now. I'm very thirsty and ask for a drink of water every time she comes to the kitchen.

She says, "In a minute" and goes 'round the house all over the place fast. She comes in to watch the water run two times.

I wonder why she don't give me some water right now. She adds ammonia in the sink. It smells awful. I ask Mommy for water again.

She says, "In a minute!" Mommy in a big hurry. She says, "I've got to get dressed and put on my makeup yet." Mommy has a slip on. She goes to the bedroom.

I'm gittin' to be a big girl now, so I can git a drink by myself! I have Celya's beat-up tin cup in my hand.

I 'cide that I can do this for myself. I stand on my tippy-toes. I dip my glass into the sink, pulling out some water. It's easy. It smells funny, but I don't care. I'm trusty! I'm mad at Mommy, so I drink the water.

The last thing I 'member is Mommy rushing toward me saying, "Now what have you done?"

[I was faulted with this little stunt for the rest of my life. My anger and my "I can do it for myself" attitude were beginning to form at this time. My keen sense of logic is off center and has not served me well.

The following happened after our move to San Pablo, California.]

∞ ∞ ∞

Carajean is my friend and is the same age as me. Her sister is Patty, and she is my sister's age. Carajean is taller than me by a whole head. Me and Celya git to play with Patty and Carajean sometimes but only if Celya wants to go to their house and asks Mommy if we can go. I can't go there all by myself. I'm too little. If I ask, we can't go.

Mommy wants to take our picture all together—Patty, Cara-jean, Celya, and me—because we are "rag muffins" with our holey clothes, dirty faces, and messed-up hair. I'm "always dirty," 'sempin' when we go to church or jest plain ol' take a bath for no reason.

After the picture, I have to take a bath because I'm "filthy."

Next door live twins who my sister plays with. I think they are better than me because they's big stuff bigger than me and don't want to play with me 'cause I'm too little. They call me squirt. I don't like that. My name is Cynthia! They teached Celya to make tiny furniture out of mud.

I want to learn too, but they tell me, "Go away." I'm sad but I want to play with thems too. I pester Celya till she teached me how make mud furniture now. I don't wanna do it no more, so I go by myself to play other stuffs that I like better.

[As a child I got into trouble numerous times because I wasn't supposed to be doing something or I was too young to try a particular task in the first place. I carried the trait of impatience and learned the art of pestering because I never felt heard or seen.

Even as an adult, not feeling heard or seen bothers me to no end. And I like to learn something new. Once I get it, I try to do it better creatively than my instructor or other people working on the same project because I become bored and disinterested. If I can't immediately accomplish the task or grasp the concept, I get angry and frustrated, and I feel incredibly dumb. But if I accomplish something easily, I feel that I must be doing it wrong because of the ease.

Also, I get bored quickly if I reach my goal or surmise that something isn't worth my time. Sometimes I set the bar higher and higher as a personal test. I get great satisfaction when I do this and succeed. I must honestly say that when it comes down to it, I'm pretty arrogant, at least internally. But I still seek positive input from others to validate my experience and bring attention to myself.

As a teen I pushed myself to the limit to make something less boring or gain the rewards that come from mastering something, such as learning a musical instrument or pulling on my artistic prowess, as in a piece of art.]

∞∞∞

Mommy wants to go Back Maine for a visit to be with her father, Aunt Cecile, Mammay, and Pappay.

She says that she misses them and wants to see them and the town where she grew up. Daddy takes a piece of plywood and other wood to make a play area/bed in the back of the car for me and Celya for the drive. The back seat has been pulled out to make room. Our bumpers have burlap water bags, whatever means, and there is blue and red letters on these, but I can't read yet and Celya don't know what the writing mean. The bags make the water taste funny but it better than 'monia.

Me and Celya gots brand-new toys to play with. Granma Burrough buys them for us. I can't believe my eyes. New toys! Celya gots paper dolls and I gots this funny face man that is magic. I can move black bits around using a pointy thing to give the face a beard or thick eyebrows or whatever I can dream up. Also me and Celya gots a cardboard thing, and we draw on it. After we do, we can gits rid of what we jest drawed by pullin' plastic up from the board.

[The younger reader may not know what paper dolls are. The main doll was backed with stiff cardboard, and there was a book full of various pieces of attire, such as dresses and purses. Everything had little paper tabs. The attire could be cut out and attached to the cardboard figure. All you did was bend the tabs over the edge of the cardboard to keep the cut-out pieces on the doll.

Both Celya and I received a waxed cardboard clipboard with an acetate sheet that we could draw on with a stylus. Then we would lift up the plastic to remove the drawing and begin anew. We were also given coloring books. We had arrived! Pay dirt! This was a child's heaven, and both of us felt very special. We had no idea that all of these toys were to keep us busy, quiet, and occupied during the long trip to Waterville, Maine.

Especially me.]

∞∞∞

We drived to "ten buck two" through the very very hot Mojave Desert, where pointy cactus is. Mommy have "conniption fits" when daddy has me and Celya git out the car so'z he takes a picture of us in front of a big, big cactus that's a hundred feet tall.

We is at Back Maine. Me and Celya play with Aunt Cecil's boys. That is lots o' fun. I'm a whole three years old now. See? This many. One, two, three fingers. Me and Celya speak French, but mostly me to Mammay and Pappay. Mommy speaks French most all times in Back Maine. Mammay and Pappay speak French all time too. Daddy don't say too much French, and when he says it, it sounds funny. But that's O.K. because everyone speaks a little English.

Pappay plays with me and tells me to go and git his pliers from Mammay. He gits a great big ol' smile on his face.

I tell Mammay what Pappay wants, and she says, "Don't know why. What he's up to now?" But she finds them pliers and gives them to me.

Pappay sits in his big ol' ugly wood-armed, plaid rockin' chair. It's ugly. I give him them pliers and he puts them pliers in his mouth and pulls out his teeth! For all the world, I don't know how'd he done that. It scares me and I know it's magic! Him and daddy laughin' hard. Pappay leans to me quick and asks if I want my teeth pulled out too. I say, "No!" and run screamin' to Mommy at the kitchen table.

Mammay give Pappay "what for." "Stop it!" she yell. "You scared this little one half to death."

Pappay says somethin' back to Mammay in French, but I can't understand one word.

In the kitchen I ask how to say the words in French, and Mommy or Mammay says it to me.

I say the words back and Mammay says, "It won't take any time before this little one can speak French well."

Mommy nods her head.

We go to New York. It very windy. Mommy and daddy talk 'bout payin' for gas to git to Statue Liberty. I *really* want to see that statue I never seen before, and Mommy and daddy told me 'bout it when we gits to here. When Mommy and daddy talk about goin' to Statue Liberty, my tummy goes flip flop. I hold my breaths. Mommy don't want to go to no Statue Liberty because we may not have 'nough gas to git back home. Me and Celya waits.

Inside my body I jumpin' up and down because daddy wants to see it, but then he says, "Yes, you're right, honey. We *really* can't afford it." The smile melts off my face like hot rubber. My stomach falls. My shoulders go down and I feel down right awful sad. These words, "We can't afford this" means nothin' good's gonna happen. I heared that Statue Liberty is *very* big, but my hopes to seein' it turn out to make me feel low down.

Finely daddy says to Mommy, "Let's take the risk and go to the Statue of Liberty, because we probably won't ever see it again."

We drived to git out to Statue Liberty and we gits out the car. I stand with my hands on the cyclone fence, hair blowin' in the winds. It tickles my face. I can see New York 'cross the water. It's tiny. That Statue Liberty ain't big at all like Mommy and daddy says it is! It's only three inches high! Little biddy. If that's what they call big, I sad and I don't thinked why daddy wants to see it so bad. I have to pay more 'tention to what big peoples say because they don't know what they talkin' 'bout.

[Grammar and structure in my world came from Dad's colloquialisms and Oklahoma drawl, and Mom's French grammar, which caused me difficulty with sentence structure, words, and spelling. Added to that, I'm a bit dyslexic too. My mind argues with itself, so this delays some of my speech patterns. While French began to fade in our home as I grew, the slang persisted for a long time. I still slip into that relaxed way of speaking when I'm tired.

Also, I hate cyclone fences and wind to this day. Once I stood with my hands on that cyclone fence in New York, my perspective on life changed. I wondered if adults told lies or just were stupid. My pattern of questioning adults began then, and ultimately I got into a lot of trouble while advancing in age. I questioned just about everything. Life for me changed dramatically at this point. Hearing the words "We can't afford this" often throughout my young life, I knew that the possibility of doing, having, touching, seeing, or tasting probably was not going to manifest. Part of this was due to our poverty, but it was also a way to dictate our behavior.

My excitement for life began to fade, and I believe that it was only during my escapades (for good or not) that I was able to experience a temporary relief from this fear. If we were going someplace special, Dad would become angry midway and say, "If you don't stop, I'm turning this car right around right now." He said this to us kids and my mother. Also I learned that "In a little bit" and "Let me think about it" really meant "No." Disappointment and my lack of sureness came from my father's and mother's anger or moods. With these in mind, I clearly saw that their anger proved just how powerful they were. A perpetual state of fear became part of my childhood. As result, fear holds me in its clutches even today.]

∞ ∞ ∞

The vacation is over and we are back home at San Pablo. We visit Granma and Granpa Burrough lots. Granpa Burrough says that I'm "full of the dickens." My mommy says she wishes she had a harness with a leash for me. That way, she says she could keep track of me when we go out in public.

See, that's because I jest love runnin' all over the place real fast and lookin' at things I ain't never seen before in my whole life, and I know Mommy and daddy can't never buy them because they don't never buy what I look at and touch. I can't help myself. I have to touch everything. If you are a 'splorer, be sure to take a map with you because you can lose your Mommy and daddy right quick. I always gits lost, and sometimes Mommy and daddy forgit me till they figger out they don't see or hear me no more. I don't know why they gits so mad because I'm right where I am.

Anyways, Granma Burrough says that I'm "a happy little bit of a thing … full of energy that wants to know everything about everything." She claims that I jest can't keep still for a minute to save my life.

I'm like that all times.

There's a way to keep track of me though. I put my arms around daddy's leg because he tells me to when we go shoppin'.

He says, "Then I knows where you are." One time I let go of his leg, then 'member to git hold of it again. But I look at his pants and I wonder what happen to his pants. The ones I holdin' don't look like the ones he was wearin'. Can pants change color like magic? I look up. It ain't daddy's leg at all. It's 'nother man's leg. "Oh no. I lost my daddy!" I say. Then I look over and seen daddy's leg.

I look up and see the man and daddy chuckle with big smiles on their faces, then daddy says, "See what happens to you when you let go of my leg?" I was ascared. Mommy and daddy think I'm tired when I tug on daddy's pants to pick me up. I'm not tired at all. I cry because my legs hurt *so* bad.

Daddy says, "Do you want me to put you on my shoulders?"

With tears in my eyes I nod my head.

He chuckles and say to me after puttin' me on his shoulders,

"Sweetheart, you can't put your hands over my eyes. I can't see, and I need to see where I'm going." It's hard not to put my hands on daddy's eyes because I think I fall off his shoulder. I barely push the side of his head when I put my hands there. I don't want to hurt my daddy.

∞∞∞

1956

Daddy has a purdy shiny black car, which he painted with a fly sprayer. The sprayer has a tin cup at the end with a cap on it with killer liquid in the cup. I can't go "anywhere near it." Daddy put paint in the cup and sprayed the car. I never seen the car dirty because daddy washes and waxes it every week. Mama vacuums the inside once a week too.

Mommy dresses Celya and me for church. While she's doing this, daddy puts on his ironed blue pants, white shirt, and blue tie. Daddy looks handsome though I've seen this outfit a hundred billion times before. He wears the same outfit to church every Sunday. Daddy watches me and Celya while Mommy dresses up in a blue-and-white pokiedotted dress. She has to take the rolled-up rags out of her hair that she put in last night after washing her hair. She has curly black hair, but she likes it extra curly because that's what the womens have for their hair now days.

Mommy is gittin' ready and tells daddy to give us girls the oatmeal she cooks up. I *hate* oatmeal! It smells bad, looks bad, and tastes worse. Daddy give me and Celya a glass of water because there ain't no orange juice in the house. I can smell the Evening in Paris perfume that Mommy puts on. I love the sweet smell, and it helps block out the oatmeal smell. My mommy rushes in, grabs a washcloth, and wipes the oatmeal off my face real hard. Then she takes my bib off and carries me to the sink, where she picks up the baby bottle filled with milk. For some reason she can't breastfeed me, so there's always milk in the house. Daddy is cleaning out the tiny pan that the hot cereal was made in.

Mommy rushes away toward the front door while tellin' daddy, "Hurry up, Billy. We're going to be late for church." Mommy grabs my hand and walks me to the car in a hurry. Seems like we are always late goin' somewhere.

Daddy says, "I'm almost done. I'll be right there." Celya wants to take daddy's hand before he goes to the door. He opens the door, stepping outside and banging the door behind him. He takes a few steps and Mommy yells at him, "Did you lock the door?"

"Yes," he says in a voice that sounds mean. But Mommy lets go of me and rushes back to the house to lock the door. Daddy and Celya are in the car now, and Mommy comes back.

I 'cide that I can git into the car all by myself. Mommy's car door is open, so I grab the car doorframe. I can pull myself up.

Then Mommy rushes back to the house saying, "I forgot Cynthia's diaper bag." Mommy comes back agin and gits into the car and slams the car door on my hand.

Bang!

My hand hurt on my fingers. The blood runs down my arm. Mommy looks down in shock.

Oh it hurt! I cry like mad.

Mommy says right quick, "Billy, go get a washcloth and wet it down with water."

Daddy rushes to the house and Mommy follows him inside. Celya, like a good girl, stays in the car waitin' for all the 'citement to be over.

Daddy comes back to car, picks me up, and rushes me to inside house. Blood drips on the floor all over. I think that Mommy is gonna be mad at me for being late to church and about that blood on her clean floor.

Daddy takes me to kitchen sink, turns the cold water on, and pushes my hand under the faucet. I jerk my hand away. I cry louder because water stings my hand. Daddy pulls on my hand and says, "Honey, we have to wash it off."

Mommy grabs a washcloth and wraps my hand with it. For a little while the cloth is white but lots of blood leaks. That's all I 'member.

One time when we go shoppin', Mommy gits real mad and tells daddy to take me to the car. I don't know what I done wrong. I'm ascared in the car alone with daddy, but at least I can sit down. My legs hurt real bad. It isn't too much longer before Mommy comes out of the store with Celya.

We go shoppin', so after a while I tug at my daddy's pant leg and cry.

He says with a smile, "I can't carry you on my shoulders any more. You are getting too big." I stop cryin' outside of myself sometimes because it don't do no good. I cry inside now, though, when my legs hurt bad. They don't never stop hurtin' when we go shoppin' now or walkin' a long ways.

We move to El So-bran-ty, Cal-e-for-n-e-a, a little town that means "the leftovers." It was created because it was the leftover land created by the borders of all the other towns. A big rich Spanish con-keys-tee-door used to own the land we live on. So is we the leftovers too? There's hills all around with lots of green plants and trees. In the hills 'cross from our house there's these cows. The man that lives in the house across our street also has chickens and a rooster that crows whenever he feels like it, but mostly in the mornin'. All the time the man's boy, Dennis, who is almost my age, has to round up a cow that walks down their long dirt driveway. There are lots of dirt roads in my life. Peoples ride all over the place on horseyback. The horsey walks slow and easy like, moseyin' up the streets.

When we move to our brand-new house in El So-bran-ty, Uncle Jesse, Aunt Carol, Patty, and Carajean move right 'cross the street in an old house. Uncle Jesse and daddy are bestest friends. Aunt Carol is Mommy's bestest friend too.

A little bit after we move to the new home, my brother, Thomas, git born. I see that everyone in the *whole world* gotta hold him when he first come home from the hospital. Everybody 'cept for me. Daddy and Mommy say, "You're too small," or "He's too big for you."

Mommy and daddy don't usually stay in bed so late as today. It's Saturdee. We all are watchin' TV. Granma and Granpa Burrough give us the TV. Mommy and daddy are laughin' 'bout what's on the TV. Mommy is propped up with some pillows on one side of the bed. Daddy is next to Mommy on the other side of the bed, layin' his cheek on his face and propping his self up with his elbow.

I wanna hold Thomas bad. "Can I please hold Thomas? I jest wanna walk 'round the end of the bed with him and give him to daddy," I say to Mommy, hoping they see how little time I'd have him. My sister is sittin' on the hardwood floor next to Mommy's side of the bed like me. She looks at Mommy as if thinkin' if it's a good idea to let me do it. Celya knows best jest 'zactly how I am.

I say again, "Can I *pleeeeease?*" Mommy git real serious and looks at daddy. He looks serious too.

Mommy says, "Should we let her do that, Billy?"

Daddy says, "Well, he is ten pounds or more. I don't know if she can hold him, let alone carry him."

I wait without takin' a breath.

Mommy says, "Yes, you're right. I don't know, Billy."

Daddy says, "Well, why don't you put him in her arms and see if she can hold him."

I can't wait!

Mommy puts Thomas in my arms. Boy he is heavy! But I want to carry him to daddy's side of the bed so bad.

I don't know if I can carry him all the ways, but I *have* to because I begged Mommy and daddy to let me carry him. I hope all my gittin' into trouble doesn't stop them from lettin' me carry Thomas.

Daddy says, "Don't drop him."

I *am* careful. Very, *very* careful. He weighs tons. He's so heavy, but I pretend that I can hold him jest fine. I'm walkin' very slow. When Mommy was at the hospital, daddy waxed the floor on his hands and knees for a present. So I'm very, very, *very* careful. The floor is real shiny, slick, and purdy. I know if I drop Thomas, it will be a long, *long* time before I can hold him again.

Mommy says, "Carry him very tightly and don't drop him."

I says, "I won't." I walk really, *really* slow. Mommy and daddy look at me walkin'. I'm at the foot of the bed.

Oh boy, I'm gonna make it all the way around! I don't know how this happens, but I slip on Mommy's throw rug at the end of the bed. I think I'm gonna drop Thomas! I hold him as tight as I can, and I hit the floor with a bang. Everything goes white. I wake up to see my daddy crawlin' real fast across the bed. Mommy is already with me. Daddy's underwears looks funny. I saw them plenty of times, but not with him in them. I hear Thomas cryin'. I'm ascared. I'm *real* ascared.

I ask, "Did I drop him? Did I drop him?" They keeps askin' me questions and don't seem to care 'bout Thomas.

I ask again, "Did I drop him?" I never shoulda pretended that he wasn't too heavy. They say, "No. No. You didn't drop him."

I was never so happy in my whole life.

[Count them. Two times I hit my head. It really, really hurts when you do that. But these would not be the last times I'd pass out or be knocked unconscious.]

I don't have too much to do with Thomas no more. 'Sides, all he does is poo-poo, pee-pee, drink milk, and throw up. Oh yeah, and snot runs down his nose to his lip, which is yucky.

I don't know 'bout why boys is boys, and girls is girls. Every other child has prob'ly been told by older childrens how childrens come to be born. My big sister is in school, and my sister's friend told her that if a boy put his wiener in your pocket, you will have a baby. I don't care 'bout *how* you git a baby, and I don't know nothin' 'bout wieners 'cept the ones I eat. You know that you shouldn't put wieners in no pocket anyways, right? It's more 'portant how someone *turns* into a boy or girl. I'm gonna figger out 'bout that if it's the last thing I do. I look high and low, but I can't find no answer.

Children are goin' to school. I git up on my bed and I look out of my bedroom windows with fingers curled on top of the windowsill, nose up against the cold glass, foggin' it up jest like in daddy's car when it's cold outside or if it's rainin'. I keep rubbing off the glass with my arm, like daddy and Mommy do in the car.

I come to figger out 'bout how boys is boys and girls is girls. On the mornin' of the first day of school, all the childrens walk up the hill by our house. There are *so many childrens* walkin' up the street to school.

I look out real hard and think about how I don't know any of 'em at all. Not a one of them childrens. This is because parents 'cide right then and there if a child is gonna be a boy or girl. When they figger that out, they cut hairs, put on pants or a dress, and that's that! If you have pants on and cut off hairs, you is a boy. And if you have a dress on with long hairs, you is a girl.

I'm so mad I could spit. I want to be a boy! From now on I'm not gonna be a girl *as much as I can*. Being a boy is much funner. Boys git better toys and clothes that make sense, and they can git dirty all they want to. Do you know how cold you git when the wind blows up your dress? Really, *really, really* cold! Humph!

Chapter 5: Mezi Mouse

1956

I'm four years old now, so I git to go over to Granma and Granpa Burrough's house with my big sister Celya. I'm all growed up now. Mommy and daddy are going someplace special, so they drop me and Celya off at Granma and Granpa Burrough's to spend the day, a night, then 'nother day. That's a long, long time.

When we git to go to Granma and Granpa's, me and Celya sleep in a big ol' bed like daddy's and Mommy's. But I start havin' awful bad dreams about someone tryin' to come git me. Lots of times I dreamed that granpa picks me up off the bed and takes me some-wheres. When the bad dreams start comin', I make sure my feet are clean before I go to bed in real life. Don't ask me why. I jest do it. I clean all the dirt from out between my toes and on the bottoms of my feet. Me and my sister wears flip-flops all the time when we play, so my feets git dirty. Seems it don't matter much that I clean my feets at nite. When I wake up in the mornin' my feet are dirty. Me and Celya don't never walk in bare feet because Mommy says "it's unsanitary." I wonder and wonder 'bout my dirty feet, but I don't never come up with why they git dirty after I go to sleep.

Me and Celya play together all the time at Granma's and granpa's, but she don't have no dirty feet like I do.

Oh yeah! There's a word that granpa says that I never heard before. I mean I heard it before but not like granpa says it. I like

49

the word because it jest sounds funny to me: *Micky.* Like Mizy Mouse. I watch Mizy Mouse cartoons on TV.

The mans and granpa sits real close to the TV set to watch boxin'. They hoot and holler all the time. The mans are granpa's friends. They look at the boxin' and says, "One, two. Would you look at that, Joe." Joe is granpa Burrough's other name. Course granpa seen it. He's right there! Grown-ups say the dumbest things. Granpa moves his fist like he's fightin' with one of them boxin' mans.

One mans says to granpa, "Did you give Ora the micky?"

Granpa shushes him and says, "I put it in her RC Cola."

Granma loves RC sody pop and drinks it every chance she gits. I ask in my reglar voice, "Granpa? What's a micky?"

Granpa looks up at me in a mean way and shushes me too and says, "Just you never mind. Be quiet and don't tell your grandma about it. It's a surprise."

I like 'prises, so I know Granma will like what granpa give her.

Then he says all smilin' like, "Cympi, if you tell her 'bout this, I'll just give you what for." And he holds up his fist to my face. Granpa's makin' funny I think, but I'm not too sure because of how he looks at me. Granpa never hits me though. Never. He jest jokes 'bout it with me. Granpa really loves me and I know that for true. I don't never hear the word *micky* agin. Ever!

The next day I ask Granma what her 'prise was, and she don't say anything, but she looks surprised.

It's time to go to bed. Granma winds the little travel clock that she puts on the tan wood headboard where me and Celya climbs into bed. The sheets are stiff, thick, and scratchy. That clock is *loud.* Granma tucks us in very tight. Now Granma goes to her own bedroom and says somethin' to granpa and winds her clock in there. Click ... click ... click.

It's so quiet and funny feelin' in this bedroom. I don't know what Granma and granpa say back and forth because they are talkin' soft like. I can't go to sleep because of the loud clock on the headboard, which goes tick ... tick ... tick... but 'ventually I go to sleep.

It's summertime and granpa comes into the bedroom where me and Celya are sleepin' and lifts me outa the bed and takes me outside and carries me to a garage. I'm so sleepy that I can't open my eyes for long. It ain't Granma and granpa's garage because they don't have no garage. There is a nice man with golden glasses that does things to me. I don't care what the man does because he don't hurt me none, and he smiles most of the time. I like him. Granpa tells me to bended over. The man is doing something that hurts me. I git ascared, but granpa is right there lookin', so I know it's alright. I'm in bare feet. Mama would have a tissy fit if she'd knowed I was standing on the concrete floor. I don't know what to do. I see my toes so I count my toes when the man do stuff to me. Celya jest teached me how to count to ten so I jest practice my numbers. One ... two ... three ... five. Oh oh, I gotta start all over agin. I do this over and over again. Granpa picks me up and carries me home after the man give him some paper money or granpa gives him money. *I'm confused.*

In 'nother bad dream, a nice mans holds my hand and walks me to a green car. Granpa is always watchin'. I'm glad he does. The seats don't look like granpa and Granma's seats, and they don't look like Mommy and daddy's car seats, neither. Granpa undresses me and lays me down on the seat. My head keeps hittin' the arm rest. It hurts so bad what the mans doing. The nice man puts me on top of somethin' then puts a white snake on my tummy. I scream because snakes haves poison in them. Now I'm up in the corner of the car lookin' down at me and the man. I don't know what he's doin', but I'm very, *very* ascared. Very ascared. That's all. Granpa puts me back in my pj's. Then granpa has a bunch of paper money, and the man and him talk about money like I told you. There is a big moon outside and it's not cold at all. The man walks to the back fence and says somethin' else to granpa. Granpa carries me to the inside of the house, takes me to the kitchen sink and kisses me on the lips, cries, then puts me back to bed. He don't tuck me in like Granma. This bad dream is the scariest to me, but I don't tell nobody 'bout what I dreamed. I try to keep my eyes open at nighttime as long as I can because of the bad dreams.

There is a loud train comin' and I know this because the bed shaked a little bit. Clickthump ... clickthump ... clickthump ... clickthump. I go back to sleep. That's all I dream 'bout at granpa and Granma's house, but now I dream that the monster is comin' to git me all the times.

[This is the second time I was molested. At this point I was confused because my grandfather looked on while the molestation was happening. I thought I was safe, and I enjoyed the special attention. But I was confused by my grandfather's stern expression. I took it as something strange. But of course, one does not have a frame of reference to know that anything might be unacceptable behavior, even if it causes physical pain.

I had what I thought were bad dreams. Only much later in therapy did I bring this "dream" up to my therapists. As I grew, shame formed around these events. As an adult, it was difficult to share what I'd dreamed as a child because I thought I was a very sick person, and I didn't want anyone to know this—as evil as it was. It was only when my therapist said, "Children don't have these kinds of dreams" that I accepted that I had indeed been molested as a child.

At that point in therapy I was still unaware that my father had also molested me. Our minds remember only when we are ready to handle something traumatic.]

∞∞∞

Mornin' at Granma and granpa's is like at home. The sound of pots and pans bangin' 'round and good smells and the sound of coffee percolatin', then the squeak of the oven door. The oven part is different from at my house, because my Granma and granpa don't have no heater in the house and Granma uses the oven to heat up the house. We have a stand-up heater in our house.

Granma comes into our room, wakes me and Celya the rest of the way up, and says, "Get up out of that bed now, wash up, and come to breakfast."

I can hardly wake up. Me and Celya eats corn flakes sometimes after we go to the bathroom and warsh our hands.

Granma always wears a clean, starched cookin' apron when she cooks. We eat high on the hog at Granma and granpa Burrough's house because sometimes Granma cooks eggs, bacon, and toast. No yucky Cream of Wheat or oatmeal like we have at home. Wowee!

Later on in the day, Celya asks fer pennies, but I *beg* for pennies from granpa or Granma. Granpa is a snap. He smiles, jingles the coins in his pocket, and says, "Well, let me see what I have here for you." He pulls out a bunch of moneys from his pant pocket and moves the coins around in the palm of his hand with his pointy finger. Then he gives us big money, like quarters, nickels, and dimes.

Granma is a different story. She always looks worried, shakes her head, and says, "We really can't spare any money." I pester Granma till finely she says, "Well, let me check and see." She pulls out her coin purse from her handbag and looks more nervous. She always looks nervous lessin' she is singin', playin' the guitar, or cookin'.

She looks in the coin purse and says, "I don't know, because your old grandpa drinks, and I may not have much more money until the end of the week. I still need to buy some milk for you girls."

I pester her and pester her until she comes up with a couple of pennies, nickels, or dimes. If we are lucky, she only has big money in her coin purse. She hands Celya a paper dollar bill, tells her to pick up a big bottle of RC sody pop, and tells us to give her back the change after we buy candy. Alls I know is Celya gives her back all the money that we didn't spend for candy. My sister's a good girl.

Anyways, pesterin' Granma is for a good reason, and she always gives in. Granma tells Celya not to let go of my hand on the way to and from the store, so Celya never lets go of my hand. Sometimes before we cross the road holdin' hands, I try to wiggle and squirm to git my hand loose and pull as hard as I can so'z Celya will let go of me. But Celya holds my hand tighter than before and tells me, "Quit wiggling around!" She says she isn't goin' to let go my hand and I better behave or she's gonna tell on me.

Sometime I git my hand loose, but Celya grabs it back right quick. "If you don't stop doing that, we will *both* get in trouble," she says. Celya don't like me trying to git away much because we are not yet safely in the store. Mama tells us to not ever go into or near *"that sinful place* next door to the store." I try to peek into that place to see if granpa is there. It's very dark and there are only a few mens there. I can see all kinds, shapes, and colors of bottles on the shelfs behind the bar man. It's where granpa drinks. I don't know what all the fuss is about, but Celya obeys every time and any time any grown-up tells her to do somethin' or other. I don't, and that's why I git into trouble so much. Granma says I'm a "handful."

Once we're inside the store, Celya lets go of my hand. Then, wowee! It's all there in front of our eyes, up on the shelves behind the store man's back: *candy and chew gum!*

Granma wants Celya to bring back some Juicy Fruit gum. Sometimes she asks for Beech-Nut gum though. I don't like Juicy Fruit so much as I like Beech-Nut gum. I like bubble gum the best, and you can git two pieces for a penny! The paper inside the wrapper has funny comic book pictures on it. Little bitty ones. Me and Celya save these papers so we can look at them later, then after we look at the comics for a long time we put them in our secret hidin' place. That's at my house, in my bedroom closet, up at the top where there's a hole between the trim and the wall. There is a big ol' roll of them with a rubber band around them.

We always ask the same thing when we come into the store and point at the same candies as usual. We git the best for our money by pointin' to bubble gum, Neccos, Chick O-Sticks, Red Hots, Sugar Daddys, Milk Duds, 3 Musketeers, taffy, or cinnamon toothpicks. And believe you me, that's not even all the candy.

There's little wax bottles you chew on with sweet juice inside and a bunch of other candies: Hershey bars, Big Hunks, and PayDays for a nickel. I like gum sometimes, but I like the candies betterer. We almost always git the same thing. We are good shoppers.

"How much are these?" We point, and the storekeeper tells us whether what we want is one penny, two for one penny, or a nickel each. I git the "two for ones" because you mostly git twice as many candies or bubble gum. I also like the candy cigarettes and the bubble gum cigars. The candy cigarettes look jest like real cigarettes.

The store man never minds us askin' how much this candy or the other is, and it's as if it's the very first time we ever bought anything from him. He's real nice. What Celya tries to figger out is how to match the money with the candy. After she makes her mind up, she puts all our money on the glass counter. The mans slides it all around to check Celya's figgers. Sometimes we git more money back than we come with, but mostly we end up using it all up buyin' more candies. Buyin' sody pop for Granma makes it 'fusing for Celya when she tries to count out the money. She's real good at countin' money though! I don't know how to count much yet.

On some days if granpa is at the store, he's usually in the small side room next to the storekeeper's store part. Most of the time Celya and me don't know if granpa is in that room.

Once granpa comes out to git me after the storekeeper goes inside the room. Granpa takes my hand, and we go into the man's room. Inside, on the windas behind a big desk, are a bunch of bottles that have different shapes, sizes, and all kinds of colors. They look purdy when the sun shines through the windas. I like the blue-colored bottles the best. The room has piles and piles of books and papers all over the place. Real high piles. Three chairs are right by the door because there ain't much empty space in the room nowheres.

Granpa and the mans drink special drinks in fancy glasses. Granpa likes beers best most of the time though. The mans isn't smiling at all like the man in the garage. This mans picks me up and sits me on his lap. I don't like that so much now that I'm a big girl, so I wiggle around and try to git off the man's lap. I feel a hard thing in the man's lap that wasn't there when he first put me there. I don't like that one little bit.

Granpa looks mean while he watches, but I tell him I don't want to sit on the man's lap no more and I want to go back to where Celya is in the store part. I pester granpa 'nough and he lets me go back into the store, but he don't look none too happy about it. Celya is left in the store all by herself. She says granpa takes me into that room lots of times, but I don't 'member. Then off me and Celya go to Granma and granpa's house. Celya makes sure that I hold her hand when we cross the street agin. I'm not as happy as I was when we walked to the store, but I have bunches of happy in me so no one can tell the difference 'cept when I cry.

Mama drops Thomas off with us the next day. Mama bring his wagon so'z we have somethin' to play with. Me, Thomas, and Celya take turns pushin' each other up and down the sidewalk. Me and Thomas have to push together because Celya is so big. This time my inside top legs hurt. I ask Celya if her legs hurt too.

She says, "No."

I only push the wagon a little bit more this time and say, "I don't wanna play no more." That's not usual for me because I like to play all the time no matter what.

I go into the house to be with Granma. She's in the bedroom foldin' and puttin' the clean clothes away. She has a bunch of scarves. I like the hot-pink one the best. She folds the pink scarf and I asks her if granpa ties up her hands like he does me.

She flutters around in the bedroom and don't say a word, then she looks mean and says, "You are a *very bad girl!* How could you ask such a thing as that? I don't want to ever hear anything more about that scarf! How you come up with such a thing is beyond me." She is mad at me but I don't understand why. This time I didn't do one little thing wrong.

One day Granma Burrough is with me and Celya in the corner

store to buy food for supper. Granma sorta moseys around in circles before she buys stuff and asks me what she should buy for supper. I don't know. I jest tell her what I like. Potatoes. I love potatoes!

This time when we are in the store with Granma, I say, "Granma, *please* tell granpa not to take me into that room no more." I point at the room. She don't hear me so we walk on to different foods.

I say to her agin. "Granma please, *please* don't let granpa take me into that room agin." Agin Granma don't hear me, but she acts fidgety.

I make a big fuss and 'ventually she says, "I'll talk to your grandpa."

"You promise?" I say.

Granma nods.

Done! It's done. I never ever have to go into that room agin.

We git home from Granma's and for some reason mama give me a spankin' when we git home. I guess Granma told her how bad I was. Granma don't spank us none but tells mama 'bout all the stuff I git into while she babysets us. Course, I'm all bruised up even before mama lays into me. Today I have to go to school, so she puts makeup on my face to hide the bruises she gave me yesterday. Sometimes after slappin' Thomas's face she has to put makeup on him too. But that's only a few times. Mostly I have to wear the yucky smelly stuff.

Celya don't never have to wear makeup.

I *hate* makeup.

Speaking of bruises, my feet git bruised jest from walking on them. The bruises are under my foot near my toes. Mama takes me to the doctor all the time because my legs are crooked and I walk funny. The doctors try to help with the braces and correct-ive shoes, but they don't keep me from gittin' bruises on my feet. I have to do regular exercises, like walking up and down our hall at home on my heels or turnin' my feet on their sides and walkin' with them that way up and down the hall over and over again. I have to wear corrective shoes to school now, along with the braces.

[I was molested by at least four men. In all cases except for when my father molested me, my grandfather looked on.]

Chapter 6: Suffer the Children to Come Unto Me

1956

Sundee school is called the children's worship service, and it's in the old white church that looks like it's gonna fall apart any minute now. The floor squeaks and groans when you walk on it. The big people have their call to worship in the new church sanctuary. At least that's what Mama calls it—the *sanctuary*. That's the biggest room in the new church, with wooden chairs stuck to the floor. Behind the pulpit and the choir seats is a big ol' bathtub where people git baptized.

For being French, Mama sure has lots of fancy English words that no one else uses for stuff. She calls it a *divan* instead of *couch* or *sofa*. Stuff like that. The children at school don't know what I'm talkin' 'bout half the time when I say certain words. No one in church ever calls it a *sanctuary*. I'm not real sure 'bout that, but I'm pretty sure. All the children meet in the old church sanctuary.

Mr. and Mrs. King lead the children's worship service. Each age group (toddlers to sixth grade) sits together for the main meetin', which is very very fun. There are always surprise prizes that are handed out to whoever wins somethin'.

Before we go to church, Mama always says, "Billy, do you have any money for the children's offering?" Mama and daddy always come up with a few moneys for us to put in the offering plate.

Daddy calls out, "Cecilia ... Cynthia ... Thomas. Come here." When we git to him and stand around him, he pulls out from his pocket his red oval-shaped coin purse with the slit in the middle. Then he squeezes the two ends in one hand and says, "Let's see." He moves the change around with his pointy finger, then pulls out a few coins and puts the change into our cupped hands. Usually they're pennies though. Nickels and dimes are what he calls "big money."

He puts the coins in each of our hands, then he says, "Girls, go put the change in your purse. Thomas, you come here." He takes Thomas's money out of his little cupped hands and puts it into Thomas's tiny pocket. "Now don't lose these, Thomas," he says.

Thomas nods with very serious eyes. Off Celya and me go, bouncin' to our bedroom.

Mr. King is the children's service pastor. He has shiny, see-through gray hair, and he is very kind and gentle. I like his smile. He has good teeth and wears silver glasses.

When we git into church, we all have to "simmer down," and once we git quiet, Mr. King says a prayer.

"Dear Lord Jesus, blah blah blah ... In Jesus's name, amen."

And we all say "amen" after he says it.

After that we have to say two pledges of 'legiance. The first one is the regular one we say in school. The next one is the Christian one. It takes time to git ready 'cause the teacher of the youngest childrens has to show them how to cross their heart. Some of them are really dim-witted, and the teacher has to help them cross their heart every Sundee. Here goes:

The Pledge of 'Legiance
I pledge 'legiance to the flag of the 'nited States of 'merica, and to the 'public for which it stands, one nation under God, invisible, With liverty and just us for all.
Anonymous, Paraphrased
Published September 8, 1892
Revision by President Dwight D. Eisenhower, June 14, 1954
Second Paraphrase 2015

Even in school, that one don't make no sense to me. Here goes the Christian one:

Pledge to the Christian Flag
I pledge 'legiance to the Christan Flag and to the Savor for whose Kingdom it stands. One Savor, crus-fied, risen, and comin' 'gen with life and liverty to all who beliefs.
Charles C. Overton, Paraphrased
September 26, 1897
Second Paraphrase 2015

I bet all you nonbelievers didn't know we have that Christian flag one. We have to say it because this is church, after all.

Our children's service is almost like the big people's service but *tons* better. Mr. King asks if someone wants to say a Bible verse by heart for the next week's service. When we git called on, we have to go to the front and say what we rememberized the week before. I don't like to do this because I'm always shakin' in my boots and hopin' I don't mess it up and not rememberize the whole verse right, but I do it anyways because we are the Burrough family and that means we are real spiritual. Mama says, "We have to set a spiritual example for others." I don't have no Sundee boots, but if I did, I would ruin them by shakin' so hard. My big sister, Celya, helps me at home to rememberize the verse when it's my turn. I do like showin' off to big people though.

Finely Mama says Thomas is old 'nough to go to our church. He is so cute. That's one thing I can say 'bout my brother. 'For we go to church, Mama puts Brylcreem on Thomas's hair. When we go to church Thomas wears a brown-and-tan little outfit. Instead of pants, he has shorts that are brown, a white shirt with a brown bow tie, and a jacket over that. The jacket is tan. He wears that outfit *forever*, but he don't seem to mind. He probly don't know no different.

One Sundee Thomas raises his hand to say that he wants to rememberize a Bible verse for next Sundee. No one believes that he can do that. For Pete's sake, it weren't that long ago when he learnt to walk and talk. Mr. King winks at him, leans over, and whispers somethin' into Thomas's ear.

Mama finds out 'bout it and says it's a secret what verse Thomas is goin' to say and he isn't suppost to tell nobody, 'cluding us girls. He smiles real big, as if sayin', "I gotta secret. I gotta secret and I'm not tellin' you."

This whole next week I pester him like mad, tryin' to git him to tell me the secret. Mama hears me pesterin' him and tells me to stop it or I will make him cry. He looks like he is 'bout to cry anyways. I stop for the day or two, then start pesterin' him all over again. I can see that he isn't gonna give in to me by Sundee. Boy, that must be *some* secret. I'm really kinda proud of him for not givin' in to me. That's hard to do even if you are a grown-up. Not give into me, I mean.

Sundee. It's finely time for him to git in front of us all and say his Bible verse. I jest know he can't git it because I never heard him practice at home and he's so young. Thomas walks to the front of the room holdin' his Sundee school teacher's hand. She lets go and goes back to her chair. I can hardly wait. It gits real quiet like. Mr. King leans over and whispers somethin' in Thomas's ear. Here it comes: the secret he kept all week long. Everyone, 'cluding the teachers, sit forward in their chairs.

Mr. King whispers somethin' to Thomas agin, but I hear Mr. King say, "Now say it real big and loud."

Thomas jest stands in front of everybody smilin' until Mr. King says, "Go ahead now." It's so quiet you could hear a pin drop. Then Thomas says nice and loud, "Jesus wept."

The older children and the Sundee school teachers clap. I'm so proud of him I could bust.

Thomas is the *youngest* to ever say a Bible verse in front of the church. After that he jest stands there and smiles till his Sundee school teacher helps him git over to his seat.

We sing too in Sundee school. I like that a lots because the songs are fun, like:

Jesus Loves Me
Jesus loves me—this I know,
for the Bible tells me so;
Little ones to Him belong—
They are weak, but He is strong.

Yes, Jesus loves me!
The Bible tells me so ...
Anna Bartlett Warner, Lyrics 1860
William Batchelder Bradbury
Music and Arrangement

Another song we sing is "This Little Light of Mine." This is my favorite. I like when we yell out "... light it under a bush oh *no!*"

Mrs. King shushes us to stop us from talkin', then Mr. King gives a short sermon and prays agin. Then the teachers take the offering. We put our pennies, nickels, and dimes in a basket that the teachers hand out then take away. I'm not sure if they take the moneys to Jesus, but I know one thing: if they don't take it to Jesus, they are gonna be in big trouble!

After takin' the offering, Mr. King says that if anyone wants to "take Jesus into your heart and become born again," they should raise their hand. I don't know why he says to do that. He shoulda said, "Raise your arm." Some of the little ones raise their arms every week, but we all know it's because they see the big children raise theirs.

Well, I know full well that I have been born once and don't wanna do it two times. I think it's silly. I guess Mr. King has to do special stuff to make these children "born again" because he always wants them to come up to him after the service. It must of hurt real bad, since Mama always says, "Childbirth is painful." Oh boy, I feel sorry for them children. They don't know what they are in for. I don't know, neither, but if Sundee school is all serious and quiet, I know they are gonna git it. And that is another reason I don't wanna become "born again."

I'm sad. I don't know nothin' about nobody else, but I think of all them children goin' to hell 'cause they don't raise their arms. I think 'bout me goin' to hell too and burnin' in the lake of fire.

In Sundee school class all the children git picked up by their parents. I'm the last and only one left with the teacher. She cleans up all the messes that we made. I start cryin' because I'm sure that Mama and daddy forgits me on purpose because I done somethin' real bad and they don't want me no more. I'm one pitiful thing, with tears runnin' down my cheeks. The teacher says that they didn't forgit me, but I know they did. My teacher has to walk with me to find Mama or daddy. I'm pretty sure she don't want me to come live with her. Mama and daddy are stuck with me, and that's all there is to that.

[This time of my life was frightening for me because my mother said that I was still too young to "ask Jesus into my heart." The seed of fear was planted quickly and began to take root. Sunday school was mixed with happy things for me, yet I believed that I would be sent to hell before I was old enough to become a Christian. Once I became "born again," an impossible list of everything I needed to do to be "good" was set in front of me.

But I could never measure up to the standard. This set me up for a life of unending failure and fear. I believed that every time I did something wrong, I'd sinned. When I was punished by my parents or teachers, I felt that I was headed down the slippery slope to hell.

I was in anguish regarding this throughout childhood.]

Chapter 7: Kendeegarden

1956

I'm a big girl now, so I can go to kendeegarden with my bestest friend, Caroljean, from 'cross the street. I walk home with my other bestest friend named Mark. He teaches me how to sneeze right. You put your fingers on your nose and pinch, then you sneeze. Mark does that all the time because he has something called algees. I sneeze like he does now because it feels good to do it that way. Brenda from 'cross the street is my bestest friend too besides Caroljean. She lives next to Caroljean, but I don't like her as much as Caroljean.

Mark makes me laugh. Kristina is my bestest friend in school, but she lives far, far away, so I don't git to walk home with her. Kristina has dark curly hair that looks purdy but funny to me. My hair is clean plumb straight. Caroljean lives with Patty, my sister's bestest friend.

Mommy's on the phone with Aunt Carol *all the time* still 'cept when Aunt Carol is over to our kitchen talkin' to Mommy, or when Mommy is over at Aunt Carol's kitchen. They talk all the time there too. Talk. Talk. Talk. Talk is all they ever do.

I don't like my little brother, Thomas, one little bit when he is first born because I don't git most of the 'tention. He smells somethin' awful when his diapers have to be changed. Then he smells even worse when Mommy or Celya opens up his diaper. It makes me gag! *And* the house always stinks like dirty diapers and 'monia. Well, I do sorta like him when he is jest doin' baby things

65

and not smellin' up the house so much.

I love the smell of finger paint. I jest *love* it. My teacher opens a jar of blue paint and lets everyone smell it. She also takes out jars of yellow and red to teach us our colors, but I already know my colors.

The day before we finger paint, the teacher says, "Now children, you will need to bring in one of your daddy's old shirts to wear, so you won't get your clothes dirty when you paint. I would like you to bring in the shirts tomorrow."

Now, we suppost to bring in one shirt or two? Big people don't make no sense. So it's a good thing that she sent us home with a note pinned to our clothes. I don't know where Mommy is gonna git an old shirt from daddy. He wears all of his shirts until they are threadbare. The other shirt besides his work shirts is white, and they are like new because he only wears them to church. I don't know what *threadbare* means, but I know daddy wears his shirts till they are all ragadee, and then Mommy takes them shirts and makes them into cleanin' rags.

So, Mommy calls around to people to find a shirt, and I ended up wearin' some other man's shirt. This is O.K. with me because daddy's shirts stink from his work even after Mommy washes them. This other man's shirt don't stink none. It's *real big* though. I have a hard time findin' the arm holes, and when I find the second hole, my other arm slips outa the first hole. The teacher has to help me put on my shirt backward, roll up the sleeves a lots, and button the shirt in the back.

Mrs. Mahoney is my teacher in kendeegarden. She is *real* old and she looks kinda crunchity. I mean, she wears clothes that are real old too. She wears the same dark-blue dress with white itsee bitsee pokey dots and a big white lace collar all the time, but she don't have to wear no shirt when we paint. She has to roll our shirt sleeves up real high over and over agin because they fall down.

Slow as slow can be, the teacher and her helper wets all the papers. "Don't start until everyone has a piece of paper and paint on the paper," she says. I can't never understand why grown-ups say that. By the time she has wetted all the children's papers, the first children have to git theirs done *agin* because their papers start to dry out. *Finely* the paint jar lids are twisted off, and my teacher and a lady I don't ever seen before goes 'round the room tappin' a spoon full of paint on the papers. *Tap, tap, tap.*

"Now children, what color is this?" teacher asks. How stupid! I already know my colors and some numbers because my sister Celya teached me them. One more time Mrs. Mahoney picks up 'nother jar, tellin' the children the color. We have to say out loud what the colors is.

Since I already know that stuff and have some of my colors, I dig in with my hands, movin' the paint every which way before everyone gits their paints. Now I got almost all my paint. It feels so good. Oozy, messy, mushy, and squishy between my fingers and fist. I splat my hand down on the paper, but I don't like the way that looks. All of a sudden Mrs. Mahoney looks at me and says that I'm "not to start." *Everyone* bosses me around. She finishes off with a jar with red paint in it and walks 'round the room with the spoon tap, tap, tappin' on the papers.

She asks, "Now children, does anyone know what color this is?" I do but I'm ascared to say anything case I'm wrong. She does the same way with all them other colors. How dumb can you be? I mean the children, not the teacher. Then she goes 'round the room with one last color. Wow. This is gonna be fun, fun, fun! Down my hands go onto the paper agin. They glide this way and that, pullin' in more and more colors until it looks all brown. Yuck. Uh oh. I gone too far, but I can't help myself. It smells and feels so good. The other children seem to know when to stop mixin' the colors. My picture is *very* ugly.

Mommy says to me sometimes, "You just do not know when to quit." Now I know she is right 'bout finger paintin'. Mrs. Mahoney hangs up our wet papers to dry on a string with clothespins on it. She takes our shirts, and we wash our hands off in a jest-our-size white sink. I watch the colored water spin down, down, and around into the drain. It's almost as fun as it is to finger paint.

Mrs. Mahoney tells me to hurry up "because the other children have to wash their hands too." It's hard to hurry up because the colors make pretty shapes in the water.

The other day we got to use jest-our-size easels with troughs in the front that holds the paint jars. The teacher showed us how to mix the dry powder colors with water that turns into paint. We didn't git to pour the powder or the water into the jars, but we had to mix the water and paint up like mad. The teacher was busy all over the place.

To my way of thinkin', the paint is usually too thin. It drips down the paper and wrecks the paintings. I like paintin', but I'm so "taken" (Granma Burrough's word) by the colors that a lots of times my paper ends up with brown paint all over it agin. Mrs. Mahoney makes us take all our papers home. I git two big ol' fat gold stars on all my papers, 'cept when I don't.

At Christmastime the kendeegarden class puts on a play that is 'Twas The Night Before Christmas.

'Twas the Night Before Christmas
'Twas the night before Christmas, when all through
   the house
Not a creature was stirring, not even a mouse;
The stockings were hung by the chimney with care,
In hopes that St. Nicholas soon would be there ...
Clement Clarke Moore
December 23, 1823

All of us have to act out the story. Sugar plums dance in the story. I do *not* wanna be a *stupid* sugar plum fairy. I pray *not* to be a sugar plum fairy. I beg Mommy *not* to let Mrs. Mahoney make me a sugar plum fairy, but Mommy says she can't do nothin' 'bout that. Oh, the *trials* (Grandma Rasmussen uses this word) of children in kendeegarden. I don't know what a sugar plum fairy is, but I *don't wanna be one!* I do *not* wanna wear the *stupid* frilly tu-tu dress. I like pants, and Santy Claus gotta wear pants. I wanna be the Santy Claus!

Guess what I gotta be? A *stupid sugar plum fairy* that don't even dance a real dance. We jest have to twirl 'round and 'round.

Soon we will be doin' the real play, in front of big people. There is some other grown-ups that help us put our costumes on for the play. *Where did they come from?* I wonder. I'd never seen them big people before in my whole life. I'm ascared.

We wait in a line *forever* and are bein' told over and over agin to "be quiet and stay in line" by the big people. More bosses! Come on now. All the childrens are five years old 'cept me. I'm four, but that don't give them grown-ups no right to point at me when they say somethin' or jerk me around.

We are finely goin' into our room. I almost fall out of line laughin' to see all them big people sittin' in our little chairs.

There are four of us that are fairies and have to twirl around wearing frilly fru-fru dresses with our hands in the air. "Mama in her kerchief and Papa in his cap" are on their pretend bed pretendin' they are sleepin'. All us fairies almost step on Mama's long blonde hair when we dance near the headboard. There is very little space to dance in. You tell me. All the grown-ups take all the extra space in our classroom! Us sugar plum fairies are payin' more 'tention to Mama's head than twirlin'. I don't know why we have to twirl. Mama keep givin' us fairies dirty looks when we step on her hair. I for one accidentally step on Mama's hair when I try to dance.

So we *don't* do a very good job. Not our fault. The teacher is doin' a crummy job of tellin' us what to do in the first place. She was rushin' around the room like a chicken with her head cut off when we practiced before the big people come in. What the sugar plum fairies do sorta wrecks the whole play because the big people laugh so hard.

∞∞∞

1957

Catalogs. I look at them catalogs 'specially when I'm doin' Christmas shoppin'. Christmas shoppin' for me, myself, and I. There's JCPenney, Wards, and Sears catalogs. Mommy's in the kitchen bakin' cookies for Christmastime, and I sit at the dining table and drool over all the boys' toys in the catalogs.

"Mommy! Look at *this!* I hope Santy Claus brings me this one."

Too bad some of the children don't believe in Santy Claus. Lots of us talk 'bout if he is for true or not. Alls I know is that I believe in Santy Claus and he brings me real good toys. Both grandmas buy us new things like clothes too. That's mostly what Mommy asks them to git for us children.

Mommy wants me to stop lookin' at the toys in the catalogs and "do something useful," so I lick some Blue Chip Stamps and put them in the special book. We git the stamps when we go grocery shoppin'. Mommy looks in a little book and saves and saves up stamps so she can git somethin' for free. We have Green Stamps books, too, but not so many Green Stamps as them blue ones.

There's one thing I think is real magic 'bout Santy Claus. When we go shoppin', Celya and me git to sit on Santy Claus's lap and tell him what we want for Christmas. By the time we git to the next store, Santy Claus is already there! He looks different, but it's him all right. I always hope daddy will drive as fast as he can to see if we can beat Santy Claus to the next store. We never do. That's why Santy Claus is magic, besides flyin' in the air and comin' in houses that don't have no chimney like at our house. Sometimes Santy Claus's breath smells real bad though.

You know? I'm never sure if Santy Claus is going to git me anything because Mommy says that I'm a bad girl all the time.

Kristina was one of my bestest friend that lives far away. Her black hair is always done up real purdy, and she always wears real purdy frilly dresses. Jest like Sundee clothes. She has a bunch of different ones too. She wears a new one every day of the week, and there's a lots of days in a week. The week is very, *very* long. I'm always funnin' with her and makin' up stories to make her laugh. Sometimes I like to make her scream too.

The other children know I'm ascared of no bugs 'cept pincher bugs, but I sure as shootin' not pickin' one of them other bugs up. We git ugly scary potato bugs up under the house, and we make daddy go and git 'em out. The children, 'specially Caroljean and Mark, call me over to see whatever big bug they find in the play yard.

I come back to Kristina and I says, "Kristina, there's a purdy butterfly over there." She comes over to see it and sometimes it's a big daddy long legs, a potato bug, or a salamander or frog that one of them children brings in a jar. She always screams and I always laugh. You'd think she woulda figgered it out that when Caroljean or Mark calls me over to see somethin' that I'm gonna git her to see what I seen to scare her. If it always scares her, she shouldn't keep a comin' to where I tell her to come. 'Ventually she guesses though, but school is almost over when she does. Then we have summertime.

One day Kristina brings a chocolate candy to school. "Just for you," she says. It's one of those fancy ones that big people getta eat from purdy white boxes. In my house we never git those 'cept daddy. He always shares some with me and Celya though. Anyways, Kristina tries to give the piece of chocolate-covered candy to me. Now, Mommy says we can't eat *nobody's* food 'cept our own because we will git germs. "You'll git sick if you do," Mommy says. So I says "no" to Kristina a bunches of times and finely tell her that I can't eat other people's food. She keeps tellin' me that there's nothin' wrong with the candy and that I won't git germs. That candy looks soooooo good, but I'm shakin' in my boots. She's my bestest friend, so finely I can't help myself. I take the candy and bite down hard.

Kristina laughs and laughs. It's made of rubber. This is how she gits me back for all the tricks I play on her. I know that is fair, so I laugh with her. It's a good joke and the funniest thing I ever seen. But I kinda feel sorry for myself because the thought of that candy makes my mouth water, and I not ever gonna eat the real thing.

I git in a real lots of trouble in kendeegarden. There's big ol' wood blocks there. Daddy says they are "eighteen inches square." Daddy knows everything because he uses wood in the basement to make things. He goes to the basement a lots.

The blocks in kendeegarden look heavy, but they're not so much if you jest push them around on the floor. When it rains outside, we gotta play with those big ol' blocks in school. One time it rains "for days on end." Mrs. Mahony 'sides to make groups of three children to play with the blocks. Each day it rains she picks some more different children. I keeps waitin' and waitin' for my name to be called. I don't want to be called because I want to play with the blocks all by myself. All the childrens are called on, 'cept me. Now it's my turn!

Mrs. Mahony asks, "Is there anyone that hasn't played with the blocks?" and my hand shoots up. I'm so happy that I git to play with the blocks alone. I want to build a pirate ship all by myself. For days I jest sat there and dreamed up all kinds of stuff 'bout the pirate ship. I dreamed 'bout bein' a pirate and yellin', "Timber me shimber!" I pretended that I was in a boat way out in the waters fishin' by myself. I thought up lots more, but these ones are the best ones. Now the time is here. I finely git to play with them blocks. No one has ever made a boat. I could show the teacher how smart I am. The teacher don't pick no other children, so I run over to the blocks even though the teacher says, "No running inside" and I start puttin' the boat together.

I begin to build my the pointy front part, then the sides, and then I put in the seats, too. Last I put on the back of the boat. It's jest the way I want it to be. The teacher don't look yet. Then a boy comes over and starts movin' *my* blocks around.

I yell at him real big, "It's my turn and you can't play with my blocks!" He's a crybaby and starts cryin'. *That's* when the teacher looks up, but the boat is all wrecked by now because of the boy.

The teacher is mad and tells me I'm suppost to share. She never spanks nobody, but the paddle is on a hook behind her desk where everyone can see, so'z we don't git bad. She sorta drags me over to the paddle. I think for sure that I will be the first one in our class to git hit.

I'm so 'prised when she says, "Sit there and think about what you just did. That was a very naughty thing to do. We *always* must share in this class."

I don't think that's fair because I waited a long, long, long time to play with them blocks *all by myself*. But she don't paddle me none, so I guess what I done wasn't so bad. Mommy and daddy paddle me lots of times.

Instead of spankin' me, she gits to her desk and starts a writin'. Then she comes over to me and pins a folded piece of paper to my dress.

When I git home Mommy reads the note and gits real mad. "How could you embarrass me in front of the *teacher?* I'm gonna give you something to think about, young lady, so you will not do this again." (She is always giving me somethin' to think 'bout. You'd think I was real smart by now.) Then she spanks me with daddy's thick belt "up one side and down the other within an inch of my life."

I don't 'member, but I think this is the first time she has spanked me for so long with daddy's belt and "I tell you me" (Mommy says that lots), boy oh boy, it hurts a lots more than when she shakes me hard and hits me with her hand.

I guess that it's bad to 'barrass her "in front of the teacher." She wasn't even in front of the teacher unless she was hiding in the corner of the room. Mommy's sneaky like that though, but she did say, "in front of the teacher." Mommy never lies, so that's that. Mommy can see me even if she's not with me. This is when the spankin's turn into beatin's. This is the beginning of when I'm bad lots of times.

Mommy don't want us children to walk in the ditch water because of polio. Course, I do it anyways. There is a boy in kendeegarden who is real cute and smiles all the time. He comes to school with braces on and crutches. He also has a hearing aid in his shirt pocket that screeches and squeals somethin' awful. He's absent a lots.

They don't have no shots for poison ivy, though, and lots of my friends git that and have to put stinky calamine lotion on.

They say it still itches after they put calamine lotion on it, so I can't figger out why the parents put calamine lotion on poison ivy at all. All us children think that you can catch the poison ivy from the other children that have it. So, the person with the poison ivy itch gits chased and yelled at because they have cooties. Cooties are yucky, blicky germs that you can git if someone with them touches you.

Calamine lotion stinks, but not so bad as Noxzema. Eileen at school has cracked, dried skin that bleeds, and her mother puts Noxzema on her sores every day. Nobody wants to be around Eileen because she smells bad. But you know what? She smiles all the time jest like Kevin. I feel sorry for her, and sometimes I ask her to play with the rest of us girls. She seems real tickled when I do that. My hands crack and blood comes out sometimes, but not because I have a disease like Eileen. Mama says we have chapped hands because we have to warsh our hands so much. Mama puts a special cream on her hands so her hands don't hurt. I put Vaseline on my hands jest when they git real bad. I don't understand, but the rest of the children at school don't have no chapped hands. Mama is tellin' the truth because the children don't warsh their hands, so their hands are filthy and they might git pinworms.

'Ventually we don't have to git polio shots. They put the medicine on a sugar cube. Yum. They also begin to put somethin' called fluoride in *our* water so our teeth won't git cavities and fall out. The water still tastes like water. I still git cavities. I don't think they put fluoride in our water.

Kevin never comes back to school.

∞ ∞ ∞

1958

Every day mama makes me take a nap. Celya don't have to take naps 'cause she's better and older than me. I hate naps. Anyways, mama lays me down for a nap.

Mama said to daddy, "Billy, Cecilia's bed is too small. She has to sleep with her legs bent up." So daddy went and bought me and Celya this used twin bed set. I git the one that has a marked-up headboard and Celya (as usual) gits the nice one.

Mama and daddy say that's because I "don't know how to take care of things." I'm very angry now because I got the headboard that's all marked up. Mama and daddy say that Celya's bed belongs to her and my bed belongs to me. So my bed is *my* bed no matter what. It has scratches and holes that form three sides of a square. Someone used a nail or somethin' like that, but anyone can see that the square isn't finished.

I jest can't go to sleep, so I look at the ceiling. Aunt Carol comes in to check on me, but I play possum. I still can't go to sleep, so I look at the wall and pretend to see all kinds of faces on it. I stare hard, and the faces change into other faces, but I still can't go to sleep! Aunt Carol comes in agin and pulls the comforter up over me. I'm still pretending that I'm asleep. Usually when I do look at the wall like that, I can go to sleep, but it's not working this time. This is driving me nuts. I want to sleep fast so I can git up and play with Patty, Carol Jean, and Celya, but the box makes me stay awake even more.

I'm jest lying here wide awake, so I turn on my tummy and lean over the mattress, where there is a small box full of green and red Man-op-o-ly houses. (That's a game.) I fiddle with those pieces for a little bit. I spot a long, thin nail up against the inside edge of the box with no head on it.

Hmm. What can I do with this? I think. I try to git the nail out of the box and I nearly fall out the bed. Finely I have this nail thingy, and I'm turning it every which way but loose. I still can't figger out what to do with it.

I roll over on my back and tilt my head up to look at the headboard. I look hard at the scratches—a dot here and a dot there, with a line going from one corner dot to the other.

This is my bed, so I can do whatsoever I want to do with it, I think. It bothers me that the box isn't finished yet, so I 'cide to make the scratch marks into a square. It's my bed, right? I'm takin' the nail, and in the lower place, where there should be a hole to match the other holes, I roll the nail thingy 'round and 'round.

"Boy, this wood is hard!" I say. As I push in the second hole, Aunt Carol comes in. Right away she sees what I'm doin' and says, "Ooooooh. Wait until your mother sees this."

Uh oh, I think. But I don't understand why I'm in trouble. I guess she does not realize that I'm makin' the headboard look alright.

Mama comes rushin' into the room.

I did it now. But it's my bed, I think.

She looks at what I did and goes rushin' off to the kitchen to git the belt for spankin' off the towel rack. She grabs me out of the bed by my arm and begins to whale on me. She tells me to stay on the bed and not move a muscle.

Those dreaded words come out of her mouth: "Just you wait until your daddy gets home!"

She's whalin' on me for a long time. She leaves and comes back a bunch of times to whack me some more.

Daddy's home now, and he comes into the bedroom. He is starting to hit on me and says, "This is the *last* time I do *anything nice* for you."

Then he goes off to the kitchen and, with an angry voice, tells my mama how mad he is. Mama comes into my room and spanks me some more while yellin' at me and sayin', "Whatever got into your head?"

I don't know what to say because I'm cryin' so hard. She leaves the room, and daddy comes in agin. I start screamin'.

I can't feel anything but pain.

After he finishes with me he says, "You will just do without dinner. Maybe that will teach you."

I cry and cry and am almost done with the cryin' when mama comes in and spanks me some more. Back and forth, on and on, first mommy then daddy spank me.

I'm so tired and hungry.

It's nighttime now, and daddy comes in and yells at me to "get into that bed!" after he spanks me some more.

I fall asleep.

Then daddy comes in and pulls the mattress clean off the bed with me on it. "If you can't appreciate your bed, from now on you are going to sleep on the floor." Then he starts hittin' on me some more. Something pops in my leg. I think my leg is broken.

He leaves, so I start prayin' to myself and God, "Now I lay me down to sleep, I pray the Lord my soul to keep, if I should die before I wake, I pray the Lord my soul to take."

I know I'm gonna die tonight.

Daddy comes back and spanks me some more. Then mama comes to the door and says to Daddy, "Billy that's enough."

He stops. I go to sleep crying.

I'm still alive.

Chapter 8: Over the River and Through the Woods

1958

It's Sundee after church, and mama calls Grandma Rasmussen (her mama) to see if it's O.K. to come over. We don't git to see this grandma much because Grandpa George and her live far away. Grandma says that we can come over, so I jump for joy. Grandma Rasmussen, Grandpa George, and Uncle Billy live in Concord, California, where it's real hot. It takes a long time to git to their house. It's right smack-dab on the private golf course. When we are at Grandma's house, she makes sure that mama and daddy don't smack me around. I love Grandma Rasmussen.

The road we take to Grandma and Grandpa's is a single-lane dirt road. Only one car can go up or down it at a time. The tire tracks from the farmers' trucks and tractors are deep because of the rain and are burned into the dirt road once it gits hot. This makes the way we go slow and bumpy. The car squeaks and bucks all over the place. This is fun until I git carsick. Celya gits carsick too. She gits sick a lots more than me.

Mostly it's hot when we go to Grandma Rasmussen's, and we git to swim in the country club swimmin' pool to cool off. Grandma is pretty wishy-washy 'bout lettin' us swim in the pool because a member of Grandpa George's family has to be there with us. Most times Uncle Billy is there. But sometimes he's not.

Grandma has to call some people to see if it's O.K. for us to go swimmin' or to check and see if Uncle Billy is there at the pool.

Grandma is really scared of water because once she got stuck in an undertow, (whatever that is) when she was a young girl and almost drowned, so it's a dark day in hell when she takes us to the swimmin' pool even if it's a short ways from her house. I think an undertow has somethin' to do with the way they measure the water. You know, like ten toes equal one foot of water, and one foot makes an undertow. Somethin' like that. Grandma's story makes sense to me once I figgered that out. Too many toes makes you drowned.

Grandpa George or Grandma never take no one anywheres in their car. Ever. All Grandma does is sit in her big chair, talk to mama, drink coffee, and smoke cigarettes. Sometimes mama and Grandma talk French when daddy and Grandpa George is not around, but mostly they talk regular.

Anyways, to git to Grandma and Grandpa's house, we have to ride on a very lumpy bumpy road. I like those words. Lumpy bumpy. The air is dry and dusty, and it smells like dry hay, weeds, and cow's poop.

Mama says, "Billy, watch out!"

Daddy shoots back, "I see it. *I see it.*"

Mama says, "Billy, you're too close to the edge." Mama has to look out the rolled-down windows to make sure we don't drive into the ditch because it could be a long time before anyone finds us on that road, and it's so hot that we might die. We pull over to the edge as close as we can, stop, and let another car, truck, or tractor goin' in the other direction go by. I'm scared that we will fall over the edge and git stuck in the ditch out in the middle of nowheres. My stomach is pretty bunched up comin' and goin' on that dadgum road.

Mama says, excitedly, "Pull over. Billy? *Pull over!*"

"I *am* pulled over," daddy says, all 'zasperated-like. He says, "We're not really supposed to be on this road."

The road belongs to the farmers, and we aren't suppost to ride on it at all. This don't never make no sense to me. How come the road is for the farmers? A road's a road, and everyone can use a road.

It takes a real long time to git to Grandma and Grandpa's because we have to go so slow as a snail on the lumpy bumpy road.

'Cept for it bein' so hot in the car, the ride is sorta fun. The car bucks up and down and side to side. If you pretend, it feels like ridin' a horse. Since we don't have nothin' to do in the car, me and my sister start singin' for all it's worth. When we wash and dry the dishes at home, Celya teaches me songs she learnt in school. So we both know the songs good. We learn songs from the radio too. We mostly like The Everly Brothers when they sing "Bye Bye, Love."

I git tired of both of us singin' the same notes, so I 'cide to go into a lower note like Granma Burrough does when she sings. They call it harmony. It's not the harmony that you eat. I don't know 'zactly what it is, but it's funner to match up the notes this way. We git asked to sing in front of the con-gre-ga-tion at church, so when we ride in the car we have time to practice a new song or go over ones we already know and try to do them better, like "Go Tell It on the Mountain." I started singin' with my sister in front of the church when I was 'bout five years old and she was seven.

It's so hot that after a while we go to sleep, and one of us goes to sleep with our head in the other one's lap. We always fight 'bout whose turn it is to do that. I lie jest so I can do it more than Celya. When my sister sleeps in my lap, I barely touch her eyelashes so she almost wakes up. I also mess with her nose the same way. It makes me laugh inside when she tries to brush away the fly that's not there. I can't understand why she don't never try to do somethin' like that to me. She is jest a nice sister, I guess.

She don't know how to change her voice like me, but she knows how to make herself burp. I make her do it over and over again till she can't do it no more. Burp, I mean. I think it's funny. Wish I could do that.

Grandpa George is a groundskeeper (whatever that is) for the ritzy golf course.

When we rolls up to Grandpa and Grandma's house, Grandma looks all real sad. I bounce out the car and run to her, and she always has a twinkle in her eyes once she sees me. She hugs me, takes my face in her hands, and gives me a big, juicy kiss on my lips. That's the only thing I don't like 'bout Grandma Rasmussen: the juice in the kiss. But it's worth it jest to be near Grandma.

My brother, Thomas, jumps out of the car after me but don't run right over to Grandma. He jest has a big ol' smile on his cute little face. I think he holds back because he knows Grandma loves me best. He comes over to Grandma, and she takes his face in her hands and kisses him with a juicy kiss too. He don't mind none though. The juice, that is. I know this because I wipe the juice off my lips and he don't.

My sister? I jest don't see much difference from her usual way, though she smiles real big. She's the last of us to hug Grandma. She don't like to be touched much, though, most the time.

Nothin' matters now because I'm "the apple of Grandma's eye." I don't know what that means and I can't figger it out none. I jest know she would do anything she could for me.

I wish she was my mama.

Finally, after all the hugs and kisses, she lets out a yell to Grandpa George. "Put those *goddamn dogs* away, George!"

Grandma sure can swear! Mama hates it, 'specially 'round us children, but that's jest the way Grandma is. "Sons of a bitches" this and "*that* goddamn" that. My other granma don't swear none because she's a Christian.

When we git into the house, me and Celya wanna watch TV, but golfin' is on. It takes a long time before it's all over, but Grandpa George really likes golfin', and heaven forbid anyone ask him to switch channels. He's always messin' 'round with this gold-and-brown box with a knob on it with two wires stickin' up in the air so he can see the picture better. This little box sits on top of the TV. Daddy tells me that there's a 'tenna on the roof, and Grandpa makes it move one way or the other by turning the knob on the box so the picture comes in clearer. Sometimes it don't work so good, and the picture is all fuzzy lookin'.

Grandpa George gives me a busted watch, and daddy says, "Let's see if I can fix it for you." Mama don't like us saying *busted*, but it feels better in my mouth than *broke*, so I watch out for when I say *busted* so she won't catch me sayin' it. We're not sup-post to say *ain't* either.

Daddy does fix the busted watch, but it don't take no time before I break it and daddy fixes it agin so it ticks. I put it up to my ears because I like to hear the tick ... tick ... tick ... tick. Here. You can listen to it too if you want to.

When golfin' is over, daddy and Grandpa George head outside to talk 'bout bees, turkeys, chickens, ducks, geese, and fruit trees. Grandpa has all these, but mostly they talk about bees and fruit trees.

Grandpa George says, "Russel says blah blah blah ..." 'bout them plums or other fruit trees. Russel is Grandpa George's brother. When Grandpa George is finely gone outside, Grandma Rasmussen switches channels on the TV and messes with the box so we can watch movies. Mama loves Fred Astaire and Gin-ger Rogers most. She loves to dance and is real good at it too. She likes Gene Kelly fine but don't think he dances as good as Fred Astaire. Me and Celya like Our Gang, Topper, and Shirley Tem-ple movies, and there's a whole bunch of other famous people movies we like too. Celya likes the Thin Man, Nelson Eddy, and Jeanette MacDonald movies. I don't so much as her.

Mama and Grandma sit, talk, and drink coffee while we watch movies. Grandma smokes cigarettes, "one right after the other."

Me and Celya sit close to the TV so we don't miss a thing, but mama and Grandma say over and over agin, "Move back away from the set because it will hurt your eyes." Never hurts *my* eyes.

Me and Celya already seen the movie that Grandma or mama want to watch, so we 'cides to play jacks. Jacks is a game where you bounce a tiny red ball on the floor, and there is these metal stars that you throw on the ground. You have to pick up a certain numbers of jacks in one bounce after you throw the jacks on the ground. It's a fun game, and Celya plays it *real* good! Celya always does stuff better than me even if I try hard.

All of a sudden we hear Grandma say loud, "It's so god ... damn ... hot in here. Why George wanted to move here is beyond me, Jeannine."

Grandma says agin, "God, it's hot!" and she swishes a bit of the newspaper in front of her face. Back and forth, back and forth, Grandma swishes the paper back and forth saying, "Damn ... it's ... hot," between swishes.

'Ventually one day Grandpa George gits a used air conditioner for Grandma, but she still says, "Goddamn it! It's still goddamn hot in here. George should have picked up a new air conditioner." But when she goes outside to cool down, she says, "Jeannine, let's go inside where it's cooler because it's so god ... damn ... hot out here."

Mama says, "Mother, don't swear in front of the children," but that don't make no never mind to Grandma because she forgits, and after a while she lets them swear words fly every which way but loose. I follow mama and Grandma inside, but they tell me to go play, so I go outside to play and stuff because I know that's what they mean. It's the "stuff" part that gits me in trouble.

Grandpa George goes inside with daddy right behind him, and they are still talkin' mostly 'bout the fruit trees and other plants around the outside of the house. I go back inside the house too.

Grandma says, "Goddamn it, George, take these children down to the garage and let them pick out a soda. It's so goddamn hot."

Grandpa George is real different from granpa Burrough. He smells funny. I don't like the way Grandpa George or granpa Burrough smells. Grandpa George smells like cigars, and granpa Burrough smells like chewin' tobacco. I don't like the way daddy smells either lessin' he wears man's perfume on Sundee.

Grandpa George is sorta standoffish, but he twinkles when he smile at me like Santy Claus. He don't wear no glasses like Grandma Rasmussen, but he has almost all-white hair. The only hat Grandpa George wears is a stocking cap. A navy-blue one. He sits way back in his chair and smokes a big ol' cigar in the dark room. The seat in his folding-out chair is round where his bottom sits and has gray tape on it so'z the torn part don't cause him to slip right down to China.

I don't like Grandpa's smelly cigar. It's all mixed up with Grandma's cigarette. This makes the house smell different from anything else I smelt. Kinda old smellin'. It's yucky.

Now I'm gonna tell you about the bees. I'm told over and over again *not* to mess with Grandpa George's bees and *not* to go near the hives *or* throw anything at them to make them mad. The baking soda come out more than once when I'm around Grandpa's hives or playin' on the clover grass in the front yard. Celya and Thomas gits stung too. I don't mess with them bees much, but I go a little too close to their hives sometimes jest to see if daddy is right. They don't sting me, so I'm not too sure daddy's right.

Mama puts the bakin' soda on the place that is stung, I guess to git rid of the hurt. I think it's a bunch of hooey though because that bakin' soda mixed with water don't make one little bit of difference. Mud is suppost to work better, but mama wasn't havin' none of that. Well, I got stung without doin' anything special to deserve it. I was scared of the bees. But really, if you are gonna git stung, shouldn't it be for a good reason?

To do or not do something takes over my mind and body as if I'm possessed by the devil himself. I go to the bee hives and look at them for a while. No one is outside with me and it feels good to be alone without someone or 'nother tellin' me what to do or not to do. I pick up a small rock that jest happens to be in eye shot. I look at it, then look at the hives. I ponder for what seems like five minutes. I ponder and ponder and wonder if it's worth it. I wanna find out if bees really do git mad and come after you.

I wonder what would really happen to me if I take the risk. I know that I'm ready for it—to find out, I mean. I can outrun the bees. It takes another five minutes of plannin'. I throw this rock as hard as I can. I hit the hive. (God ... damn ... it ... George), I was good. One bee comes at me. Then two or three more. All of a sudden bees are all around me, darting at my head. I bat, scream, and run as fast as I can after seven of the bees sting me on the top of my head.

Boy, I will *never, ever* never throw a rock at a bee hive ever agin.

I finely am in the house with bunches of bakin' soda on my head. Daddy asks, "Did you throw something at the bee hive?" I nod with tears runnin' down my cheeks, and he says, chucklin', "Didn't we tell you not to mess with the bees?" I nod agin.

Mama flutters around. Actually, mama never flutters. A runnin' stomp is more like it. She says, "Whatever possessed you to do such a thing, after all the times I told you *not* to mess with the bees?" She's madder than a hornet. I could have told her that the devil made me do it, but that wouldn't matter to mama. I don't know why *she's* mad. I'm the one who got stung, and let me tell you me, one bee sting hurts a lot less than seven.

Bad hearing can git you into a lots of trouble if you're me. People say, "Don't mess with this, that, or the other thing," and I hear, "Mess with this, that, or the other thing, but don't git caught." It's part of me. They shoulda given me hearin' aids when I was first born though. You can't really help it if smellin', touchin', sniffin', and lookin' at stuff jest come natural. I say, and will say agin and agin, "I jest couldn't help myself." But if I'm gonna git a beatin' anyways, I can't ever think of a thing to say. I freeze.

Grandpa George takes me and Celya to the garage where the golf course trucks, tractor, and other big machines are. They are all painted a lightish, ugly greenish color. Grandpa says every time, "Stay away from those machines. I don't want you to git hurt on them."

I hear, "Don't let no one catch you on those machines, but you can climb all over them and push all the buttons."

He says, "Now, I'm not supposed to let you children have a soda from this machine." He would take out a key chain that has a whole mess of keys on it—more than I ever seen in my whole life! Me and my sister nod.

He opens the door of the machine and says, "Go ahead and pick out the one you want." Cecilia chooses a grape sody pop this time, but most of the time she gits root beer. I always take the orange sody pop, 'cept when Celya gits root beer, then I sometimes git root beer too. The root beer bottle is spelled "MUGS" and has all kinds of bubbles on it.

After we pick out the sody pop, we watch Grandpa pull out the bottles. We hear the glass bottles move down. Then he shuts the door of the machine, locks it, takes our bottles, and pries off the caps with the bottle opener on the front of the machine. Clink. The cap falls into a little box under the bottle opener. Then Grandpa gives us our bottles back and leaves to go do work on the golf course.

Me and Celya take a drink and feel the cold sody pop go all the way down to our tippy-toes. Not really that far down, but all the way to our stomachs. If you drink a sody pop too fast, you can burp real big. Me and Celya laugh when one of us burps because it's not ladylike. We are never 'llowed into the house with the sody pops, so we sit on the metal lawn chairs on the porch, in the porch swing seat, or on the wood steps. If we 'cide to sit on the swing, Celya has to move the seat back and forth because my feet don't touch the wood porch floor yet. We both like the squeaky sound that the swing makes. Squeak, groan ... squeak, groan ... squeak, groan.

Grandpa goes to go inside, openin' the screechy screen door. It slams shut behind him like it always does, then we hear Grandma yellin', "God ... damn ... it, George! Do you have to let it slam like that?" Grandpa never says anything back but goes to his brown chair or to the inside back porch where the dogs are. The lady dog is called Duchess and the boy dog is named Duke.

'Ventually, when Celya gits older, Grandpa gives Celya the keys to open up the sody pop machine on her own. We have to take the keys right back to him though, because he has to have them for work. Me and Celya sit on the steps drinkin' our sody pop, feelin' *real good.*

None of the grandmas or grandpas spank us, but Granma Burrough don't wanna babyset me no more because I'm "too much of a handful." Yep. I did jest say that. My mama says I'm changed and she jest can't figger out why. "Just all of a sudden, you changed. Where is my child that I used to know?" she says, sad like. I don't know what she means, because I am here. I do the same ol' thing, 'cept I sit in my swing and talk to myself for a long time when no one is around. Sometimes I jest swing a little bit and think about nothin'. I never done that before when I was real little.

Chapter 9: Sweet Dreams

1959

Mama spanks me hard for a long time most every day unless it's Christmas or some other holiday.

Every year I always wonder if Santy Claus will bring me anything for Christmas because I've been so bad. I count if I've been good enough more times than bad. I try to count it out, but it always seems I'm more bad than good. I hold my breath on Christmas morning, and I wonder if he will add and subtract better than me and bring me anything. But he always does, and I'm always surprised.

One day, out of the blue, mama asks me if I feel loved.

I think for a minute and 'cide I should lie but I also think, "Well, she hurts real bad lots," so I 'cide to tell her the truth.

"No," I say.

I think it's a funny question and wonder how she came up with it. She looks sad and never asks me agin. This doesn't change anything because she still spanks me hard for whatever I do that's bad. I guess it's right that I don't feel love because I'm an awful person, and I deserve to be spanked so hard and so much.

I git bored or sad in school, so I daydream. If I don't understand somethin' right off the bat, I daydream. Most times the teacher don't catch me, and that's jest fine by me. The good thing 'bout day dreamin' is that you don't have to sleep in the dark and be ascared that someone is gonna git you. The best kind of daydream is when I don't dream nothing.

Most of the time, my nighttime dreams are 'bout some monster tryin' to git me. I run and run as fast as I can, but the monster goes to reach right out at me. I try to scream so someone will help me, but I can't scream. Jest air comes out of my mouth no matter how hard I try to scream. I try to wake up, and most times when I do, I'm still ascared and I cry. My body shakes, I can hardly breathe, and I can hear my heart thumpin' fast in my ears.

When I was littler I would go to mama and daddy's room for help. Mama tried to calm me down so'z I'd go back to sleep. Mama would take me back to bed and tuck me in. We didn't pray because we already prayed before goin' to sleep at night.

Most times after a while I can go back to sleep.

I'm older now, but I still pee my bed. I can't help it. I wake up when the pee gits cold on my pj's and sheets. Mama don't make no fuss 'bout it no more. I guess it's 'cause I do it all the time and she's tired of changing the sheets. Most of the time I try to hide it by makin' my bed. One night I had a bad dream, and I went to mama and daddy's bedroom but I couldn't git in. I kept callin' out for mama and cried, but she never came out. I turned the doorknob to come into their room, but the door wouldn't open. I knocked and knocked but they didn't hear me. I thought they had left me, Celya, and Thomas all alone.

Next day I went to their room and saw this little funny, gold metal thing that swings like a door. It was on the molding right by the door. It's little bitty, like the size of a half candy bar. I can flip it back and forth with my finger, but I can't figger out how to make it do anything. Celya and Thomas sure as shootin' can't figger it out neither. I'm the one who always figgers out how stuff works.

Daydreamin' is the best place to be no matter where you are, and no one is there with you. You don't hear no one 'cause you are away. I'm away, I mean. I dream about ridin' a horse and goin' fast as fast can. I dream that *that* Randy at school don't tease me and follow me all over the place. I will tell you 'bout him later. There are big ol' clouds outside, and I dream I can fly and go up to the fluffy clouds. I dream that it's jest me on the playground at school and I can play and play and no one stops me or teases me. Sometimes I'm part of stories I hear 'bout. Celya reads to me and Thomas in the car when we have to wait for mama and daddy when they go shoppin' on Friday nights. I dream that I'm in them stories.

I dream that I'm in TV stories too.

Chapter 10: Spare the Rod, Spoil the Child

1959

Mama does lots of shakin' and bakin', and it isn't the chicken whose goose gits cooked.

Nope. Most of the time it's me bein' shaked and screamed at. I'm thinkin' she thinks screamin' is better than a spankin', but it's not. The spankin's come later anyways, dependin' on what kind of trouble I git into.

This time she grabs me by the shoulders, shakes me but good, and asks kinda calmly, "What in the world were you thinking?"

I'm thinkin' and 'bout to tell her, but for no good reason she asks the same question, but louder. Whatever kind of answer I'm 'bout to give her is long gone. Next, as she says each word, she gits louder and louder and shakes me back and forth real fast. My head bobs like one of them dolls with a spring for a neck that I saw in San Francisco. A bobble doll.

'Ventually she lets go and all out screams at me real close to my face with her eyes goin' real fast. Back and forth, back and forth.

How does she do that with her eyes? I wonder. She is so close that I can smell her coffee breath, and I want to back up real bad, but know better than to do that. That would git me into more trouble. She scares me half to death almost all the time—even when I'm not in trouble.

She asks, "How many times have I told you *not* to do *that*?"

I wonder if I should answer her.

"*Tell me!*" she screams.

Ah, well, this is a harder place to be in. Do I or don't I answer her?

"I *asked you* how many *times* have I *told* you *not* to do that?" Now she full out yells. "I've *told* you *over* and *over again!* I've *told* you until I'm *blue in the face!*"

Now I'm thinkin', *Do I answer her this time?* I try to count the times she told me not to do what I jest done.

She says, "This will be the *last* time you *ever* do *that* again. Do you *hear* me?"

Do I hear her? How can I not? She's yellin' for all she's worth right in front of my face, nose to nose. I jest barely nod. I don't wanna add a face slappin' to all of this because I'm *smartin'* off or *sassin'* her back. I really don't know the difference between those two words, but I do know that whenever I say something sassy or smart, I git a face slappin' or have to suck on soap. I don't know which one is the worst.

I think the soap is. Yep. The soap for sure.

She moves even closer to me. As if there was any room left! *Now how does she git her eyes to go back and forth so fast like that?* I wonder. Jeez. I really, *really* want to know. Once I tried it, and all I got was an eye-ache. I better listen.

"Now you *sit* in your *room and you think* about *what you* have *done, young lady! Do you hear me?*"

This is an even tougher place to be in.

I wanna yell back, "Yeah I hear you! You're standing two inches away from my face!" But I jest nod for the second time. That is a safe thing to do. This is no time to make mama madder or make her laugh. Believe you me!

Now she starts spankin' me and screams, "You *stay* in *that room* until I *tell* you to *come out*." She hits me each time she says each word. As she walks away she sorta says under her breath, "I don't *care* if you *stay* in that room *all ... day ... long ... Why, I ought to ...*" Then she's off into the other room, talkin' to herself. Well, compared to the yellin' it sounds like she is sayin' it under her breath.

I'm worried that she will come back after talkin' to herself and beat me some more. Sometimes she does that. Sometimes I think she forgits all 'bout me 'cause I'm in that room a *long* time.

Sometimes she comes stompin' back and says those awful words: "Just you wait until your father gets home!"

Nowhere to run and hide with daddy comin' home. He has a temper on him, and you don't wanna be at the other end of *that*. When daddy's home "after a long, hard day at work" and after mama tells him what I been up to, the belt comes off the towel rod in the kitchen or he makes me go fetch a fruit tree branch to use as a switch. "It better be a good branch too," he says. I brought in a short, limp, broken branch one time, and that was the last time I did that.

Branch or belt don't matter because the beating begins. Jest be glad if you don't have an orchard anywheres near your house.

I know that Carol Jean gits hit as bad as me because I hear her screamin' from across the road, but it's only a few times that that happens. I jest figger all parents beat their children, but I'm really bad so I git it much, much more, and more, more times. What mama and daddy gives is not no spankin'! Believe you me.

Today mama comes into my bedroom and says, "I don't know why you are crying. I haven't even started in on you yet." She grabs my arm and says, "I'm going to tear you up one side and down the other. I'm going to spank you until you can't see straight."

I start runnin', but I only go in circles because mama's holding my arm hard. Around and around I go. I'm runnin' as fast as I can. I'm trying to git away from her, but I can't. I *always* know before she starts in on me what it's gonna feel like. If you don't have a mama who tears you up one side and down the other, you don't know what I mean. You don't *wanna* know what I mean!

I scream like mad.

[With each beating I got, I crawled deeper and deeper into myself. It was as if my will was slowly being taken away from me. As if my soul was being crushed down on a daily basis. My spunk was being torn away from me. It's clear to me that at this point the abuse was so severe that I was suffering from PTSD.]

Chapter 11: Mercy Me

1959

Sometimes after a long rain we go home from church up a steep, winding road. Daddy points out a house and says, "That place is gonna slide down the hill any day now. They built it with fill on top of the slide area. That dirt won't hold it."

Next big rain the house slides down the hill. I don't git it. With all this sliding, why don't we ever *see* the house slide down a hill? I'd jest say sadly, "Oh yeah." I'm so forlorn, he probably think I feel sorry for the people.

Speakin' of church. We're churched to death. Evangelical free-churched to death. We have to go to *every single service and function* that is put on up an over at church. We go to Sundee school, big church, evening church, prayer meeting, youth group, and any other meetings the grown-ups can think up.

People raise their arms and give testimony all over the place. At prayer meetings is when the pastor asks if anyone wants to share their story of salvation. To testify. Those stories git boring after a while because the same ol' people say pert near the same thing *every time*. And believe you me, there aren't a lot of people there, so the same ones testify *over and over* agin.

Before kneeling to pray in the prayer meetings, people give prayer requests. You know, like, "I would like to pray for Sister Mildred, who is having a wart taken off her nose on Friday. Pray that she comes out of it O.K. God bless her."

I think if I had a wart on my nose, I'd put up with almost

anything jest to git it off my face, but I sure as shootin' wouldn't tell nobody to pray about it.

Every adult is Brother blah blah or Sister blah blah blah. That don't make no sense to me either.

When it's time to pray in prayer meetings, you have to turn around and put your knees on the floor facing the seat of the chair in front of you. It makes my knees hurt, so I can't stay still. This is jest like when mama punishes us (me, mostly) and makes us stand on our knees facing the wall at home. We have to do this for ten minutes, and if she catches you (me) slouching, she adds on another five minutes. Most times I have to stand on my knees for twenty minutes. This is all on our bare hardwood flooring too.

Back to the prayer meeting. 'Member I was talkin' 'bout that? It's funny to hear all them noises the grown-ups make. Celya and me have to face the chair seat, put our knees on the floor like I told you, close our eyes real tight, and fold our hands. Jest like the grown-ups. When my knees start hurtin' too much I weave back and forth and *pray* that the meeting *ends soon!*

Someone prays out loud for one of the prayer requests that someone shares, and you can hear people mumble, "Praise God," "Thank you, Jesus," "Amen, hallelujah, praise the Lord," or "Oh yes, Lord," and other stuff like that. It's creepy because they don't never talk that way in regular life. I hold my breath when daddy starts to pray out loud. He sounds so uppity, and he don't never sound like that in real life. He prays the same words *every time*. And when he gives his testimony, he always says the same words every time too.

Along with all of them meetings, mama and daddy drag us to all the meetings for grown-ups, like board meetings and deacons' meetings, elders' meetings, Bible study, and plannin' meetings.

I lied. Only daddy goes to the deacons' and elders' meetings sometimes. There was a man's Bible study *and* a women's Bible study and a women's sewing group. Not to mention vacation Bible school and pioneer girls meeting.

But I jest did mention them. Sorry.

I have to go to the women's ones though. I think whatever cottonpickin' meeting they make up is jest to make me wiggle. We also have to deep clean the church every so often. As usual, my job is to collect all the trash. I go to the men's restroom, and it smells up a storm and has funny toilets in it.

Being in a fun-da-ment-list church, you have to do all of this stuff, like goin' to meetings and passing out tracts. The people who go to these small meetings are more spiritual than the rest of the church. If you have to pass out tracts like me and Celya do, you go to *every* door in the neighborhood, ring the doorbells or knock on the doors, then hand the people this little folded piece of paper so they can "find Jesus." (He's not lost though.) Handin' out those tracts was pretty fun when I was a little girl, but it gits old fast after the first few times. And it's embarrassin'. Mama and daddy jest stand on the street when we have to do this. We don't have no sidewalks in most of El Sobrante. I guess that's 'cause the horses have to walk down the streets, and cement or blacktop is hard on their feet.

Lots of times I git yanked out of my seat by daddy or mama and whipped in the church vestibule, or outside if I'm really gonna git it hard. This is because I wiggle around, fight with someone by pushin' up hard against them, or whisper to Celya or Carol Jean. I whisper a bunch of times in church. I try to git Carol Jean or Celya to giggle. It's very embarrassin' to be smacked at church because other children in the church aren't yanked outa *their* seats like me. Carol Jean does if Uncle Jesse catches her talkin' to me, but most times it's me.

Mama and daddy take services *very* serious and, like I said, go to all of them services and meetings, which means me, Celya, and Thomas git dragged right along behind them. Mama and daddy don't pay no babysetters when they have to go to church. We are lucky if a grown-up wants to babyset us in the Sundee school room. Then we don't have to go to no big church service or prayer meetings.

Linda is our best one for babysettin' at home. We like her

bunches. She plays the piano at church.

At nighttime in grown-up church, someone from time to time clips their big ol' fat fingernails, which makes a loud popping sound that sorta echoes. It's *real* quiet in church, so the sound sticks out like a sore thumb. It makes me giggle, so I git into trouble. Mama or daddy gives me a dirty look, so I try to stop. But sometimes I have to hide my laughing. If I try not to giggle, it makes me giggle more. So I have to think of something awful so I won't giggle. I'm gonna figger out who it is that's cuttin' their fingernails, but I still haven't found out who does it. That man should pray to God and ask for forgiveness because everyone can hear that he's disturbin' the service when the preacher is preachin'. *He* should be taken out to the vestibule and git *his* bottom spanked!

Another thing happens when it rains on Sundee: we don't git to go see Grandma and Grandpa Rasmussen near as much as we see Granma and granpa Burrough. Mama has to call to see if the roads are too muddy. We don't want no a chance of daddy's car gittin' stuck in the mud. I always cross my fingers when mama calls Grandma because I really want to be with Grandma.

1960

We are not so poor that we can't have some special things. Mama makes sure of that. She scrimps and saves even though we don't git 'nough to eat. I don't mind that none because it's worth it. That's the only way she can save. The one thing I don't like is how mama and daddy fight on Fridays after daddy gits paid from work. Mama wants to save every nickel and dime, and daddy likes to spend money, so they fight.

Me, mama, and Celya wear hand-me-downs. A mother and two sisters (who I don't know) give us some of their old clothes. It's like Christmas when we git them clothes. It really is! The mother and sisters git new stuff to wear, so the mother gives their old clothes to mama.

These clothes must a been the ones they didn't like so much or grew out of, because they look brand new. Mama and Celya wears the clothes first, and I have to wait a while before I've growed 'nough to fit into them. By the time I git big 'nough to wear the clothes, some of them are fourth-me-downs. Sometimes I never am big 'nough to wear the clothes. Good thing I don't care how stuff looks so much.

Jest kiddin'. These are real good clothes that last a long time. I hate havin' to wear the same ol' clothes all the time till I grow out of them or they start gittin' holes in them. How stuff looks is 'portant to Celya and mama. They call it "fashion." It also means, "Can you believe what people are wearing nowadays?" Grown-ups say that when they go shoppin'.

Aunt Carol and mama look at the Sears and Roebuck's, Ward's, and JCPenney's catalogs, but they jest look and hardly buy nothin'. Those books are *heavy*! The catalogs are 'bout three inches thick each. I don't care much 'bout clothes so long as I have my play clothes. When I finally outgrow my clothes, mama puts them into brown paper grocery bags and takes them up to the school so poor people have somethin' to wear. Mama likes to share the clothes that "the good Lord gives to us."

∞ ∞ ∞

I dream about Disneyland at nighttime and when I daydream. We are on our way driving to Disneyland now. It's takin' forever. Mama and daddy have saved every dime hard so we and Uncle Billy (mama's half-brother, who is only one year older than Celya) can go to Disneyland. We pray that daddy gits a cheap hotel or motel with a swimmin' pool. I git these two names mixed up: *hotel* and *motel.* If a place is cheap, mama always goes into the room to check for cahcahroaches and to see if the room is clean before daddy pays anything.

We children also hope that daddy can git the big ticket book at Disneyland, but we git the littlest ones with less tickets in them 'cause they are the cheapest. The books have tickets from A to D. The A tickets are for the best rides, and the D tickets are for the rides like the merry-go-round.

Daddy has to give me a boost up for some rides because I can't git on one all by myself. Mostly us kids git to 'cide what to ride. There aren't so many A tickets for the really good rides like the Madahorn, so we have to pick and choose what rides are the best. The Madahorn is a scary ride, so I don't care if I don't ride that one. Celya and daddy stand in the very long line for the Madahorn because they like rollycoasters a lot, and the Madahorn is like a rollycoaster that goes way up into a mountain. Later, Tinkerbell flies off that mountain.

Mama and daddy have to talk the men and ladies into letting me ride some rides 'cause I'm not tall 'nough for all of them.

The hotel we're in now has a *swimmin' pool!* Mama made sure we took swimmin' lessons at the Richmond Plunge so we won't git drowned. So we all go swimmin' when we are back from Disneyland, then we have to take a long trip to go back home. All that scrimpin' mama does is worth it. Oh yeah, we go to Knott's Berry Farm too because it don't cost no money and we park in the free parking lot. Knott's Berry Farm is like Old Western times. I like it a lot.

We git to go to Mount Hermon in the Santa Cruz Mountains almost every year. It's a Christian camp. On the way there, daddy laughs at the people who have their windows rolled up when it's hot outside. They have air conditioning. There's a big, steep hill that the cars have to climb. The hill is so long and steep that regular cars heat up sometimes, but the cars with their air conditioners on heat up a lots more, and the people have to pull over to let their cars cool down. I keep my fingers, toes, and body parts crossed when we go up the hill. Our car is old, so it "may or may not make it up the hill without overheating," but we make it up the hill every time without havin' to pull over.

The first thing we do when we git there is go to the real 'state office. Mama and daddy pick the cheapest cabins for us to stay in. We go to look at the cabins, then 'cide which one to pick. Everything is like goin' to church, but it's in the redwood forest, so it smells good and almost every meetin' is outside.

∞∞∞

Daddy fixes all the stuff that's broke in our house, 'cluding the car, in order for mama to scrimp and save. We can't afford other people to fix our broke stuff anyways. We wear our school shoes till they git holes in them, then mama takes them (and us) to the shoe repair shop (which smells bad) and has our soles or heels replaced over and over agin until the shop owner says, "Mrs. Burrough, I just can't fix those shoes anymore." Inside I says, *Whoopee!* because that means a new pair of shoes has to be bought for *me!*

Sometimes mama and daddy can't afford to git our shoes fixed or git new shoes, so me and Celya wrap the floppy soles of our shoes with masking tape, and sometimes I put cardboard inside the shoe if the holes go straight through to the ground. Daddy has to take his "hard-earned money" to buy us stuff we need, and sometime there jest isn't enough money to go 'round.

∞∞∞

Daddy gits mad, 'specially when I do something I *know* he told me not to do. This is 'specially true when it's Saturdee. He comes in the house after mowing the lawn or doing woodwork in the basement and the rest of us are gittin' ready for Sundee church the next day.

I don't know 'bout you, but our house is all ablaze on Saturdee. Hair has to be washed and rolled, clothes have to be cleaned and ironed, and shoes have to be polished—school shoes *and* Sundee shoes. Daddy gits tired after fixin' our car and doing all kinds of other stuff daddies do before he comes into the house. When he comes in, he don't want to have to wait on me to bring him the shoeshine box or bring him my shoes, because he's plumb tuckered out. He made the wooden shoeshine box when he was in shop class at school. He polishes our school shoes and Sundee shoes with us in 'em. Granma Burrough buys us new shoes for Easter, which we wear all year 'round for church. If I don't bring daddy my shoes right quick, or if he sees mud on any shoes, he hits the roof.

"I told you that I didn't want you walking in the mud, and then there you go, off walking in the mud!" he yells.

Now, I know I walked in the mud on purpose, and he knows I walked in the mud on purpose. I say, "It was an accident."

He says with tight lips and eyebrows pinched together, "I know it weren't no dadgum accident. You did that on purpose! And you are lying about it on top of everything." He rips his belt off of his pants so quick you would think his pants would catch on fire. It would make your head swim.

Daddy spanks me as hard as mama does, but it don't last so long unless I do something real bad. But it hurts bad too. He also yells at me to stand still, or he gits shoe polish on my socks. Sometimes he's real nice when all this happens and he don't give no one no spankin'. He jest chuckles. Like with mama, I jest don't know which way he's gonna be. I plumb clean don't understand. Sometimes he laughs at what I've done, and other times he beats the fire right outa me.

Celya don't hardly ever git a spankin' 'cause she's a good girl most of the time.

Chapter 12: Quit Schooling Around

1960

Daddy does somethin' that would scare the pants right off of you.

We children fight or what have you in the back seat of the car when we go someplace. I mostly cause the shovin' and hittin'. Then Celya and Thomas shove and hit right back. Daddy tells us to stop. We don't.

"Stop!" he says agin.

We don't. There's always that one last hit we want to git in.

If we don't stop fightin', he reaches 'round lickety-split and starts slappin' whoever he can reach, and with each slap he says, "I ... told ... you ... to ... stop!"

It stings if he hits you. The car goes every which way but loose on the road 'cause he's tryin' to slap the smarts right out of us. When he's slappin', the car weaves all over the place 'cause he's not lookin' where he's goin'. Well, I tell you me, we stop fightin' right then and there. Not 'cause of the slappin' but 'cause we are so ascared that the car will crash.

But even with all that slappin' in the car, daddy's not near as hard on us as mama is. She says to us *before* we git in the car, "I do not *want* to *hear* a *sound* out of you. If I do, I will *pull* this car *over* and give you *such a spankin'* that you will never forgit it. I will knock the socks right out from under you."

And she means it! She may be little, but she hits real hard! When mama gits like that, she's real scary.

She says, "I'm doing this only because I love you." But gittin' a spankin' don't make me feel very loved.

She says, "I'm doing this for your own good." I don't think that makes sense either. I can tell you that sometimes I really, *really* deserve it though. I know I'm a bad person, but I can't seem to change no matter what.

Celya says, "You better not do that. You going to git in trouble." Sometimes I listen to her. Sometimes I don't. I don't lots more times than I do. Guess what? I pert near always git in trouble. I git into trouble even when I don't think I'm in trouble. It sorta depends on mama's mood. Celya knows 'zactly what mama's mood is, and that's how she knows when I should watch out. Most times mama is in a bad mood now, and if she isn't, she turns into a bad mood when I do something bad.

Mama can "beat you senseless." She says, "I'm gonna beat you until you're black and blue all over," or "You're going to wish you've never been born when I git through with you," or "I'll beat you till you can't see straight." And she does what she says she is gonna do! When she hits me, I git black and blue where she hits. When daddy spanks me it only turns red where he hits me most of the time, unless he uses a switch. Then where he hits me turns red or opens up the skin.

I *love* to play. I *l-o-v-e* to touch things, pick stuff up, smell it, and taste it. I don't like school very much though 'cause I can't do that there so much. Now that I think of it, that is not the whole reason I don't like school. The times that I *do* like in school is when I git to do art and music. When we do art, lots of the children eat the paste that we use to glue stuff together. When we children found out that it was made of horses, I got sick to my stomach. Yuck! That put an end to eating paste for most of us. But some don't believe that, so they keep eating the paste. Dummies! I could always see that dead horse in my head with flies buzzin' all 'round it, and it ain't pretty. Besides, I love horses. I love animals and hurt inside when I see one of 'em hurt. They don't do nothing to deserve to git hurt.

My friends git to go to school early and play in the play yard before school starts. Pract'ly everyone at school gits to play before school and at lunchtime. Most of the children eat lunch at school too. That makes them better than me. I usually don't eat lunch at school. Mama's ascared I might pick up pinworms or git into trouble, I guess. She is wrong or right. I don't know. I couldn't tell one way or the other if I git pinworms from school. We can talk 'bout that later.

I do git into trouble though. Most all the children don't play with me no more 'cause I cheat, lie, and git mad real easy. Mama makes me wait to go to school and sometimes makes me late. Before school starts she talks on the phone to Aunt Carol while she does my hair. It hurts when she yanks out a tangle or pulls it too tight when she braids it. When she does that, it hurts all day long. Sometimes I wiggle while she's workin' on my hair 'cause it hurts. And I know I'm goin' to be late for school and git in trouble with the teacher. That's usually why I'm late to school.

When mama thinks I wiggle too much, she yanks my hair hard or hits me on the head with the brush and yells, "Stop moving!" I sit as still as I can, and she still hits me and says I'm wigglin' 'round. Sometimes she hits me with the phone. I think she makes me late to school on purpose to punish me.

I'm also late because I have to sit and sit at the breakfast table to finish what I have for breakfast. I hate—*h ... a ... t ... e*—oatmeal or soggy corn flakes, and sometimes I can't eat it all. I don't like orange juice none neither. It makes me wanna gag.

Mama says, "You will *sit* there and *sit* some more until you finish what's in your bowl." Or she says, "You're going to *sit* there until the cows come home."

I put my orange juice into my cereal to make it taste better, like ice cream, but it's *worse!* If time is runnin' away and it's too late, mama puts my cereal with orange juice into the 'frigerator and says I have to eat it later for lunch, and I do. Ick.

My face gits all hot and turns deep red when the teacher asks me why I'm late. All the children stare at me too. When mama makes me late, I play on the way to school. I mean late is late, right? I like bein' by myself. One place I love to play in is a swimmin' pool that don't have no water in it. I pretend I'm swimmin'. Mama says that she don't want me playin' in it because it used to be a septic tank. She tells me what a septic tank is, but I don't see no poop, pee, or toilet paper in the swimmin' pool, so I play there anyways. And I pick some flowers for the teacher so I won't git into so much trouble. Pickin' flowers on the way to school for the teacher *would* make me late, so the teacher don't git too mad at me. It *always* works most of the time.

I *love* playin' in the ditch when it rains real hard. I see the bubbles and hear the gurgle as I stand watchin' the water run down the hill. The water gits real deep in some places, so I try to guess if the water will go over the top of my rain boots. Most of the time it's deeper than I think and the water goes into my rain boots, but I like that jest fine. I walk slow and watch the water and small sticks run down the ditch. I watch the leaves float by too.

Mama don't want me to walk in the water. She says, "It ruins your shoes and you might get polio." My shoes look the same to me after they dry, so I keep walkin' in the ditch and guessin' how deep the water is before it comes up over my boot tops.

When we start a new year in school, I'm put up front near the chalkboard because I'm the shortest one in the class. But if there are a bunch of troublemakers, then they end up at the front of the class. The janitor has to come in and fix my seat so my feet will touch the floor. He makes it so the desk's not up too high too. Sometimes I git to sit at the back of the classroom when the teacher sits us in alphabetical order because there are a lot of As and Bs and my last name starts with Bu, but by the time school ends I'm sittin' in the front with the other troublemakers. I talk in class and I'm not suppost to. That's why I git put in the front row.

1961

In reading there are three groups. One for the very smart children, one for the sorta smart children, and one is the group I'm in, which is for the dumbest and stupidest children. It's awful hard to be in the stupidest group. Being in the dumb group makes me mad. I *hate* that. I'm a big ol' fat dumbo. On top of that, I can't spell right, do 'rithmetic, or read, so it must be true. I always git Ds for very bad work. When mama and daddy see my papers or report card, they look at me sad and say, "I know you can do better." They are wrong. I *can't* do better than I do now. It's a good thing that I never git Fs though. F means flunk. I don't know what they would do to me if I got Fs. I think teachers give me Ds jest to be nice to me, but I know I deserve Fs.

The teacher tells our class that her son went deep-sea diving and brought back some things that he thought our class would enjoy. Oh, the stuff is *very* purdy. The best one is the bright-yellow coral. Everyone likes that one the best. I wish I had that one for myself. We pass the ocean stuff—shells, rocks, and coral —all around like the teacher tells us to. Then she puts all of the stuff on one of the short tables so everyone can keep lookin' at it.

In my dumbest group for reading, I sit real close to the little table where the ocean stuff is. I really want to git back at my teacher for always puttin' me in the dumb group. I jest have to have that bright-yellow coral. I jest have to! If I take it, the teacher won't know it was me. I'm never gonna be able to git a piece like that in my *whole* life!

Everyone else sits on the floor and crosses their legs Indian style. But I can't. My legs won't bend like that. I always sit with my legs out flat in front of me on the floor. Sometimes it's good to sit like I do. You can't skooch good when you are sittin' Indian style. If you try, you have to sorta push up off the floor and go backward or forward. People could catch you if you did it that way. I'm lucky for once that I can sit with my legs out. Most times I'm 'barrassed that I can't sit Indian style.

This day, I sit in the perfect place. Course, this isn't by accident. The children in my reading group have to make a circle. I'm the first one on the floor, and I don't budge even though some of the children try to push me over. Not this time! I planned it out to the end.

Once everyone is sittin' down in the circle, the teacher sits in one of the chairs with a book in her lap. When she looks down at her book, I skooch backward toward the table. I do this very slow, inch by inch, till I'm in the right spot. It's a *perfect* spot—inches away from the table where the yellow coral is. I reach up real quick and grab the coral when the teacher is looking down at her book. I hide it good in the pleats of my dress.

When we go back to our desks, I raise the lid on mine and put my *dumb* book into the desk, and also the coral, as quick as I can. I can't wait to git home to add the hard, bumpy coral to my rock collection. I know that someday it will be worth a lot of money. I was told if you collect stuff, one day it will be valuable. That's how I know gittin' the coral is big stuff, and I git away with it! I'm smilin' in my tummy, but also my tummy is bunched up. I can't tell anyone in the whole wide world that I took the coral because it was wrong for me to take it.

The next day the teacher says to the class, "Someone took the yellow coral." She looks straight at me. My face gits hotter and hotter. My heart is beating so fast, loud, and hard that I jest know the teacher can hear it. I'm hopin' and prayin' that my face don't turn red, but I know that it has. When I git home, I think on givin' it back. If I put it back, my teacher would know it was me that stole it, and I sure as shootin' don't want her to know it was me that took it. I think and think till my brain hurts. There is only one thing I can do: *keep it.*

I feel bad that I have to do this. I put the coral with my rock collection, which is in a shoebox in the attic. No one looks in that box. I don't know why, because I have a rock that is round like a baseball that Carol Jean give to me, and it's worth bunches. Now *that is* something to see.

Well, I tell you me that *every time* I look into my special rock collection box, I see the coral and think 'bout what I done. *Every time* it makes me feel bad 'bout myself. I tell myself that I coulda put it back. I say to myself, *You're jest chicken!* These words cut through me like a knife.

Mama and daddy never find out what I done. I'm sure not very clean after doin' this because "cleanliness is next to godliness," and I'm sure I'm gonna go to hell for what I've done. I'm sure God is nowheres near me too, even if I did ask Jesus into my heart. He sure isn't there anymore. The grown-ups say that once you ask Jesus into your heart, He will never go away. I know that is not true. I know He knows everything I do. So does mama. All she has to do is look at my face to see if I done somethin' wrong. And she's always right, so she has a right to beat me.

This yellow coral starts me on a life of crime. I lie all the time now so I won't git hit or nothin'. And 'member: God knows everything. Mama gits irritated at me no matter what I do. I can't even breathe without gittin' into trouble. When mama's on the phone, that's when I do somethin' I know I'm not suppost to do. I figger she won't catch me, but she always does. I don't know how she does that—how she sees me when she can't see me. If I ride my bike down the hill when I'm not suppost to, she screams at me to come home, then I really git it. I don't understand why one time it's O.K. to ride down the hill and 'nother time it's not O.K. Mama screams at me a lot 'cause she wants to know where I am at all times and what I'm up to.

I'm not the only one who gits into trouble. We have a party line. That's when all sorts of people can talk on the telephone to each other at the same time and you can listen to someone talkin' when they don't know it. When two of the people are on the phone, mama tells them to git off the line 'cause she has to make a 'portant call. She does this all the time. One time mama picks up the phone by accident and hears two ladies talkin'.

The first one says, "Those Burrough children are *so* sweet, but that mother of theirs is something else."

Her friend says, "Yes, it's horrible how she screams at her children."

Then first lady says, "I don't know what's wrong with that

woman."

Well, mama gits off that phone and starts askin' me and Celya if she's bad. Course, we don't know if she is or isn't, but Celya tries to calm her down by saying, "No, mama. You're not bad like those ladies say." Celya is always tryin' to calm down one or the other of us in the house. She tries this with me, but it don't work so good.

I cry and stuff all the time, and I git angry at the littlest thing. The children at school call me a crybaby. I am, but I don't want to be one. Sometimes when mama gives it to me bad for nothin' I do wrong, I go into the closet, close the sliding door, bury my head in the clothes, and softly talk back to her while I cry. Celya guards the door so I won't git into more trouble, and she tells me if mama is comin'. Sometimes I stay in the closet a real long time and cry. It hurts Celya when she sees me git a beatin'.

Mama and daddy work with me every time after dinner with the flash cards so I'll git better at reading and 'rithmetic. Grandma Rasmussen give mama those cards that Uncle Billy used 'cause he had trouble with 'rithmatic and reading too. And I thought I loved Grandma. Foo-wee with her!

If I git an A in the classes like art and music, it's sorta like cheatin' 'cause it's so easy to do music and art. I can't wait to git a bunch of As on my report card. You jest wait and see. Someday I will! I only have a year or so of private piano lessons, and I play special pieces I make up. So anyone can see that I can do music easy.

I have to learn spellin' *pho-ne-ti-cal-ly*. That's stupid. Take this word for instance: pho-ne-ti-cal-ly. I know the word now, but I sure don't when it's on the flash card.

My parents say, "Sound it out." Then they show me the card with the word on it.

I say "Dah ... dah."

They say 'citedly, "That's it! That's it! Now sound out the next letter."

"Oh ... Oh."

"You got it! Now sound out the next letter." They are *so* happy.

110

"Gah" I says. "Gah."

"That's it!" They are so happy, I think they are gonna git up and dance the jitterbug. Their voices go higher and they say, "Now put it all together."

"Dah ... oh ... gah."

"That's it. Now say it faster."

"Dah ... oh ... gah."

"Now faster."

I say it faster and faster. "Dah ... oh ... gah. Dah ...oh ... gah." I don't know 'bout you, but I never heard no one nowhere's that knows what a dah ... oh ... gah is.

"What is it?" they ask. I want to please them. I really *do*. So I don't say a thing. Finely, all 'zasperated like, they say, "Dog! It's *dog!*" If they had said, "It rhymes with *God*," I woulda got it right away!

I think they are gonna hit me upside the head, which most times would be the case, but they don't. On we go to the next word on the flash card, and on and on. I figger *flash* means "quick," but I go slow as a turtle, so that's 'nother word I can't understand.

They give up on me, sayin', "We just don't know what we're going do with you. We give up."

Later one night I hear mama and daddy talkin'. Mama says, "Billy, I just don't know what we're going do with her. Try as we might."

Daddy says, "Honey, we are doing the best we can."

I think, *I'm doing all the work! What's wrong with you people? Spellin' and readin' is stupid!*

I'm sure you wouldn't wanna hear 'bout no 'rithmetic. It's pretty much more of the same. I'm better at it though because I sit on my hands and count with my fingers. Once the teacher switched from apples and oranges to jest real numbers, I was lost. There aren't any pictures I can think up to match the numbers to. Most of the time I jest guess, hopin' that I will land on the right answer, but usually I guess wrong.

I learnt to do something pretty tricky 'ventually. Did I tell you 'bout my brown rain boots? Yeah, I told you about the boots, only I didn't tell you they was brown, I don't think. We put those rain boots on over our reg'lar shoes. It's real hard to put them on that way, but that's what we are suppost to do. Now I sometimes git Fs. 'Specially on my spellin' papers. Well, I figgered out that I could put my F and D papers, all rolled up tight, into the toe of my boots, where they were sittin' when it wasn't rainin'. Lots of days go by before it rained agin. When it finally *did* rain, first off I tried to put my foot into the boot with the papers in it, but it was too tight. So my foot didn't go all the ways in. So I learnt to bunch up the papers even tighter and put them in my raincoat pockets. (This was Uncle Billy's old yellow raincoat with a matchin' hat.)

The first time, I throwed them papers into the ditch, where the water was runnin'. But that was risky 'cause the children comin' behind me might pick the papers up and tell on me even if I was tricky 'bout it. So I switched my plan. I figgered that 'nough days had gone by in school, so if the teacher looked in the big gray garbage can, she wouldn't 'member the lesson that I got the F or D in.

It was hard to git to the garbage can to throw my papers away because the teacher would watch us *real* careful when we played outside and when we filed into the classroom. Sometimes I would raise up on my toes when I got to the garbage can so I would be taller. I would put the paper in sneakily, holdin' my arm straight down. I'd hold my arm real stiff and drop the papers down slow and easy. Sometimes I make myself late for school so I can throw the papers in the big garbage can without nobody catchin' me. I even make sure that the custodian don't catch me doin' it. Being yelled at for being late to school is a whole lots better than mama findin' my F and D papers. I usually lie to the teacher and tell her I'm late because of mama. My face gits real hot when I do this, and I'm sure the teacher is gonna figger it all out. So far I'm O.K. No grown-up has caught me yet.

Now, no one in the class can diagram a sentence as good as me. The whole class is lost. I want to stand up and yell, "Now do you know what I've been going through? You sure are dumb! 'Goddamn those sons of bitches, George.'" I don't know what *sons of bitches* means. I only know that when Grandma Rasmussen says it, she is madder than a wet hen and means business. Grandma says the most wonderful words. And Grandma is real smart too. My mama can't stand her.

Mama says, "I just don't understand *that* woman. We give her something nice, and she tucks it away in a drawer somewhere. She knows we don't have much money. Why she does that is beyond me." Then mama says the list of the "nice" things she gave her mother. By the way, she never calls Grandma by the word *mama.* She always uses *mother.* Daddy does that too with his mama. Now *that* sounds strange to me.

Anyway, I'm gittin' older and the whoppin's are more like beatin's. Mama gits madder than a hornet's nest and comes at me swingin'. She don't care where she hits me or what she hits me with, but it usually is on my head, face, or the top of my legs. When she is in a certain mood she says things like, "You're never going to make anything of yourself," or "I wish I'd never had you." I don't really understand what she means so much, but the other thing she says is, "This hurts me more than it hurts you." *Now that's a big ol' fat lie!* It hurts lots when she's hittin' on me. I know she says these kinds of things when she's mad, but it kinda hurts my feelings, and sometimes I think she is right.

She's at me all the time now. I never know when she is in a good mood or a bad mood. Like I said before, Celya can *always* tell one way or the other what kind of mood mama is in.

Do you wanna hear something strange? The belt on the towel rod in the kitchen is gone. No one says they did it. If I threw it away, I don't 'member that I did it. Mama is *sure* that I threw it away, so she made me git my special spaceman belt that I love and put it on the rod. I didn't throw the old belt away, honest, but I don't know who did. I thought mama threw it out. I sure was glad when I didn't see it hangin' there though. I thought that would be the last of the beatin', but that didn't stop mama none. She jest kept on using her hands till she got the idea of using my belt. Now she don't care which end of the belt she grabs, and sometimes the metal buckle hits me but good.

I think mama loves me, but I'm never sure. Sometimes she's real kind and nice to me and listens when I tell her about someone from school that doesn't like me and hurts my feelin's. But sometimes she jest says, "I've heard it all before," then she tells me to go do homework or do some errands for her.

Celya don't mind doing stuff for mama unless it's something she don't want to do, but she tells only me that. She hates washin' and puttin' the dishes away, but she still has to do that because I'm not tall 'nough to put the dishes in the cabinets or wash them. But I dry them. I jest don't seem to be growin' much.

Well, I'll tell you what. At least Celya don't have to take out the garbage at nighttime anymore. Me and Thomas have to do that every other night. In other words, I take the trash out one night, and Thomas takes it out the next night, then back and forth. He's afraid of the dark too. If I'm sick, Celya does it, but then she says that she don't understand why I git so ascared when I have to take out the garbage. She don't understand why things scare me, and a lot of things scare me. If it don't scare her, she thinks it shouldn't scare me. That's good thinkin' for you.

I told you that I don't like school much. *Yes I did!* In a manner of speaking. I *hate* school! There's 'nother reason I don't like school and don't like to go to school late. And that's because of *that* Randy. He is a demon. Why he choosed me to pick on and bully, and no one but me, is beyond me. But I jest know that I will 'member him on my dyin' day because he makes my life *miserable!*

He lives at the end of my block, so he plays anywhere he wants to on our street. He says mean things to me and says mean things 'bout me to everyone, then they show bad 'tention to me too, like *that* Dennis, the boy that lives across from us and has cows. Now he is with Randy and teases me jest the same. Randy is cute, but that's all there is good 'bout him. Every day he spits on me, throws sewer water on me, and hits or kicks me. He also pushes me over when I'm on my bike. *I hate that Randy!*

It's Valentine's Day. I don't never git no Valentine card from *that* Randy , though I hope each year that if he gives me one, it means he won't pick on me no more. Practically no one gives me cards 'cept Carol Jean. This makes me feel bad.

There is a big, purdy box that the teacher made. It's at the front of the room with a slit on the top like a big piggy bank, but bigger. Every teacher has one of these no matter what grade you are in. There is all kinds of store-bought hearts on it too. A teacher can wrap the whole box in white or pink paper from school, but sometimes the teachers wrap the whole box in store-bought wrapping paper. At home we write, "To ... blah biddy blah from ... blah biddy blah" on the Valentine cards we exchange. When one of us children finish fillin' out our cards, we drop them in the box. On Valentine's Day the teacher pulls one card at a time outa the box, says whose name is on the card, and hands them out to us one by one. We walk up to the box every time the teacher calls our name. Some children git more cards than other ones. It takes a long time for the teacher to git all the cards passed out because there are thirty-seven of us in the class (no matter what grade we are in), and we all give one card to *even the teacher!*

You can tell which child comes from a rich family because those cards are always nicer than the rest.

For years, *that* Randy don't never ever give me a card. I don't care because I *hate* him. At least I think I do. Mostly I'm scared of him, and he hurts my feelin's. I never give up hope, though, that someday he will stop pickin' on me. Randy has been pickin' on me for *years*! He makes me cry lots of times and does things to my bike, like lettin' the air out of my tires at school.

I'm in fifth grade now, and lo and behold, I git a card from him. So I think maybe this will be the year that he will stop pesterin' and bullyin' me. Anyways, I git a card from Randy, then the teacher tells us we can open our cards. I leave Randy's card till the last. I'm smiling on my inside. I open his card slowly. I do not scream. I do not gasp or pass out. I'm jest hurt and angry.

He put a worm inside my card.

It's all dried up. When I git home, I cry and cry and tell mama what he done. I would tell the teachers what he done, but they don't care none 'bout me. He teases me, calls me names, and makes my life a livin' hell. Even if I'm late to school he hides and waits for me to come up the street. Then he does mean things to me after all the other children are gone. I don't like school no more, and I don't like home no more either.

We are not allowed to fight, or I would knock Randy's block clean off. I know I'd win in any fight with him even if I'm smaller because I'm so very, *very* mad at him.

But one mornin', I'm late to school. Randy comes and pushes me and my bike over one too many times. I run after him and push him down. I'm sittin' on his chest and raisin' my fist. I can tell he is scared to death.

Then I hear mama say in my head, "If you ever get into a fight, you will get it twice as bad when you get home." I lower my fist and git off of him. I know right then and there that I made an awful mistake. He starts laughin' and callin' me names, and he shoves me and my bike all the way to the bike rack.

After that, his bullying gits worse.

I ask mama what I can say back to him when he calls me names. I say what mama told me to say. I say to *that* Randy, "Sticks and stones may break my bones but names will never hurt me." That's not really true, so I stop sayin' it. I can't think of anything else to say, so I ask mama to figger out what to say. Mama is at her wit's end.

Days and weeks go by, then mama says to me when I git home from school, "I know what you can say to Randy. 'I use Dial. I sure wish you did.'"

There's a commercial on TV that the soap people made up. The person on the TV at the very end says, "I use Dial. Don't you wish everybody did?" Well, since it's the only thing I know to say to Randy, I yell it at him almost every day. One day he comes up with "You smell like poo-poo."

I stop saying the commercial to him.

Mama goes to school once to tell on him and git him to stop pickin' on me, but the teachers and principal don't wanna do anything 'bout it because they don't really like me. They say, "Boys will be boys." They also say that Randy likes me a lot. How can they say that? What would it be like if he hated me? I know grown-ups can do jest about anything, but they won't help me because I'm bad. I jest have to put up with *that* Randy.

The other children are startin' to do the same things to me that he does. Mostly boys.

Grandma Rasmussen says to mama, "If she was my child I would march right up to that school and tell those sons of bitches to take goddamn care of it!"

Mama says softly and sheepishly, "Mother, I did."

I jest know that Grandma could make *that* Randy keep from bullyin' me. I *know* she could.

Chapter 13: Cleanliness Is Next to Godliness

1961

I f cleanliness is next to godliness, then my mama would be sittin' at Jesus's right hand. Father, Son, Holy Ghost, and mama.

My goodness, but mama can clean, clean, and clean some more. You really can eat off the floor at our house, though I don't know why anyone would wanna. Cleaning is mama's purpose, her mission, her all-out war, and her life. Us children are drug kickin' and screamin' as little godly things, picking up the spiritual banner in mama's war.

Our house in El Sobrante is built on what used to be a cow pasture. The soil is as rich as anything. Least, that's what daddy says. It's easy to pick up all sorts of bugs and things if you play in, on, or near the dirt. Course me, Celya, and Thomas play on the dirt all the time. And well, we got dadgum pinworms.

These are tiny, little white worms that git inside you and cause itchy bottoms. Dr, Greenburg (our family doctor) tells mama not to worry because the eggs could be found anywhere (even in the air), and gittin' them was not due to dirtiness. He is the same doctor that told mama to keep an eye on me when I flew over the embankment on my tricycle. He's also Grandma Rasmussen's and Uncle Billy's doctor.

Once mama's mind is made up 'bout anything, no matter

what, no one can convince her of anything else. *Even a doctor!* To her, these bugs (I guess you can call them bugs) mean ... *all ... out ... war.* Like a general layin' plans for the enemy's capture, mama plans her attacks, and me, Celya, and Thomas are little soldiers marching to the tune of *her* own drum. That is, we have to clean as much as she does every single day. Well almost. On Sunday we don't 'cause "God rested on the sabbeth day."

Out comes the 'monia, (which is never really put away), Comet cleanser, and rags. The house is cleaned from top to bottom. Scrubbed, rubbed, polished, washed, rinsed, dusted, and vacuumed—and all this is done day after day every day 'cept Sunday. Thank goodness God rested on the seventh day, 'cause if He didn't, we would have to clean on Sunday too.

We children have to run around like chickens with our heads cut off. Floors are scrubbed, and toilet and bathtub are hit with Comet and 'monia. Mattresses are flipped and vacuumed with a heavy Kirby vacuum cleaner. The furniture is dusted, along with any other wooden thing. Actually, *everything* gits dusted daily, even the baseboards and door trim. Mama has a big canning pot, and she boils the sheets with 'monia and water before washin' 'em in the regular washin' machine.

Mama is a rushing whirlwind of activity. Git out of her way, 'cause no one can stop her attacks. Even daddy can't stop her. Or maybe he never tries 'cause he doesn't know 'bout what she's like when he's not around. Like I told you. It is her life. It is her way. It is her mission to find and kill those teeny, tiny worm eggs.

Dr. Greenburg prescribes a deworming medicine, and off she goes to the pharmacy. After the medicine is brought home, poured into a tablespoon, and swallowed by us three children, we are lined up like the Von Trapp family, bent over and grabbin' our ankles with bare bottoms a floatin' in the wind.

It is, after all, a military action.

My sister is first. Mama examines Celya's rectum by pullin' apart her bottom and checkin' for worms. Each of us learns to examine each other's rectums 'ventually. It's a horrible thing to have to do, but it has to be done for the general's all-out war on filth.

I think mama snapped. In other words, not all her cookies are in the jar. Maybe the cleaning fumes got to her.

There is a little, white, triangular-shaped Tupperware container with a lid with water, a rag, and 'monia in it set beside the toilet. We have to wash the toilet after we use it. This is done with the bathtub too, adding Comet cleanser to the mix. Only this time we have to use our washcloths to wash the tub down.

Things are washed out, turned upside down, inside out, and around daily to kill the horrid pinworm eggs. If fruit from our orchard or the store is to be eaten, we have to wash it off with Comet cleanser before eatin' it to make sure that no crack or crevice contains any kind of germs whatsoever.

We have to tell mama and git her permission when we need to go to the bathroom *every time*, *all* the time, *no matter where* we are, *even at home*. Goin' to the bathroom at school is out of the question unless we can't hold it in no more, whether it's pee (number one) or poop (number two). We can't sit on any public or private toilet; we have to stand up when we go.

After every bowel movement, we have to call mama. She sorta bends forward a little and stomp-runs into the bathroom to check the toilet bowl for any forms of life. She takes a piece of toilet paper, twirls it to make a point at the end of it, then dips it down into the water to move the poop 'round inside the bowl for 'spection. All of us children 'ventually have to do this too—examine our own poop.

Thank goodness the rectal exams are no longer needed, but we are not to sit on any toilet for number two 'cept our own. And we must *always* pee standin' up, no matter what, making sure that not one piece of our clothes touches the toilet.

Come to think of it, we are told that germs can git on our clothing. So what? If it happens, what am I suppost to do 'bout it? Go runnin' and screamin' from the bathroom, yellin', "Unclean unclean!"? People with leprosy in Bible times had to yell out "Unclean!" so that no one would git too close to them and catch leprosy. That leprosy is awful stuff 'cause your nose can fall off your face. I can't say I love my nose, but I'm pretty 'tached to it.

After the pinworm stage, the thorough cleaning becomes a way of life. Me and my sister still have to stand up to pee. We sure have great thighs, though, after all that peeing standing up. Unless we have to go real bad (number two), we aren't allowed to go to the bathroom in most private places, like a person's house. *Ever!* In an emergency, mama checks first to see if a bathroom is filthy or not, then we can pee if it git the O.K. stamp of approval from the queen bee mama. At Grandma Rasmussen's, it *has* to be an emergency 'cause mama says that Grandma's bathroom looks like it has never been cleaned. Sometimes at Grandma Rasmussen's, mama goes into the bathroom and cleans the toilet and sink with Comet before we can go in.

Daddy never has to follow these rules. I don't even know if he knows that there are any rules about germs or if he jest tolerates mama's idiot-sink-rassy. (I learnt that word from my sister.) And mama has a *lot* of idiot-sink-rassies. There is a lot of stuff that mama makes us do that she never makes daddy do. For instance, 'cause of his work as a tool-and-die maker, and from workin' on our car, his hands and fingernails are always filthy, but mama don't send him back to the bathroom to scrub them better. He does use Comet cleanser on his hands though. Does that mean that daddy is "unclean" and we shouldn't git near him? If this was true, he wouldn't be allowed to git close to us to spank us. *That* would be good. I'll betcha daddy don't know half the things that mama makes us do 'cause he is in la-la land most of the time. Daddy don't touch us anyway unless he's gittin' ready to spank us.

[This was a particularly difficult time in my life. While Mom had always been abusive and emotionally unwell, the pinworm incident turned her into a raging maniac. Nothing she did could ever be construed as being mentally stable. She, indeed, was very sick, and we children were expected to stand under her nightmarish umbrella. It was only when she was in a very good mood that she would hug and kiss us, but that faded away once she had to keep an eye on Dad to make sure he didn't stray away from her. In retrospect. I think that this was a valid concern.]

∞ ∞ ∞

Daddy's one job in the house is to hand wax and polish the hardwood floors once a year with paste wax. He also works on our car and gits lots of grease on his hands and under his fingernails. Mama makes us use a fingernail brush loaded with Comet cleanser, like he uses, to be sure that the undersides of our fingernails are clean. We have to clean our fingers like this every time we eat, come in from outside, or go to the bathroom.

There is an inspection before any food comes anywhere near our mouths. For all us children, that is. Daddy don't never ever git no inspections. If our fingernails are not as clean as mama thinks they should be, we are sent back to the bathroom.

Mama sometimes says, "I'll come clean them for you!" I tell you what, if she says that to me, I almost run to the bathroom. I hold my breath when I have to hold my hands out to mama for a second check. My hands shake 'cause I don't want mama to clip my fingernails no more than she's already clipped them. The only good thing 'bout all this is that all us children could be doctors right then and there 'cause our hands are so clean. I seen how Dr. Ben Casey on TV has to scrub his hands before operations. My sister likes Dr. Kildare on TV best. He has to scrub his hands lots too.

Washin' behind our ears isn't no problem 'cause we never have to do that, though I wish we had to do that *instead* of our fingernails. Our fingernails have to be e-macu-lately clean. That's mama's word for it. Yuck! Yuck and double yuck!

It's not like we can't git dirty. The good Lord knows *I* do. But we can't stay dirty for longer than necessary. Mama makes sure of that. If she has to come in after a second inspection, she cuts our close-cropped nails to the quick. We have to wash our hands with cleanser after that to catch all them bugs and germs that no one can see 'cept mama. I wish that mama's eyes were covered with a blindfold! When there isn't any more fingernail left, she holds my hand over the toilet bowl 'tween her legs to cut more of the nail off. It hurts so bad by then that this is the only way she can cut them without me wigglin' and pullin' away from her as hard as I can.

"Stop wiggling and pulling!" she says. "It will only make it harder on you." She tugs hard on my arm and puts it even tighter between her legs over the toilet bowl so that the nail won't fall on the ever-so-clean floor that never ever is filthy. Lots of times she makes my fingertips bleed, but after that I have to wash my fingernails with Comet *agin.* After she cuts my nails and I have to go to the bathroom, the 'monia stings more than before. My fingers hurt extra bad when I have to use the 'monia and cleanser on the toilet or bathtub.

I guess Granma Burrough washes her hands before she fixes supper 'cause we eat over at her house all the time after church on Sunday. I love Granma Burrough's cookin'. She takes out a fresh piece of steak from the 'frigerator and pounds and pounds the stuffin' out of it with the edge of a plate to make it tender and make it go more far. I suppose she's right to do this 'cause it always is tender and there is plenty to go around. She turns the steak over in flour after dippin' it in liquid, then she throws the steak into the fryin' pan. As that steak sizzles and cooks, she makes cornbread while mama peels potatoes. Then she gits the potatoes goin' in a pot of boilin' water. Granma flips the steaks and opens a can of string beans or corn. Sometimes both. I hate slimy cream corn and okra, but mama makes me eat a little of it sometimes.

I don't know how Granma does it, but with all of this cookin' goin' on, she makes a choc'late pie. The potatoes are smashed with a heap of butter, and canned milk is added. My job is to shake a jar of water and flour as fast as I can for as long as I can. This water and flour is used for the gravy, which is made from the meat drippin's. I think I'm given the shakin' job so mama and

Granma knows where I am "if only for a few minutes." That little house is filled with wonderful smells and wonderful sounds. All the grown-ups are talkin' all at once, and the TV is on, too. It's a fine celebration! My stomach hurts bad from hunger, but help is on the way.

When I was little I used to have to go potty before we ate, so I sat on a one-pound coffee can in Granma and granpa's bedroom. Granma came in when I was done and said, "Oooooo wee! For such a little thing, you sure can stink up the house."

Me, Celya, and Thomas wash our hands real good. Thomas is still too little to wash his hands, so Celya hikes him up on her knee and washes them for him. Sometimes I do too. Wash Thomas's hands, I mean. We all sit down at the dinner table, and Granma asks what each one of us wants to drink. Granpa, daddy, and Celya want buttermilk, and they put chunks of cornbread into the glass with the milk. Yuck! Mama gits coffee while Granma pours out a glass of RC sody pop for herself. Me and Thomas gits regular milk.

Granpa asks, "Cympi, do you want some buttermilk and cornbread?" He laughs when I shake my head wildly to prove I mean business saying, "Nooooo."

Granma asks, "Virgil, would you like some hot peppers?" And everyone knows that that goes without sayin'. He loves them hot peppers.

Once he has a few on his plate he asks me, "Do you want a taste, Cympi?" He knows how I *hate* those hot peppers. He asks my sister too. I tasted a pepper once on the tip of my tongue and I *never ever will agin!* Them peppers would burn the hair off a cat!

Daddy 'cides to say grace. We all fold our hands, bow our heads, and close our eyes. Sometimes, like at prayer meetin's, I peek to see if everyone has their eyes closed. Granpa is not a Christian, so he jest stares out in space.

Well, after a while Thomas is so tired, goin' without his nap, that he falls asleep on his mashed potatoes. It's loads of fun to watch him nod off, wake up, then nod off agin before he hits the potatoes.

'Bout once a month there is a potluck dinner at the church after church services. All the families in the church bring food and put it on tables that are put down end to end in a row. You never seen so much food in your whole life! Mama tells us to eat only the food she makes 'cause of them germs that might be on the other people's food.

"People don't wash their hands before cooking," she says.

How come? I wonder. Other people put the food that they touched in their mouths, and they don't git no germs that make them sick. They don't even go to the restroom to wash their hands like mama makes us do. Mama says, "They are *so* unsanitary." That means they are filthy. I jest don't understand it.

Mama says, "And don't you put anything into your mouth but what we bring. Even the precooked dinner rolls." These are the store-bought rolls. She says this every time, but we all know ('cept daddy) not to do that before she says it for the um-teenth time.

Daddy eats whatever he wants to. I feel ashamed to have to eat only mama's food at the potlucks. I'm scared that someone will see us do that and think we think we are better than them. We also have to wipe off our silverware before our first bite. We have to do this even in restaurants, though it's far and few between that we git to go to a real restaurant. It's forty times more 'barrassing to have to wipe off my silverware in public.

When we go out on a Friday night before goin' shoppin', we git the special if it's six burgers for a dollar. Mama says before we go out for food, "Now don't touch a thing until we get there." And we don't. We are never allowed to touch our food in public. We have to eat the food with the wrapper still on it. In other words, we peel the wrapper down and hold onto the food where the wrapper is. Mama gits french fries, which she 'ventually shares, and daddy gits two hamburgers. Even though we always git the same things on our burgers, daddy gits our order wrong *every single time*, then mama has tizzy fits.

Eatin' at Grandma Rasmussen's is far and few between because she always has dirt under her fingernails. She also has gigantic blackheads on her face. Her fingers git black from reading the newspaper, then she touches her face.

"She is just filthy," mama says. Mostly we have fried egg sandwiches to eat at Grandma's, 'less Grandma gits a bucket of "broasted" chicken. That's what mama calls it. 'Cept for the bread, Grandma don't touch the food none. Mama tries to beat it into the kitchen before Grandma has a chance to touch any of the food. I don't know if Grandma knows that that's what mama is tryin' to do.

Sometimes the eggs are rotten because no one knows how long the chicken or duck eggs were in the sun before someone carries them into the house. Mostly Celya and me fetch the eggs from outside. Some of the insides are green. Blick! And they smell terrible too. Mama always tells us to watch out for the spoiled ones when we eat. Not all the spoiled ones look spoiled, but you sure know the difference after takin' a big ol' mouthful. Some of the eggs have blood in them. Grandma says that's because a baby chicken is inside, but you can't see the baby yet. Under no circumstances are we allowed to spit out our food, but this is one time when spittin' out our food is O.K.

Mama says *lots* of times that Grandma's house is filthy and we are not suppost to touch anything in it. Maybe it is filthy, but I only think the air is filthy 'cause Grandpa George smokes them big ol' cigars and Grandma smokes tons of cigarettes. She smokes Chesterfields, Lucky Strikes, or Kools. Mostly Chesterfields. Her ashtray is always clean plumb full to the brim, but she manages to squish one more cigarette out with her pointy finger. I usually dump the ashtray out. It's a flat bowl that sits on a metal stand. Grandma painted it gold. She paints everything gold and dark green around the house to make the old stuff look new, but it don't look too good. Mama is "disgusted with" Grandma's painting.

Mama is a kick sometimes. It's easy to make her laugh, and I do that as much as I can. It's my protection against her. Thomas takes over wherever and whenever I leave off. He learnt from the best. Me!

Daddy gits a bee in his bonnet and 'cides that no one is gonna talk at our supper table. I think that is the stupidest thing I've ever heard. He is never with us anyways. And even if he is with us, so what's that rule 'bout, anyways? I mean, at breakfast he stares straight ahead, plops his spoon down into the oatmeal, scoops the cereal up slowly, raises the spoon to his mouth, takes a bite, then does it all over agin until the cereal's all gone. He's jest not with us most of the time. So how can he even tell if any of us is talkin'?

In the case of the no-talkin' rule, the trick is to git mama to snicker or laugh. This time it's trickier than usual. I have to do this without sayin' a word and without daddy seein' what I'm up to. Boy oh boy, this is gonna be fun!

We all sit quiet and stiff, like we're in church. That alone is makin' us almost giggle. Oh goody! Mixed vegitables. I hate mixed vegitables, mainly 'cause of the lima beans in the mix. My sister loves lima beans, so as always I sneak them over to and under her plate, and she sneaks them onto her plate. This time I make sure mama sees me do this.

Between actin' like we are in church and the lima bean trick, in no time I git mama to snicker. She has to leave the table 'cause she don't want daddy to see that *she* is disobeying him. She covers her mouth and is jest pretending that she has to go to the bathroom or git a handkerchief to blow her nose. She comes back in, tryin' to be serious, but once she sits down I take a lima bean off my plate. But this time I push the bean right onto Celya's plate.

Usually, if mama giggles or laughs hard enough, she has to leave the table like I told you so she don't pee her pants. This is funny 'cause she pees her pants lots of times. She has some sort of condition that makes her pee her pants easy. I swear she can sneeze and pee her pants at the same time. She got this problem 'bout peein' her pants after she had my baby brother Thomas. He was too big or something like that when he came out of her. Where he came out I have no idea, and don't care either.

When I can make her laugh, it's even funnier to see her leave the table 'cause she stands up, crosses her legs, and bobs up and down. Then she uncrosses her legs and puts her knees together, crouches down, and walk-runs to the bathroom while she is gigglin' or laughin'.

We children pass silent bets on whether she's gonna make it to the bathroom on time or not. Tears go rollin' down her cheeks if she is full out laughin'. I have to make her laugh as much as I can 'cause she's really, *really* fun to watch, and she don't git angry when she's laughin'. Duh.

This time mama has to turn right around and pretend to go to the bathroom or blow her nose again. When she comes back, we jest can't help ourselves. We are all laughin'. All 'cept daddy. He's madder than a wet hen. He jest gits madder and madder. This makes it even *more* funny 'cause his face is bunched up like *he* has to go to the bathroom and suck on a lemon at the same time.

I planned. I saw. I won! And I don't git yelled at or anything. Well, that's not totally true, 'cause daddy yells at all of us for "ruining a perfectly good meal."

Anyway, after supper is all done, mama talks to daddy and says that the rule is stupid jest like I said. Well, she doesn't 'zactly say that. She does a lot of sweet-talkin' and says that dinnertime is a chance for all of us to be together to catch up on what happened during our day. He don't want to, but he caves in pretty easy this time.

He is six feet and three inches tall, and mama's only five feet and two inches short, but when she starts in on somethin', you'd think she is ten feet tall. I think she thinks she *is* that tall. Now that's funny. Size don't mean nothin' to mama.

Daddy gives in 'cause with mama it jest isn't worth havin' an argument and gittin' yelled at unless it's something really, *really* 'portant. She's always yellin' at him, so he gives in lots of times without much fuss. If daddy wins an argument, she goes around tightlipped and angry and says digs to him till she gits her way anyway.

The no-talkin' rule lasts less than one half of a suppertime.

Havin' mama on your side is very, *very* 'portant, and gittin' mama on your side goes to the special few and the chosen. In other words, Celya. For instance, my older sister, Celya, is good at gittin' mama and daddy to do something that we children want them to do. Havin' daddy on your side is like wavin' a wet noodle in front of mama's face to show her you mean business.

When mama and daddy are yellin' at each other, us kids know to shut up, scatter if possible, duck, and cover. If you are the reason for the yellin', hide real good, 'cause you don't wanna be 'round to find out what they 'cide to do 'bout you. I'm usually the one they are 'cidin' what to do 'bout.

Most of the time us children huddle together, sit on the hardwood floors, bend our knees, and hold them up to our chests with our backs to the wall, and shake. At least me and Thomas shake. Celya jest puts her arms around us and makes sure we stay quiet so she can hear what mama and daddy are yellin' 'bout so we won't git into trouble. Or at least, not into more trouble.

Now, Celya knows 'zactly when and how to git close to mama or daddy to ask for somethin' and not cause them to start yellin' at her. She knows 'zactly how to git us children what we want. She gits what we want most all the time too. She hardly ever gits yelled at anyways. I'm terrible at that. I pick the wrong time and place to talk to mama and daddy and usually git yelled at. Pesterin' is my magic wand though. I try to wear them down until they say yes. I have a real knack for that. They'd soon as give me what I want jest to shut me up.

All the yellin' that mama and daddy do at each other sorta trickles down to us kids. We yell at each other too when we git mad. We punch each other a lot too. Then we git yelled at by mama and daddy and told to "sit down, sit still, and *shut up!*" There is an awful lot of yellin' goin' on in our house now.

I mean *all-out, full-out yellin'*.

Chapter 14: Pot Markers

1961

It rains lots in El Sobrante, and there are lots of hills here. 'Cause of the hills, ditches fill up, then there is flooding. I think the rain is fun, but the grown-ups don't like it much. We are on the way to Granma and granpa Burrough's house, goin' through a foot of water in the low area. This is fun! The water comes clean plumb up to our car doors.

Daddy says, "The trick to not getting stuck is to go slow. See that car over there? See how fast he's going? Bet we'll see him stuck when we come back. When you go fast, the water gets into the engine and you stall out. There's no starting the car again until the motor dries." Sure as shootin', he'd be right. Back we come and there'd be that same car stuck in the water, not goin' anywhere.

We drive though the deep water and there are those black pots with fire comin' out of the tops beside the edge of the road. They look like cartoon bombs. They are called pot markers. They put them up so the cars know how to git through the water and not fall into a big ol' hole or ditch. 'Cause the water is up near the motor, daddy has to keep comin' up over the steerin' wheel, wipin' the windshield with his arm 'cause it fogs up. The foggy windows keeps him from seein' good.

Daddy says, "I can't see a thing when it rains."

"Here it comes," mama says.

"What?" Celya asks.

"That old Catholic cemetery where they bury people. There was a bad mudslide there the other day, so some of the caskets slid down the embankment and opened up. You can see dead people inside some of the coffins," says mama.

Now, I know that what they taught us in church is true. The Catholics are not real Christians, and until they "get right with God," they will end up slippin' down the hill and slidin' right to hell. The Catholic cemetery is scary anyways, but wild horses can't keep us all from lookin' out through the fogged-up and rainy windows. We pull down the sleeves of our coats and rub the windows so we can see out. Lo and behold, there they are, all slippin' down the side of the embankment. Caskets! I've never seen one in real life. These are old wood ones. I look and look for dead people, but there aren't none that I can see. Shoot!

"Where are all them dead people that fell out of the caskets?" I ask.

"Those people were probably the first that they took care of and hauled away," mama says.

I feel cheated. "What ya mean, hauled away? Where'd they take 'em?" I ask.

"I don't know," mama says. "The papers didn't say."

I jest know that is something a paper wouldn't leave out. Mama jest didn't read it right.

"I suppose they were buried right away somewhere else in the cemetery. These graves are really old, so there are no relatives to speak of," daddy says in his Oklahoma drawl.

I'm mad at daddy. He don't read the newspaper right either. Everyone has relatives somewhere, someplace.

Shoot! There is no more stuff 'bout the caskets, but every time we go to granpa and Granma Burrough's I look at the cemetery place to see if they have forgotten to take a body away. That's one of those funny words that mama says. *Cemetery. Graveyard* is easier to say. I look real hard for a long time and I never see *one* dead body. *Not a one!*

∞ ∞ ∞

I graduated grade school and now I go to De Anza High School 'cause there's no junior high school yet. Half of the children here go to Pinole (Pin hole) High School, and the other half of us go to De Anza High School. They are buildin' a junior high up the street from where I live, where the cow pasture used to be. I'm going to the real junior high next year if they finish the buildin's on time.

At De Anza I feel like I walk around in the land of the giants, and the big kids laugh at how small I am. Classes are a lot harder. It's as if between grade school and now there are a bunch of classes I've missed. Some kids my age are real brainy. I keep an eye on them to see what they do so I can look brainy too. My grades are worse than in grade school, so I don't know who I'm tryin' to fool. Maybe that's why I'm tryin' to at least *look* smart.

There's this one girl named Mona who's real pretty, and I like her a lot. I think about her all the time, and I follow her around when I spot her. I know she knows I'm doin' it. The more I follow her, the less she likes me. I feel pretty strange about followin' her, but I can't help myself. Every so often I give her a note about how I feel so down, but she never writes back. I feel pretty strange around my classmates too, like I don't belong anywhere. I have all these special feelin's about Mona. I don't think they're normal, but I don't know how to make them stop. I used to have these feelin's in grade school about the teachers, but I don't tell anyone 'bout them. All I do is think about Mona.

Most kids seem bent on jest going to classes, and most of them carry a lot of books around from class to class. So I start doin' that so I look like them. I write notes to some of the other girls so they know how down I feel, but that doesn't make them friends with me. They have their own friends to hang out with.

Celya goes to De Anza too, but I don't see too much of her. She has her own friends all to herself. I jest don't know how to make friends, and this makes me feel odd, sad, and very alone. Sometimes I git to walk home with her, but it's hard to keep up. She only lets me do this when her friends aren't able to walk with her, and most times she reads a book while we are walkin'.

I'm learnin' to play the oboe at school in my music class. I 'cided to pick the oboe to play 'cause the teacher, Mr. Bee, says it's the hardest instrument to play 'cause of the ambiture. I take the oboe home once in a while to learn it better. Most of the kids sound awful on their instruments, but they don't practice none either.

∞ ∞ ∞

1962

Here's somethin' I *do not like* 'bout Grandma Rasmussen. It's when she says that us kids are all peaked lookin'. Well, Granma Burrough actually says *peaked,* and Grandma Rasmussen says *'nemic.* (I lied. I lie a lot now. It saves me from gittin' a spankin'.)

So out comes the yucky liquid vitamin, and we have to swallow a tablespoon of the greenish-brown stuff that smells and tastes bad. We have to do this every day till the bottle's empty. There is this chalky milk of magnesia that tastes terrible too and is given for who knows what. Of course, the pink Pepto Bismol tastes like candy—like pink Necco wafer candy. Grandma sends home liver pills for mama. These pills stink too. Mama is 'nemic lots. I suppose she looks peaked sometimes too.

Grandpa George raises turkeys, geese, and peacocks (which scare me to death when they call out at night). The geese are mean. All of these jest wander around the huge yard as pretty as you please, 'cept for the turkeys. Thomas tries to pet the geese, but they snap at him and he takes off runnin'. Then a goose bites him on the bottom. Poor Thomas. I pick on him all the time 'cause he's littler than me and everyone picks on me.

Daddy says, "You better watch out and stop picking on him

because one day he's going to be bigger than you, and then he's going to clean your clock." That means Thomas is going to hit me so hard that I'll see stars. I don't see how he's ever going to be bigger than me, so that don't stop me none.

The turkeys are big and I'm very ascared of them. Grandpa George put chicken wire around them where the pond is. I'm *never, ever* suppost to go down and play around the pond 'cause the bank is real muddy and slick and I might drown. But you know me. One time I went down there and slipped on the muddy edge and nearly ended up in the water. That was the last time I ever did that.

It's kinda crazy 'cause there's no fences on the property and all the animals stay inside the yard, 'cept for the chickens and ducks that wander into the next-door neighbor's yard. They git side-tracked when they are eatin'. Uncle Billy has to shoo them back over to his yard 'cause the neighbors "don't want no chicken crap on their lawn," as Grandma says. The peacocks are the 'ception to the rule. They can go anywhere their sweet little hearts desire. Who says beauty don't count for somethin' in this world?

Grandma never has anything to do with these "god … damn … animals." She's jest not an animal person, I guess. Well, maybe that's not true, 'cause *everything* to Grandma is "god … damn" this or "god … damn" that. I think it's funny how she talks, but mama don't think so at all, 'specially since we go to church. Grandma says, "George, git those god … damn … animals out of the neighbor's yard!"

That's if Uncle Billy isn't around.

Chapter 15: No Laughing Matter

1963

Mama and daddy argue even more now.

One Friday Celya is all excited 'bout listenin' to the radio at a certain time to hear the Beatles. I've heard of them, but I never heard them sing and stuff. We are at Raley's grocery store waitin' in the car as usual while mama and daddy shop for food. Mama and daddy give Celya special permission to turn on the radio to listen for the Beatles to come on. I hate beetles and wonder why they are THE Beatles. Yuck!

Finally they come on and sing a real simple song. The fun part is that they sort of sing-yell at the end of some sentences. They do have a different sound from other rock 'n' roll singers nowadays. I like it. I think they should change their name though.

At school, girls are trading bubble gum cards of the Beatles. The names of the Beatles are Paul, Ringo, John, and George. We have our favorites 'cause of how they look. They have bangs, you know, and they shake their heads to move the bangs a lot. I like Paul, but hardly anyone chooses Ringo. He's really ugly.

The Beatles sing, "I Want to Hold Your Hand" all the time. They sing that and a new song on *The Ed Sullivan Show*. Mama and daddy make a special exception to go home right after church to see the show. Usually they talk to other people for a long time before we go home.

We all gather around the TV set watchin' the show, and finally the Beatles come on. You can hardly hear the Beatles sing 'cause all the girls in the audience are screamin'. Everyone is all worked up. Even me. Their clothes are different too. The Beatles, I mean. They all wear the same clothes, but their clothes are different from any you've seen. I don't mean they all wear the *same* clothes. That's ridiculous!

I want to take guitar lessons. I wanted to take lessons a long time ago, but I was too small and the teacher that my parents talked to said that if I wanted to play one, they would have to have one specially built for me. But mama and daddy can't afford that. They talked to me about it and said that even though piano is not my first choice, I should learn to play it while I'm growing. They said that once I get bigger I can learn to play the guitar. Piano's not that hard and, like Celya, I play solo for the El Sobrante children's programs and for the choir on a song or two.

∞∞∞

Mama isn't too happy right now. I mean more than usual. I try to cheer her up, but nothing works. Mama says I "have a chip on my shoulder." My grades aren't that great, but the good ones don't impress her.

Daddy's more excited if I do something good. He says, "*See! I knew you could do it!*" or, "You're going to make my buttons pop right off my shirt, I'm so proud of you." But mostly he says that 'cause I perform a lot doing music stuff. He also makes sure I don't act like I'm "getting a big head." He seems pretty happy most of the time now, but then again, he's off in la-la land most of the time too. That would be fifty percent one way or the other.

Mama is happy (if you can call it that) about ten percent of the time. She looks like a sad dog when she is walkin' 'round. She looks like she's off somewhere far away. She hates it when I "get too smart for my britches," or "too smart for my own good," or when I jest plain ol' smart off to her or daddy. And she hates it more when I talk back to her. But when she says something stupid, I gotta say something back to her. Right? It's jest natural.

We've gone to dinner at the Blevins's house a couple of times. One time I go with daddy, jest the two of us. Mr. Blevins works on the Golden Gate and San Francisco Bay bridges. He paints them! (Oh, by the way, the Golden Gate Bridge isn't gold at all. It's reddish-orange. They *should* paint it gold though. The San Francisco Bay Bridge is mostly gray.) I asked Mr. Blevins if he painted the Richmond Bay and San Rafael bridges too, and he jest chuckled and said, "No." By the way, those bridges are also gray.

Some of the men at church are helping Mr. Blevins build a retaining wall on the side and backyard of his house. Mr. and Mrs. Blevins have a girl that's in high school, but most of the time she's not at home when our family goes over to their house to visit. But this one time I'm talkin' 'bout, she's there.

All the men are standin' 'round at the bottom of the Blevins's driveway talkin'. I'm with them. One man asks, "Where's Billy? Anyone see Billy? We were supposed to keep an eye on him."

No one seems to know where daddy is.

"He was working on the retaining wall in the back last time I saw him," a man says. "He's probably there." Then the men start talking 'bout what the Bible says and what a verse means. There is absolutely nothing for me to do, so I listen to them.

Another one of the men says, "Billy should be done by now. I'll go get him." Off the man goes to the side of the house, where the wall is being built. The man comes back and says, "He's not there. I wonder what he's up to."

All of a sudden the Blevins's daughter comes shootin' out of the house screamin' and cryin'. Whatever he did was bad, 'cause sixteen-year-old girls don't run to the outside of a house screamin'. Daddy follows her out with a big ol' grin on his face.

I sure as shootin' don't ever find out what happened, and the men don't want me to know. But one man says, "This isn't the first time Billy has done something like this."

I never tell mama 'bout "this" 'cause there's nothing to tell. I don't know what "this" is. I figure daddy's happy, so it's O.K. But it seems strange 'cause the men get so worked up after that happens, and right away everyone goes away.

[In retrospect I believe Dad exposed himself to the young lady.]

∞∞∞

The people finished buildin' the junior high school. Before school starts, mama says I can pick out two new outfits from the catalogs. I'm excited 'bout gittin' new clothes, but what do I know or care 'bout fashion? Clothes are clothes when you git right down to it, and all of us are naked under all the clothes, aren't we? We really are all the same.

Celya is real keen on fashion, but she don't git any hip clothes 'less she makes them herself. She's good at pickin' out stuff that's in fashion. But back to me. Yep, I don't give one hang 'bout how to dress. There is always JCPenny, Sears and Roebuck, and Wards that I already told you 'bout. They tell you how to dress, right? No? Never mind. I never heard of no other places that show you what to wear. Oh, O.K. JCPenney, but that's 'bout all.

Oh that reminds me! The *catalog!* Celya comes home from school all excited one day. As far as I know, she still thinks babies come from your pocket. I told you 'bout the wiener in the pocket, didn't I? That's how she and a friend think you git babies. I *think* (and it makes more sense) that if you swallow jest the right watermelon seed, it grows inside. And that's how you git a big stomach and that's where babies really come from. At least I used to think that. I don't know now where babies come from, and I jest don't know how all of a sudden you have a big stomach that goes mostly flat when someone come home from the hospital with a stinkin' baby like Thomas. I'll work that out someday. He's not a baby anymore, of course.

Back to the story. Celya came home from school and said that a man in the catalog had something stickin' out from under his underclothes. When mama and Celya found the page they were lookin' for, they got all red in the face, too, so I didn't dare ask them to show me what they were lookin' at. They wouldn't let me see it. They hid in the bedroom and closed the door so I couldn't come in. I went through the catalog 'bout five times, and I didn't find the man. Mama is jest as excited as Celya, and they giggle up a storm when they look in the catalog that we keep in our linen closet. That's where we keep all our catalogs.

It was all hush hush for me. *Finally*, all by myself, I found the picture in the men's underwear section. Men's briefs really are brief. I always git embarrassed when I look through the catalog and I come to that part. I mean, it's like they don't have much on when you look at them. I have no idea what the fuss is 'bout. I didn't see *no* wiener, jest a wrinkly piece of skin hanging out from the guy's leg from under his underclothes. It looked ugly to me, so what the fuss is 'bout, I'll never know. I usually turn the pages as fast as I can to git to the toy part anyway.

When daddy heard 'bout the picture, he got all mad. Celya and her *big mouth*. He told mama to "get rid of that filth."

That shocked me.

To make a long story short (too late), I git to pick two outfits from out of the catalog. I've wanted a blazer for a long time. Mama had one when she was in school. Finally I can git *two*. Mama don't want me to git a white one 'cause she said I'll git it dirty and dry cleaning is expensive. Finally, all she says is, "All right then. Are you sure you want blazers?"

I say, "Yes!" I git to git a red one and a gold one.

She figgered I had to git a pleated skirt (one gold and the other one red) to go with the blazers and two dickies to match the skirts. I bet you don't know what dickies are. They are like a turtleneck without the bottom. Them's them little things that fool someone into thinkin' you have a full turtleneck sweater on. The dickies are cheaper than real turtlenecks, too. *A lot* cheaper.

I'm beside myself waitin' for all the new clothes that mama ordered. After two weeks, we go to pick them up from Wards. I have to wait until we git home to open the boxes. Mama says it don't do no good to open the boxes then and there in the store 'cause I can't try the clothes on.

We *finally* git home and lo and behold, all the stuff is right there! Folded up real nice in the boxes and wrapped with white tissue paper. Now that's as fancy as all git out. Next step is to see if it all fit. I carefully take out the red jacket first, then the gold skirt and white dickey. Mama says we would have to send all the cloths back if the stuff doesn't fit.

I hold my breath. It's been so long that I've waited for new clothes. I put the skirt on first. I put it on from my head down. I zip it up with the zipper on my left. Then I pull the dickey over my head. So far so good. Now the all-important most favorite part: I put on the red blazer first.

I slowly put one arm through the sleeve. It feels so gooooood. Then I put the other arm into the sleeve. The jacket is lined with satin. Wowee! This feels better than anything I ever wore. It's a little big, but I hope mama will say, like she always says, "You'll grow into it."

I hold my breath again and walk into the kitchen where mama is. Will we have to take it back? Oh my. Mama fiddles with the skirt and turns the zipper to go in the back. She pulls down on the skirt. It slides down a little.

"Well, the dickey fits sure well enough," she says, "but the skirt is a little big. Hits your knees just right though." (We Christian girls have to wear our skirts or dresses two inches longer than the regular girls do.)

It sounds good so far. Sort of. Now the all-time favorite blazer. She pinches the shoulder seams and moves them back and forth. She pulls down hard on the jacket, then pulls on the skirt again. It shifts a little. She stands back and eyes me top to bottom.

"Turn around," she says. I slowly turn around with my arms out away from my sides like I always have to do when we go clothes shoppin'. She tells me to turn back around and put my arms down.

She shakes her head slowly. "I don't know, Cynthia," she says after a pause. "It looks too big for you. Both the skirt *and* the jacket are too big."

I wait and she shakes her head again. Then I say, "I'll grow into them." Did that actually come out of *my* mouth!? If I ever wanted to grow into any clothes, it's these.

Then she says, "Well, you don't have much growing to do now."

Uh oh. I said the wrong thing at the wrong time. It's over for sure. This was the smallest size I could git, and if we send these back, that's that. No blazer. No way. No how. I would have to settle for some other outfits. I jest knew she was gonna say we had to take them back.

"Well," she finally says, "you do have a little growing left to do. These may fit you after a time."

I'm close. Very close. I'm on pins and needles.

"I'll have to ask your father about it," she says.

I try to act all grown up and say, "Yep. I'm sure I'm gonna grow more. We could keep the clothes in my closet until I grow into them."

She shakes her head again and says sadly. "I don't know. Daddy used his hard-earned money for these. We can't afford to just hang them up in the closet. And you don't have enough clothes to take you through the next year. I just don't know what to do. You may not grow anymore."

She had to be kiddin'! I'm a shrimp, a pipsqueak, practically a dwarf! I jest have to grow more, with or without the clothes. *This* is gittin' serious. I already feel bad about the money that is bein' spent on me, and I thought I could show the other girls that I was jest as good as them. I can't help it. I start cryin'.

But I cry all the time, so this isn't helpin' any. I say, "I'm gonna grow. Jest you wait and see."

Then mama says those most horrible of horrible words: "I'll think about it." Every child in the world (at least to my way of thinkin') hates those words 'cause what parents really are sayin' is "No" in a very polite way.

I slowly walk back to the bedroom and undress. That's it. It's all over.

Once I change into my play clothes, come back into the kitchen, and sit down in my chair at the kitchen table, mama says,

"Your daddy and I talked it over and agreed that you will keep the clothes because you're bound to grow into them. You will start wearing them as soon as school opens. You don't have very many clothes, so you will have to wear these a little big."

I nearly jump outa my seat. All I can do is smile and smile some more. A victory! I don't see those very often when it comes to mama. Celya sees more, but this time I won. I actually won! No one will tease me at school for what I wear, except for my shoes. I still have to wear dumb ugly corrective oxford shoes with braces. Still! But I don't care so much 'bout the shoes 'cause I will actually be in style!

Mama says after dinner is over, "Now, go put the clothes on and show them to your daddy."

I hate this part. Showin' daddy how I look in new clothes feels awful. I do not want to show off my clothes to daddy 'cause ... well, it's jest creepy.

Celya hates to do this too.

∞∞∞

1964

Juan Crespi. It's the name of the new junior high school, and it's on a hill they built up. I go down the hill by my house. There's a long, flat part, then I go up the steep hill to git to the front of the school. Besides that road, there's a steep embankment runnin' along the side of the school.

I like the school plenty, but I hate that they took away the cow pasture and the field that we played on. I should say that it's the field where Celya got to play with Patty. Mama would pack a lunch for them, and they'd ride up to the field on their bikes and go all over the field. That's jest one more thing that Celya gits to do that I don't. Not that I didn't git to go up there, but I sure as shootin' didn't git to go up there with a lunch. Daddy would go up to the field with us kids if it was a windy day and help us fly our kites. We sure had a lot of fun way back then.

I don't know what it is about me, but if I git somethin' nice or git a "privilege," then I mess it up and either git the nice thing taken away or I don't git the "privilege" at all. At least that's the way it was in grade school. Now I mostly jest lose a "privilege" of some sort or other. I should have calluses on my legs by now for all the whoppin's I used to git.

Course, mama used to paddle me but good, but like I've said, I deserved it most of the time. The other day she hit me on the face with her hand a few times, and later that day she came up to me and showed me her hand, which was all bruised.

See what you did to me?" she said as I looked at her hand.

I felt a little sorry that I made her hand all bruised, so I jest said, "Yeah. I'm sorry."

Then she walked away. When she was gone, I said under my breath, "Now *you* know how it feels!"

Now that the junior high school is finished, we youngest students from De Anza and Pinole are moved to the new school. Mama says to be patient 'cause they haven't been able to hire all the teachers they need. I don't know why she said that. It don't make no never mind to me. As far as I'm concerned, one teacher is one too many teachers. Jest jokin'. Some teachers I like. I heard Aunt Carol and mama tisk-tiskin' over the fact. 'Bout not havin' enough teachers, I mean.

Mama says to be *real* careful when I walk to school 'cause buses will be comin' by. Lots of 'em. I don't listen much to my mama anymore 'cause she says the same dumb things over and over agin, and it don't matter much what I do—I git in trouble no matter what. These days, mama says, "I will take those clothes right back if you don't straighten up."

But when she catches me not listenin' or *thinks* I'm not listenin', she grabs my chin hard, gits two inches from my face and yells, "You *look* at me when I'm *talking* to you!" Then she does what she's gonna do whether I look at her or not. I don't understand why lookin' at her makes a difference. But I do what I'm told to do anyways, or I git more and harder punishments and everythin' else, like a face slappin'.

I have three new friends now and they like me pretty good I guess. We are in the same classes and sit near each other. Guess you could say that we are only classmates. All the other kids in school still don't like me. I don't know why. I thought with *that* Randy gone, things would be better. He has to go to another school. A military school for bad boys, I think.

Chapter 16: From the Fire into the Pan

1964

I hate walkin' up the road beside the school 'cause the kids stand all along the top where the school is and yell at me and make fun of me when I walk up the hill. There's no way to go a different way, so I'm stuck. Today they all stood up there and threw rocks at me and laughed. Two rocks hit me, and it hurt pretty good.

All the kids try to hit me, but most all of them don't throw too good. I'm real glad 'bout that! They had to stop yellin' at me and throwin' rocks when a teacher came out and stopped them. While it was happenin', one of my friends slowed down and I caught up to her. She's my safety this time.

Once I'm in school, I sorta dodge around so the worst kids can't catch me. Jest like in grade school, when I jest don't have it in me to be teased or made fun of, sometimes I lollygag around so that I'm late to school and no one can hurt me. I'm glad I have friends now. Carol Jean is still my friend, but she's in different classes, so I don't hang around with her much. Also, my parents and her parents don't git along no more. Right? So Carol Jean and me don't do nothin' together no more.

Boy oh boy, I wanna be a hall monitor, but you have to have good grades to do that. The monitors hang around in the halls at lunchtime so the kids can't come into the halls without a pass. My friend Marilynn that I know from P.E. (physical education) class is a hall monitor from day one, and she don't have to eat lunch with the rest of the kids. That's what I like the most. No one can pick on me at lunchtime if I'm a monitor.

I sit by myself at lunch now. I'm workin' real hard so that my grades come up. I have to have a 3.0 grade average to git the privilege. Math is the class I have the most trouble with, jest like when I was little. I have some trouble with history too 'cause I can't remember all the dates that things happened on. I don't care when somethin' happened in the past.

Numbers are my downfall. That and spellin'. We don't have spellin' classes in junior high, but when I hand in the dadgum papers, like for English or history, my grade goes down 'cause I still can't spell worth beans. I look up every word that I know or think is wrong, but I miss a bunch of words anyway. I feel stupid 'cause I can't do numbers and spellin'. I feel like everyone else does a whole lot better than me.

I'm a hall monitor now. Me and Marilynn got in trouble right off the bat by runnin' 'round in the halls. She started it! She said it was O.K. to do. She still gits to be a monitor, but I can't be one no more. That really stinks! And it's not fair! I figgered something was gonna happen like that. I mean gittin' in trouble. I always git in trouble no matter what. The fact is that when we were runnin' around, I knew that we'd probably git in trouble, but a part of me trusted Marilynn and wanted her to be my friend when she said it was O.K. to do. So I followed along. I mean, she's been a monitor forever, so she shoulda knowed for sure what we can and can't git away with. I don't like her too much anymore 'cause she blamed me and said I started it, and I didn't. So I got blamed for all of it as usual, and that is that. Mama always says, "Just because someone jumps off the bridge, it doesn't mean you should jump off the bridge too." Well, heck yeah, I would if it's fun to do. But I know good and well that that's not what she means.

I play oboe good now. Music is one thing I'm good at. But it's true! Most everythin' else I jest git by with. In band I always win first chair. Every so often another chair in the same section can challenge first chair. The teacher gives you some music to learn and play in front of everyone, then he picks the person he thinks plays the best. Or he lets the other kids decide. Now, I'm not tellin' you that my stomach don't git all tight and that my fingers don't shake when I have to play a challenge. They do! But no matter what, I always keep first chair, except for one time.

I'm always breakin' my oboe reed 'cause I accidentally jam it into my teeth. Oh, you don't know what a reed is? A reed is the little bamboo mouthpiece that you blow into. You don't blow into it the same way you blow into a clarinet. An oboe is nothing like a clarinet. Well anyways, you have to tighten your lips and roll them over your teeth and blow. Everyone says they don't know how I ever learnt to play the oboe. I practice a lot, jest like I practiced piano and guitar. I'm big 'nough to play guitar now. I forgot to tell you that.

Somethin' real funny happened. Mr. Boyle, my music teacher in school, handed me a Mozart quartet music sheet at the last minute before a performance. He said that the girl who plays second chair oboe was home sick, so I had to play her part for the special performance that evening. I told him I never played a Mozart quartet any, but he told me I could do it and jest to practice now. Wowee! Fifteen minutes before the performance was all the time I had to learn it. I know it's easy for me, but I always git so nervous in front of people, even though I've been in front of them doing music since I was four or five years old.

Anyway, I practiced and, jest before we went to go on, I broke my reed. I rushed up to Mr. Boyle and asked for another one, but he said he didn't have no more. I figgered he jest didn't look hard 'nough 'cause all the other kids were pesterin' him. So I waited a little bit and went up to him to ask agin if he had another reed in his office.

He said, "No," and looked real nervous. Well, I coulda gotten by with another reed that I have at home, but it was too late to go git it. Before we went on the stage, I played the piece one more time. Every tenth note or so the oboe squeaked like a clarinet does when the person don't know how to play it good.

Mr. Boyle set up the chairs and music stands for us, and we

four students walked up in front of everybody. We began to play Mozart. I couldn't help it. I squeaked. Well, the other girls looked at me every time this happened and I got the giggles. Everyone looked so serious that it made me giggle more. I jest couldn't help it. I was soooooo embarrassed. But it was funny too.

After I got home, I asked mama and daddy if they heard the squeaks, and mama said, "I knew something was off, but I couldn't put my finger on it." Boy, mama sure is dumb sometimes. One thing that mama and daddy do good is that they come to *every single* performance that me or Celya have, and there's a lot of those!

I had to stop takin' piano lessons so I could learn to play the guitar. I never wanted to learn piano in the first place. You know what? My guitar teacher looked funny. Daddy's pretty tall, but my teacher was a head taller than him. The funniest thing 'bout my teacher was he wore his hair all gathered up into a big pin curl on the top of his head. He even used bobby pins, and boys *never* use bobby pins. He had a lot of hair, but it jest wasn't in the right places. He sure looked silly to me.

It's not too long after I started takin' lessons from him that I told mama that I needed a new, better teacher. She said she'd "priced them all out" and they were too expensive. She asked me to hang on with this teacher "for a little while longer" until she found another house to clean. Mama cleans houses so that we kids can take private music lessons and go to special concerts.

I didn't have to hang on that long 'cause in a month she took me over to Scalles's music store and let me see the man that might teach me. I had to go in and play the guitar for him right on the spot! Yikes! I use my wrist to stop the sound between chords when I play, and he said he didn't ever see no one play like that before, but he never told me to stop either. I was sure that 'cause of that he wouldn't teach me. I played a bunch of stuff and held my breath, then he left the room to talk to my mama. I don't think I'm good 'nough to take lessons from him. Turns out that I am, though, and I start lessons with him next week.

He has a real good electric guitar and also a cowboy country-

and-western one that lays down flat when you play it. A steel slide guitar. I'm too scared to ask him to play it. I mean, it took a lot of nerve to work up to askin' him to play it one time. You know what I mean? Anyways, he plays both guitars real good. I wanna play real good like him, too, and also I wanna learn how to play like Chet Atkins. He's my favorite. We have two of his records at home. Granma Burrough gave me her guitar. I practice and practice, and don't you know it, I've worn finger grooves into the guitar neck jest like Granma did, but more of 'em. Someday mama and daddy are gonna git me a brand-new guitar jest like Celya got a new piano, but I've got to "prove myself." I have to prove myself all over the place.

I wanna tell you a secret, but you can't tell anyone else.

I'm not a very nice person.

I know, I know. I git mad a lot and hurt peoples' feelin's I don't mean to. It's jest that somethin' snaps in me. I git really down, and after that I git real mad. Seems I'm one way or the other. If I'm sad, I git real quiet. And after that I git angry. Then I feel ashamed and git sad again. Most of the times I don't like me, which is funny since mama says all I do is think of myself.

Daddy says, "You know the sun don't rise and set on you." I try to be good, honest I do, but the thing is that I don't know how to be good unless I jest sit still and keep my mouth shut. At least that's what mama and daddy say is being good. "Keep your mouth shut, sit there, and don't move a muscle. Just sit there," is what they actually say. It's hard to sit still for very long, so I guess they are right. That's all I have to say. I treat my little brother Thomas real bad too.

Speaking of bad. I *still* pass out all over the place. I've done that since I was little. I went to P.E. today after being out sick for a week. The teachers made us stay in the locker room 'cause it was rainin' outside and they haven't finished making the gym yet. I musta been real sick, 'cause mama don't normally let us stay home from school, even when we are sicker than a dog. Anyways, I passed out and the teachers got all excited 'bout it. I felt real bad 'cause a girl tried to help me up when I was out and said

I kept yellin', "Leave me alone, leave me alone," and swingin' my arms every which way but loose. At least that's what the girl told me afterwards.

I hit the edge of a metal locker door when I passed out, so the teachers got me into their office and made a big deal out of the cut over my eye. I didn't want no fuss made over me 'cause it would be somethin' that the kids would tease me 'bout. 'Ventually mama came by to pick me up from school, and the first thing she did was feel my head. Guess I still had a fever.

The teachers and mama said I passed out 'cause I was still sick, but I know deep down inside that it was 'cause of somethin' else. I jest know it was the same way as it always is when I pass out. I have the same sort of thought, then *blamb!* I'm out like a light. But I don't know what that thought was or is when I come to. Well, not really *blamb*. I see stuff fade out and hear a buzzin' sound, then there is a whitish light. And then I'm out. Mama says I still have convulsions when I pass out. The doctors can't figger out why I pass out even though they ran all kinds of tests on me.

One thing I'm doin' to git smarter is teachin' myself how to read better. I took Mark Twain's *The Adventures of Tom Sawyer* from the library at school, and I'm gonna check out *Huckleberry Finn* by Mark Twain next. But I'm still tryin' to read the first book. I sit on the floor, in a corner of the bedroom with our great big ol' dictionary to look stuff up. I don't know how to read all the grammar markin's very good. Once I git those, you know, I sorta guess at the words and re-read what I read and figure out if I got it right. Sometimes I pester one person or the other at home ('cept for Thomas), askin' what a word is. Mostly I pester Celya. She's real smart. But when she don't wanna help, she says, "Look it up in the dictionary!"

I say, "I *did* look it up in the dictionary and it didn't help none" (which is true). I can't find the word.

When I try to read, I sit scrunched up between the wall and the twin bed. I like that 'cause it makes me feel safe, and I feel happier sittin' like that. I'm "snug as a bug in a rug." I sit almost on top of the floor heater between the bed and wall 'cause it's really, *really* cold even if I wear all kinds of clothes.

Daddy's on strike now and has to work a late job 'cause we can't live on jest the strike money. Mama has to cut the heatin' bill in half.

We have to wait till daddy gits home after his job to have supper. I don't know what shift he has, but it's much later than his regular job. By then my stomach hurts real, *real* bad. More than it usually does before regular dinner.

∞∞∞

1965

Things have gone from bad to worse at home. Mama is more melancholy more of the time and gits irritated lots of times over nothing. How come she's like that? I can't figger it out. She used to be so happy most of the time, unless I did something bad. That's not really true. She always is angry a lot. She's in la-la land like daddy is most of the time, too, and it bums me out. She don't even answer me when I'm right in front of her askin' a question. I git mad when that happens, then she gits mad 'bout me gittin' mad.

Mama and daddy argue a lot more now. It's mostly 'bout money, and usually on Friday night before we go out shoppin'. Oh well, they always did this before. It jest seems worse. Both mama and daddy are unhappy for some reason. They fight with each other all the time now.

Mama makes sure that I go to home education class so I will learn how to sew and cook. Our teacher is a real crabapple, and almost everyone does the wrong things when they're cookin' or sewin' clothes. I made a dress, and it was real good until I did the almost last thing on it: I cut into the dart. If you don't know what that is, maybe you don't sew anythin'. The dart is a sewed triangle to make your bust look right and fit the dress better. The teacher fixed it for me, but she wasn't none too happy 'bout it.

It's hard to sew 'cause I git things upside down and backwards. Cel helps me out a lot. Granma Burrough taught her how to sew.

I like junior high school 'cause I don't have no spellin' or readin' classes now. One thing I like about school is vocabulary. Jest 'cause I don't know how to spell somethin' don't mean I can't say a word and know what it means. People sometimes laugh at how I say words, but at least I'm beginning to learn a lot more of 'em. Also I'm learning new words 'cause I read more and look stuff up.

In English, the teacher, Miss Christman, gits mad at me for not lookin' words up, but I tell her I can't find the words in the dictionary. She don't believe that I try to look up the words.

I like that the school is new, and the books and some of the teachers are new, too. We had a teacher who teaches French that got real bad sick, and so now we have a substitute teacher. She's Chinese. She said she didn't know French, but she could teach us something very important. She teaches us 'bout the stock market. I love learning 'bout the stock market. She has us pick one stock that we like. Then we watch it in the newspaper to see how it goes up and down. I chose Scott Tissue. My stock market number *always* goes up or stays the same. I figured toilet paper is a good thing to pick 'cause everyone *has* to use it and there are more and more people in the world. If I had money to put in the stock, I would be rich right now. Wish I could play the real stock market, but we don't have no extra money at home, as usual. Shoot! We barely have 'nough to buy the newspaper I use to check my stock.

Next year I will be back in De Anza High School, and I will git to walk to school and home with Cel. Oh, by the way, don't you dare call Cecilia Celya or Cel. She hates when people nickname her. She wants to be called Cecilia. I'm the only one that she let's call her Celya or Cel. I don't have no choice 'bout my name 'cause everyone nicknames me. It's funny though, 'cause they never call me by my real nickname (Cyndi). They jest call me everything else under the sun like George, Bug, Shrimp, and other names. I *did* tell you 'bout that, though. No? I'm all mixed up now 'bout what I have and haven't told you so far.

Me and Celya have to practice our instruments and do homework right after we do housework every day. Me and my sister have done housework since we were little. Mama makes sure we clean everything *real* good. I mean real good. She inspects every little thing in the room we clean. Sometimes she wipes her fingers over, let's say the top of the molding over the door, to see if we cleaned it right.

She says, "If it isn't done right the first time, I'm going to make you go back and do it *all* over again." I had to do the bedroom over again once, and *never* will have to do it wrong again. I learned my lesson. What I do, though, if it takes a long time, is sing while I work. Sometimes I even pretend that the top of the vacuum cleaner hose is a microphone. On Saturdee, Cel and me have to deep clean our bedroom. Like, we have to turn our mattresses over and vacuum them, plus a bunch of other stuff that we don't do during the week, like polish all the wood furniture. We take turns, though.

Seems I never git to play much anymore. It's hard to stay awake when I do homework. I fall asleep on the books all the time. I don't know why. It jest happens. It's pretty bad when I drool on the book, though. Don't laugh! Yep. Fun time is all but over, 'cept for weekends. If we aren't going to school, we are going to church, and if we aren't in church, we're studying something or other.

I keep puttin' my hand up to be saved by Jesus. I don't think it's taking, 'cause I'm so angry inside.

I talk back to mama in my head, and she says I'm "beginning to git a bad attitude." So now she's punishing me for that even if I'm not talking back to her. I git punished for jest how I look at her now. I don't care no more, anyways. She also says that I have a bad attitude 'cause I'm "hanging around with the wrong kinds of kids." I'm not! The kids I hang around with now are good kids!

I don't know why I'm so bad and have a bad attitude. I jest do. Maybe it's partly 'cause I have to do homework all the time and can't play as much as I use to. Maybe it's 'cause I'm jealous of Cel 'cause she gits to do all kinds of things I don't git to do. I DON'T KNOW. Maybe it's 'cause mama is jest plain ol' stupid. She says one thing then says another different thing, and I have to figure out which thing I'm supposed to do when. I usually git it wrong. I think maybe and probably the best reason is that I can't stand her no more. Don't tell no one that! If you do, I will really git it at home.

There's one service at church that scares me to death. It's the New Year's Eve service. We have that service once a year. (Bad joke, I know.) It's kinda like the prayer meetings, but they build a big ol' fire in the fireplace in the youth group room. They don't never light the fire in there, and so this means they mean business. At the first of the service, we kids can't go in. All the doors are closed too, so we kids can't look to see what the grown-ups are doing. Mama and daddy let me wear play clothes and play all over the place. I guess God's parking lot is God's only on Sunday.

As us kids file in, we're quiet. I smell the firewood and hear the crackle and pop while shadows dance all over the walls. I don't know what goes on before we kids go into the room, but it jest feels scary. I think they talk about the Rapture, which I'm afraid of 'cause I don't think I'm going to heaven. I'll be left alone with all the other sinners. There aren't any lights on, which makes it ten times more spooky.

After we come in, a person stands up and tells their story about receiving Christ into their hearts and throws a faggot into the fireplace. That's a little slip of wood. After someone shares, the people pray silently. I jest know I'm going to go to hell, and the fire makes me scared of that. I'm gonna burn in the lake of hellfire for sure.

Everyone is very serious, which also scares me. They always talk about how the Christians will be raptured in a "twinkling of an eye" and how "those left behind" (the sinners) will have to go through really bad stuff till the end of the world, which is supposed to be awful. Then they will be burned in the lake of fire for all the rest of time. So that's why you have to turn to Christ.

All of this has always scared me to death!

∞ ∞ ∞

I feel sad for Miss Christman at our school. One of the boys' fathers saw her picture in an old *Playboy* magazine. That's the magazine that has pictures of naked ladies in it. I know this 'cause I used to look at Uncle Bill's *Playboy* magazines. When I looked at the pictures I was careful not to let anyone see me do it, and I got hot on my face. Even I was embarrassed, but I couldn't stop looking at the pictures.

I know Miss Christman looks pretty, but saying she was in that magazine might be a lie. After all, who cares what she did in the past? Even if it's not the truth, the boys act like it is. Everyone talks all the time in class, so Miss Christman can't teach. Also, the boys (as usual) make paper airplanes and throw them all over the room when Miss Christman turns her back to write on the green blackboard. The boys shoot spit wads at her when her back is turned too.

They shoot spit wads all over the place. There are tons of them on the ceiling. To make a spit wad, you wad up a small piece of paper, put it inside your mouth, chew it till it's sorta mushy, spit it out, and roll it into a tight ball. Then you put it inside a straw and shoot it out by blowing fast and strong into the straw. I only saw one that hit Miss Christman, and she started crying and left the classroom. Another adult came in to watch us and told us to open our books, be quiet, and read the lesson. It got real quiet, and the kids started to read their books. Miss Christman didn't come back to teach until the next year. I hate the boys for being so mean to her. I hate it when *anyone* is picked on.

[I believe that when I thought I was making a friend, Mom would call the girl's mother and could get the mother to stop the friendship. I think that, in a very sick way, Mom was jealous of me and/or refused to let me grow. Other than church and musical events, I couldn't spread my wings and try out things in the real world. I also think that my anger stemmed from my young life of being abused.]

∞ ∞ ∞

The whole family, except for me, aren't no friends of Uncle Jesse and Aunt Carol no more.

Mama says, "They always have to buy the same things we buy right after we buy them, but of course they have to get a *bigger* and *better* one. I'm just sick of it!"

Mama gits "sick of it" for lots of stuff now. Of course, she don't take into account that Uncle Jesse makes a lot more money than daddy. They think that Uncle Jesse is rubbin' our noses in it that we are poor. I don't think they are rubbin' our noses in it that we don't have a lot of money.

I like Uncle Jesse and Aunt Carol jest fine. No skin off my teeth. I have to keep my mouth shut about this though. I think mama downright hates them. Daddy don't say much about it either, but I know he's thinking jest like mama 'cause he says "Yes" and "No" when mama flies off the hammer at them. Which is almost any time.

She also says (most 'specially to my sister) "... and *that* Patty is jealous of you too, sister." She calls me and Cel *sister* instead of our real names. She's done this for as long as I can remember. Both me and Cel tell mama that we don't want her to be our sister or friend, but she jest laughs and does what she wants anyways. That's the way she is. We have to toe the line, but she does anything she wants to. She says, "Don't do as I do. Do as I say." How she comes up with all these sayings, I'll never know. She's always saying sayings, and I don't hear no other mamas say that stuff.

Daddy jest says things when he's mad, like, "I'm going to tar you up!" or "You better not act that way with *me!*" when mama tells him what I've said to her and how I say it. He don't mince no meat about it. Daddy scares me. Sometimes he says, "You're going to wish you never been born."

It's real bad around our place now. Mama screams all the time, and daddy talks loud. Course I'm always being yelled at or hit. Daddy says, "You're not too big for me to put you over my knee and spank anymore." He never does anything about it, anyway. That don't stop mama any from knocking me around though. When it comes right down to it, I'm very afraid of mama too. I always have been.

Us kids all pitched in and gave mama a mood clock for her birthday. It looks jest like a regular clock, but mama can turn a dial to say whatever she wants. Like "angry," "loving," and "moody." Well, you know what I mean.

I'm always sneaking into the kitchen and switching it to "angry." Mama gits mad and says, "Who moved that dial?" I don't say nothing, but I smile inside. To make her so mad on purpose is a treat if she don't know I did it. Thomas and Cel don't say nothing either. They probably thought to switch the dial but were too chicken to do it.

∞∞∞

Hey! Can you tell I'm talking a little better? I've been working real hard on that. I'm back in De Anza High School. I listen hard to the teachers and how they say stuff, then I try to copy them as best I can. I think reading books helps too. I read a lot better now. On the other hand, I still can't spell to save my life, no matter how hard I try and as many times as I look up a word. Nothing has changed. Nothing changes that don't change. Soooooo, I'm as stupid as ever.

I'm *sick to death* of church and wish I could do more school things. Dating is out of the question. Mama thinks that if you go with a boy in a group, then that's a date. Cel and me both feel that it's not a real date even if mama says we can date like that. Not like anybody asks me out, anyway. That will be a cold day in hell 'cause I'm different than most all the kids except for the really smart ones.

There is this one boy (that is always in a crowd of other boys) that's cute, but I jest walk by the boys and look at him. One time all those boys were looking at me and laughing, so I thought that they were making fun of me behind my back. But as it turns out, the cute boy came over to me and asked me out. Like an idiot I started crying and said that I wasn't allowed to go on dates. It hurt to have to tell him that. I was so embarrassed.

I get to sorta walk home from school with my big sister now that I'm in high school, but she walks so dadgum fast that unless it's jest the two of us walking together, I can't keep up. She walks with her friends most the time, with me following way behind.

For the past few days it's been different walking with her because she got to go see *Camelot* the movie at the theater. She tells me the whole story of King Arthur and Guinevere and Sir Lancelot. She likes Sir Lancelot a lot! Hey, I jest made a joke. A bad joke. Cel says that the actor that plays Sir Lancelot is *real* handsome. She says Guinevere is real pretty too. She likes King Arthur alright, but he's not much to look at I guess. She feels sorry for him though 'cause Guinevere and Sir Lancelot fall in love and have an affair on the king. I ask questions and she tells me the whole story without skipping a beat.

She knows that I won't ever git to see this movie, so she tells me every single detail. She got to go 'cause it was *educational.* We are Christians, so we don't go to movies no more. We used to go to the drive-in movies when I was real little, but the preacher got a bee in his bonnet and now it's a sin to go to the theater. Mama says that even though she don't think it's wrong to go to the movies, someone from church might see her in the theater if we go.

How stupid. If someone from church is there, they are sinning too, right? Daddy jest thinks it's sinful to go to the movies 'cause the pastor says it is. So Cel going to see this movie with her class is a *big* deal. I think that they let her go 'cause it was a school assignment.

I wanted to see *Peter Pan* real bad on TV, but I didn't get to see the special because I acted up, and that was the punishment I got. Not getting to watch the special show, I mean. I wanted to see Peter Pan fly. So, as usual, I had to stay in my bedroom while everyone else in the house got to see *Peter Pan*. You know, I don't understand what the difference is watching an old movie on TV and watching a new movie at the theater.

I daydream 'bout flying like Peter Pan and flying far, far away from this house. No kidding. I get to fly in my dreams at night too, but at night I don't fly away from home. I jest fly instead of running from a monster or the kids that tease me. Most all my dreams have a monster in them. When I fly, the kids try to get me when I'm close to the ground, but then I think hard and I can fly up higher. It feels real, and it feels like magic. In the dreams I feel panic when I start to fall too low, but it's nothing like when there is a monster in the dream.

So here goes. Hope you listen good 'cause I'm only going to say it once. This stuff is not even in my diary:

I worry 'bout stuff all the time.

Good grades, mama, daddy, Cel, and Thomas. Mostly I worry 'bout me going insane. No, really. It's true. I think mama and daddy are going to give me over to Napa, the place where they put crazy people away. Mama even says she will, or send me to juvy hall. Both those places scare me.

I git depressed more and more of the time now. I feel down when I'm walking to school 'cause no one really loves me. I'm not saying anyone should love me, but it sure would be nice. So I don't feel like sticking around is worth too much. Yeah, people say they love you, but those are jest words. Real love don't knock you around like you don't matter. I so wanna feel love and be loved.

No one really understands me, but I write down what I feel in my diary. I've thought about killing myself, but I'm chicken. I guess I'm more chicken-serious than killing-serious. Also the Bible says not to kill yourself. And if I'm not a Christian, I would go to hell.

I think 'bout how'd I'd do it. Kill myself. The best way so far is pills. You sort of go to sleep, I think. So that's it: sorta an easy way to do it long as no one catches you. Then they pump your stomach. I found out that that's no picnic.

So I decide to go into the bushes on the freeway to die. Then no one would find me and no one would be that hurt.

Chapter 17: No Man's an Island

1966

No man is an island,
Entire of itself,
Every man is a piece of the continent,
A part of the main.
If a clod be washed away by the sea, Europe is the less.
As well as if a promontory were. As well as if a manor of thy friend's
Or of thine own were: Any man's death diminishes me, because I am involved in mankind,
And therefore never send to know for whom the bell tolls;
It tolls for thee.
John Donne
From Meditation XVII
1624

TV is different for me from movies. I always got to watch TV, even when I was a little kid in kindergarten. I would try to do exercises with Jack LaLanne but couldn't bend my body like he did. I'd watch Korla Pandit, who was dark skinned, wore a turban on his head, and played the organ and piano at the same time. And I watched Liberace and stuff like that when I had half days in kindergarten. I like Chocowskee the best, as far as music goes. Now that I'm older I can't watch TV until my homework is all done, but that's pretty normal.

Did I actually use the word *normal*? Dang! Our family is nothing but abnormal. Cel is real quick with her homework, but I'm not. I'm real slow, and it takes time for stuff to sink into me. I read slow too. Cel feels sorry for me, but that don't help none. We do get to watch special stuff on TV though. On the weekends, mostly. But most times I don't git to 'cause … you know why. Like I told you.

I'm picking up words that the kids say in school, like *neat*, *groovy*, *cool*, *bug*, and stuff like that. At Christmas and Thanksgiving after we eat, I usually git bored and I don't want to be around nobody. So I watch TV all by myself. I get bored with all the Christmas choir shows and end up watching Shakespeare shows and *Doctor Who*. At first it was hard to understand the actors in Shakespeare, but now I can usually watch them and tell what they are saying and what the story is about. Don't take no genius to figger *that* out. You know?

I'm pretty much by myself most of the time. No one wants to be with me, so I just stay to myself. I'm lonely and it hurts real bad.

Like I told you, I'm going to De Anza High School. Well, it feels like I walk around in the *Land of the Giants* (that's a TV show) at school. The older kids call us younger kids Crispy Critters. I don't mind that.

I hate lunchtime, though. I have to sit by myself away from the other kids. I don't have any friends no more. Nobody wants to sit with me 'cause I'm like a leper. I think I'm ugly like a leper, so I don't blame most of the kids so much for not sitting with me.

There's always a bunch of empty chairs all around me. But it does hurt. The snotty "in" group is different. They hate me and I hate them. Sometimes a girl in the popular group will look at me as if she feels sorry for me, but she don't ever come over and eat with me. That's Kristina from grade school. Do you remember her?

I try to eat as fast as I can so the kids won't look at me and make fun of me for very long. Then I go to the music room to practice or to the girl's gym to play. I don't git to buy school lunches every day like the other kids do. The popular kids, I mean. All us dorks bring lunches in bags. We can't afford to buy lunches, but when I was in grade school, I got to get a hot dog and milk on some Fridays when mama was off doing something and I couldn't go home for lunch.

Daddy never really had 'nough money for milk or a hot dog. When someone was absent and the teacher asked if anyone would like the absent person's milk, I was the first one to shoot my hand up. Then I'd get a free milk. The teacher always picked me first. I don't know why. All the teachers did, and I'm sure glad they did.

Thomas says I chew like a cow. At lunch I try to eat proper so no one will make extra fun of me. This is *so* hard to do that I can't hardly swallow what I eat. It hurts to swallow 'cause my throat is so tight from being nervous. Sometimes people walk to my table like they're gonna sit down with me to eat, but they just laugh and walk away.

You'd think I would be used to teasing by now, but I'm not. It hurts even more now that I'm in high school. In high school it's a big deal if you get teased and made fun of, but there's nothing I can do about it. I get mad and hurt inside though.

I try to make friends, but no one wants to be my friend. All I can do is write notes to some girls and tell them how I feel. Like that I feel down. I watch to see how they change towards me. Mostly I think they feel sorry for me, but they don't wanna be my friend. No one does.

I don't go to the bathroom unless I really have to. If I wanna go to the bathroom, I get a permission slip from the teacher and go when no one is in the bathroom so no one can tease me or make fun of me in there. The clicky girls smoke in the restroom, and you can smell the smoke from outside in the hall. They are not supposed to, but they smoke something furious in the bathroom, and sometimes a teacher will go in one door to catch them, but the girls rush out the other door. I wish they'd get caught and have to go to detention or get suspended. Suspended would be the best, but popular girls *never* get suspended. For that matter, they don't have detention, either.

I get a permission slip from the teacher to go to the library during class, but what I really do is go to the bathroom. No one can tease me or make fun of me when I go in there by myself and cry.

Kids kinda like me in music class 'cause I'm a lot better than all of them. But they act nervous when they ask me a question about the music. That proves to me that they don't like me but *have* to ask the question when the teacher is not there. They seem sorta shocked when I make up music on the spot. It's really not that hard to do if you just try. Well, maybe if you don't have talent or don't practice much you can't do as good in music.

Mr. Bee is one of the teachers for music. He teaches orchestra and band. Our band at De Anza High got to play in the Rose Bowl Parade in Los Angeles one time. I was still young when they did that, so I obviously didn't go. But it was a big honor for the school. Mr. Bee is fat with a big, red, pitted nose like W. C. Fields. He's also balding, but what hair he does have is gray. He don't hardly smile much, and he's real mean. If someone accidentally drops their instrument, he yells, "Now step on it!" I almost dropped my oboe a few times, but boy am I glad I didn't. I don't want any teacher to yell at me.

'Cause I'm so good in music, I daydream about becoming a big, famous star one day when I leave home, and *boy* do I wanna leave home. If I'm a star, no one would make fun of me and everyone would like me. I could say to the click, "See, I made it and you didn't."

I think I can be an actress even though mama won't let me take drama classes. I guess she thinks it's sinful, 'specially since we don't go to movies. The kids in drama put on two plays a year. It's always the same ol' plays (*Annie Get Your Gun* and *Bye Bye Birdie*), but I don't ever get to go see them, even if I ask to. I think, *Maybe next year I'll be old enough. Then I will git to go see the plays.*

Cel gits to see the plays. Cel gits to go to football games too. I don't go 'cause mama won't let me. Actually, the plays are musicals and I know I could do the singing *and* acting real good. Anyway, that's never going to happen for me, so I might as well get used to it.

Mama says, "I wish you never were born." Daddy don't give me attention anymore and is always saying, "Get away! You're always in my way!" I think that I wanna be a movie star so I will get more good attention and I will be loved. Or at least liked real good.

Cel's in orchestra. She plays the viola and piano. She's also in Mr. Grey's (the other music teacher) regular and super choirs. Super choir is an honors choir and is considered a privilege for anyone.

∞ ∞ ∞

I'm making better grades, so mama and daddy say I can take this elective class or another. I sit next to Kamm, who plays the bassoon. She plays real good too. I talk under my breath to her all the time. You know, making jokes and stuff. I know Mr. Bee hears us 'cause he sometimes smiles when I make a joke. Sometimes the other kids will play the wrong note, be really out of tune, or squeal or something, and I can't help myself and say "Yikes!" out loud. Everyone laughs except the person that made the mistake. I don't want to hurt their feelings. It just comes out of me. Mr. Bee will look at other sections and say, "No talking," but he don't never say that to Kamm and me—and we sit right in front of him. But we also know when to shut up.

Kamm is sorta funny looking 'cause her fingers don't stand up straight and she walks pigeon toed. That's when your feet turn out far. Now, why do they say *pigeon toed* when it's actually like pigeon feet? People are dumb. But I have no room to talk because I walk funny and have to wear braces.

Chapter 18: Shine and Rise

1966

E ven though Cel teases the heck out of me, I still love her. She loves to make me angry. When she does, I go at her with my fists flying, but she just falls on the bed and holds me back with her with her feet on my chest while I swing at her like mad. She thinks it's hilarious to put her hand on my forehead when I try to swing and hit her. I hate her when she does these things.

I joke and tease her a lot too, so I suppose I deserve it. Cel used to play piano for the orchestra when Mr. Bee needed the piano in a piece. She also played viola. (That's an oversized violin.) Cel's gone now (she graduated and is in college). I'm gonna to miss her something awful.

Mama just can't stand to have me out of her sight. She used to scream my name from the house and tell me I better snap to it the instant she called me to come home.

I would ask, "What do you want?"

She'd say, "Nothing. I just wanted to know where you were. I couldn't see you." She never did that with Cel or Thomas unless she really needed them.

Anyway, I don't know why Mr. Bee wants me to play in the band, 'cause there's a perfectly good oboe player there. Besides, mama and daddy won't let me take the band class. They say I'm already taking too many electives. If no one is on drums or piano, Mr. Bee has me do those instruments too in orchestra.

The year my sister was in orchestra, choir, and super choir, the kids were good enough to make a record. The record is excellent, with orchestra, band, choir, and super choir music on it. There's a music award named the Pamela Knight Award. It goes to the senior who is best in musical abilities. Cel and me thought for sure that she would git it, but to the family's surprise it went to someone seemingly less deserving. Cel was very hurt, and I vowed to myself that I would win the award in her honor when I became a senior in high school. My mind is set and just you wait. I'm gonna win that award!

Mr. Grey is the vocal music teacher. He's real nice and has two fingers missing on his hand like daddy does. (Daddy cut his off when he was working on a tool-and-die machine when I was very young.) I can't wait to get good enough grades so I can be in the orchestra, choir, and super choir. I will have to audition for the choir and super choir, but it will be a snap. Mr. Grey does auditions for two reasons. One reason is to see if a person can carry a tune (duh), and the other is so he can decide what section the person will be in, like soprano, alto, tenor, or bass.

Cel has a *beautiful* soprano voice.

I'm a junior now, so because I make straight As, mama and daddy said that I can be in the orchestra. I sit next to Kamm, who plays the bassoon. I play the oboe, which I learnt last year. Kamm plays real good too. The bassoon is that big, long, skinny instrument with a curved tube in the middle that a reed fits in. I talk to Kamm under my breath all the time. She and me have a good time. Doing the joking around with side comments makes me feel special. No one can do the piano part except for me. Mr. Bee wants me to play in the band too, but mama won't "have any of that."

Kamm seems to like me, but she don't eat lunch with me. She has friends that live in her neighborhood that she likes to eat lunch with, like Neva (who plays the flute). Neva goes to our church. I wish Kamm would eat with me. I look up from time to time to see if she is making fun of me, but she never is.

Cel took confirmation classes at church. I have to go to these classes in two years. More church stuff. She completed the course, so she got a brand-new Bible with her name on it in golden letters. Mama and daddy have big Bibles with the Old and New Testaments. Daddy's Bible has red words and tabs too. The red words are when Jesus is speaking. Cel had a regular Bible, but it was wearing out, so it's a good thing that she got a newer, nicer one. I have a pocket-sized one with just the New Testament in it. I'm glad it's a little one because I would hate lugging around a big Bible at church.

Every week, everyone except for a few people bring their Bibles to church to look up verses the preacher talks about. The preacher says something like, "In John 3:16 the Bible tells us ..." and everyone scrambles like mad through the Bible to find John 3:16 even though they practically know the words by heart.

We have a huge family Bible at home but not too many other books around the house. I mean next to none. We do have encyclopedias from the grocery store, but that's about it. Cel and me check out books from the school library if we want to read or research something.

Being a Christian is kinda funny. We think our church is the only one going to heaven. The Baptists are sort of on-and-off-again Christians because they think they have to keep coming to God after sinning and get saved all over again. Our church (the Evangelical Free Church) thinks getting saved one time is enough. They say, "Once saved, always saved."

Guess I'm a Baptist.

Our church also thinks the Catholics are going to hell in a handbag because they worship statues. Mama used to be a Catholic.

I don't want to wear makeup ever. It stinks! Smell-wise, I mean. Daddy doesn't want us to wear makeup either. All the snobs in school wear makeup and nice clothes. What drives me mad is our crazy dress length that the church orders us to have. If everyone is wearing their dress one half inch above the knee, some of us Evangelical girls have to wear our dress one and a half inch *below* the knee. If the regular-school girls wear their dresses well above the knee, we can only wear ours half way up the knee. "Holier than thou" takes on a whole new meaning when it comes to dress lengths.

We Free Church girls are always way behind in fashion because of this. Not only that, I can't understand why one year the dress length is considered sinful, but the next year when the length is raised at school, you are not walking in sin when you raise your dress length to try to catch up. It's crazy-making and just one more reason for the girls at school to make fun of me. They whisper to each other, then point at me and laugh.

When I'm at school someone grabs the back of my bra, pulls it out, lets go, and makes it snap across my back. It stings when they do that. I always look around but never know who's done it. That makes me really mad. It's just one more thing that the kids do to make me mad. Angry. The kids laugh when I get mad.

I know one thing for sure: the boys pull my ponytail. Since grade school, the kids pulled my hair. It's *very* long. I can even sit on it when it's not braided if I try hard. I've always wanted short hair like a boy's. It just makes more sense. You don't have to fiddle faddle with it and wear curlers to bed. Boy, those curlers can pull your head at night when you're sleeping, and it hurts enough to wake you up. I mean me, not you. But I don't never hardly wake up for much of anything even if I want to. I don't want to get up out of bed because life is so painful to live in. I don't know what's worse: nightmares or daymares.

When I was in junior high, mama said I could cut my hair short, but she ended up talking me into just having the front part cut short. I hate that because Brenda (Carol Jean's cousin across the street) wears her hair like that, and it makes her look like a dork. I suppose having it that way is better than nothing though. I think sometimes mama goes out of her way to make me and Cel look dorky. Why? I'll never understand. Cel didn't care much because she didn't get teased none. Cel had a bunch of friends.

I wanna be in G.A.A. (Girls Athletic Association) doing sports, but mama and daddy say my grades aren't good enough yet.

Mainly I just want to be anywhere but home. I wanna be in the regular and super choir too, but they say the same thing. They say, "You bring those grades up, and maybe we'll think about it." Guess you know what that means. That means I probably won't get to do it.

Whatever "it" is, I don't git to do anything extra right now. No clubs or nothing. Sorry. I keep saying that, but it's true—and it's a big deal to me. I don't get to do all the things that Cel got to do when she was my age. It makes me hurt all over not to be able to be a part of something that is special to me. Sometimes I get down. I think that's what you call it. It's not the same as melancholy. That just means you have a sad spirit in general. Depressed or being down means you're sad all the time about pert near everything.

I've been depressed for as long as I can remember. I wonder what it would be like to die. I'll bet people would miss me then, but it would be too late. I just wanna leave home is all. I don't really wanna die, but I don't know where I would go if I left home. I just wanna stop hurting inside of myself. Also, I'm not too sure if I would end up in hell if I died right now, and I sure don't wanna do that. People say that if you commit suicide you will go to hell.

I've always idolized my teachers, and mostly I idolize the pretty ones. Now, pretty is what I think of them, not how they look body-wise. But there are some special teachers that I try to get close to because I want special attention from them. It started in junior high school. In P.E. (physical education), I liked Miss Cooper. She's real pretty, but she didn't pay me no never mind. She almost seemed mad when I tried to do something nice for her like take in the balls and bats from outside. I put the sack holding the sports stuff where it was supposed to be, then waited by her desk to see if she wanted me to do anything else.

Mama would say to me, "Just stand there until I think of something else for you to do." If I ever asked her, "Is that all," she usually gave me something else to do. So that is what I learned at home.

Finally Miss Cooper would look up and say, "Do you need something?" I would say, "No. I just wanted to know if there was anything else you wanted me to do." She always said no, but I kept asking. I don't understand why Miss Cooper seemed upset with me just because I stood near her desk. She was a brand-new teacher. So maybe she didn't know what I should have done. I always walked away befuddled.

I would talk to someone about this, but I don't have the right words to talk about it with.

I have Mrs. Rice for P.E. now. She always smiles no matter what, but I don't want to do much of anything nice for her. She grabs me up anyways and asks me to help her out from time to time. She's nice, so I don't mind. I like helping people. It feels different from when I *have* to help mama.

I like helping daddy out too, but he pretty much don't want my help no more. A long time ago I used to hang out with daddy in the basement or when he worked on stuff to fix. I'd hand him the right tool when he asked for it. Once Thomas got old enough, he started doing the same thing. So daddy up and told me to get outa the basement because Thomas was going to help him from then on. I asked why I couldn't help him no more, and he just said, "Because I tell you. That's why." That weren't no answer at all, so I asked again and he said, "Because this is man's work. Thomas is a boy, so he needs to help me now. I don't need you anymore."

That hurt real bad, but I never helped him no more. I guess in my mind daddy never existed no more. I didn't matter no more. Mama worked me to death, and daddy didn't want to have anything to do with me ever again. I still try to get mama and daddy's attention (in a good way), but it don't work with mama. Daddy (when I perform) smiles, and I guess that's all I need. I guess. Mama looks dadgum mad when I perform. Mama says, "I'm certainly not going to brag on you in front of other parents. *That* Neva's mother won't stop talking about her children. 'They did such and such or they did this or that.'" Mama just plain ol feels it's not right to brag on your children to other people. "My children are much more talented and smart, but you won't see me bragging on them," she would say. That's for sure, Sherlock! Mama and daddy always get me real nice presents though.

Daddy and I pretty much argue over the sermon from church. He gets too mad and says, "But that's not what the preacher meant."

I say, "It is so," and he says, "No it's not."

We do this over Sunday dinner until mama puts a stop to us and tells us, "No more arguing. I don't want you two to ruin our dinner. So just stop it right now"! And of course we do. What would you do?

Daddy's just not that bright because mama and Celya say that what I'm saying is right. Oh well. It's fun to make daddy mad. He's pretty confusing sometimes though. He will laugh when I tell him something I figgered out, and he will say, "You're so bright we have to put a tub over you to let the sun shine." He means bathtub. I just walk away mad because he makes fun of me. That's one thing mama don't ever do. She don't make fun of me.

I think mama loves me, but I'm never sure. Sometimes she's real kind to me and listens when I tell her about someone that doesn't like me and hurts me. But sometimes she just says, "I've heard it all before." Then she tells me to go study or do something for her. Celya didn't mind doing stuff for mama unless it was something she didn't want to do, but she told only me that. She used to hate putting the dishes away, like I told you, and still does too.

Kamm is teaching me all kinds of slang words and helps me understand some things I just don't get. She don't mind. We practice using the words (slang or other types) when we talk.

One day mama got twelve inches from my face and started yelling at me about my attitude. Well, I can tell you how happy I was that I'd learned a new word from Kamm. Mama's eyes went back and forth real fast, like I told you about already, and finally she stopped yelling. And I said as calm as you please, "I think you're schizophrenic."

She jumped back and said, "No I'm not." There was a space of quiet, then she said, "What's a schizophrenic?"

I wanted to say, "Why don't you just look it up?" but I just walked away from her as pretty as you please.

Kamm busted a gut when I told her about this. It's getting to be fun getting back at mama and daddy for all the stuff they did to me. Kamm thinks of ways to get back at them, but most of the time I tell her I can't do one thing or another even though it's a groovy idea. She asks, "Why," and I just say, "'Cause I will git it twice as bad as regular if I do this."

More and more, though, I do stuff that I know would piss my mama or daddy off. I love using slang around them because they never know what I'm talking about. Unfortunately, I have to tell them what some words mean when they ask.

Kamm is telling me about pot and acid (LSD) and says she don't know too much about drugs but knows where she can get them. She knows a lot as far as I'm concerned. She says that there are different kinds of pot but only one kind of acid. Acid sounds fun to do, but she tells me that some people have bad trips and that you have to be careful.

We talk about how to get high, but the only thing we try is medicine cabinet pills. She gets to go to all kinds of friends' houses and smuggles drugs from out of their cabinets. I try some but don't feel much of anything except when I feel sick. It's not worth it because if you don't feel high, there's no point to taking the pills. We talk about if we had more of a certain kind, maybe they would make us feel high. Kamm knows I want to kill myself and says she does too, but I don't understand why she would want to commit suicide. The only thing she don't like is that she's adopted. I don't talk too much about my past to her. Just never think to.

I just don't want to be at home lately. I act all smart to impress the teachers mostly. But each of my teachers know just how dumb I really am.

Chapter 19: "If Mama Ain't Happy ..."

1967

For crying out loud, mama is real upset about something. If it's not one thing, it's another. But this time I can't figure it out. Why she's upset and down, I mean. She's been upset for days now and cries. She's angry most of the time. I seen her like this before when she's lost in her thoughts, like daddy is most of the time. Cel has always had her head stuck in books, so I wonder if she even knew about mama.

Mama sort of sighs when we need to buy something for school. She says, "You'll have to do without that for a while. We can't afford it." Or she might say, "Do you think you could do without that for a while?"

Most times I tell her that I can wait even though that's not really true. Ever since that home education class I took in junior high school (they should call it juvenile high school), I make some of my dresses. This way mama and daddy don't have to buy any new clothes for me, which cost more. Still, mama looks sad when I ask for new material to make a dress with. Then I feel bad for asking for the material.

Mama listens to Dr. Narramore, a psychologist, on a radio show on the Christian station KEAR. His show is on *all the time* in the house. I listen too when he's on the radio. He uses psychiatry to help Christian people solve their problems. He reads letters that mostly women send to him, then he tells people what "God would want them to do." Nine times out of twelve he sounds like he might know what he's talking about. When he don't know the answer, he says something like, "God will reveal that in His own good time."

Or maybe in His bad time? Maybe God gets into bad moods too, since we are "made in His likeness and image." Just read the Old Testament. God gets pretty worked up sometimes.

At other times the doctor says, "Pray about it, and God will answer your prayers." Why does God say no a lot when I pray? That's what I want to know. No one asks that question. Ever! They usually say that the person doesn't have enough faith, but that's not a real answer. Guess they do have a lot of faith for when God says no *and* yes. They cover all their bases by adding, "Or sometimes He says wait." That just don't make no sense. And how can that doctor say for sure that "God's gonna reveal something in His own good time?" When is it *that* time and how do you know if it's *that* time? It seems like Jesus is angry most of the time. Same as me a lot of the times. He sure don't answer *my* prayers. That's another reason I don't think I'm saved.

Anyway, mama told me to tell her when the show was on today. She runs around like a chicken with her head cut off in the house or outside and in the basement if she's putting clothes in the washing machine or dryer, and she don't think to remember what time it is. Mama has me watch the time for all sorts of stuff, like when she bakes cookies (oh, I told you how she ends up burning food) or is cooking one thing or another that she *and us* don't want burned again. She sets the timer but forgets to listen for it.

I told her that the show was on, and I listened with her. She said that she sent in a letter to the doctor and shushed me when the man was talking. I didn't know what her letter was about, so I didn't know what answer the man was gonna give her or if it would be the right one. Oh well. I did my part.

When the man started talking again, Mama started crying. *Oh boy. Now what is she gonna be like?* I wondered. I've waited to see if he helped her, but she's still down all the time. *Still!* What a bummer. I would be glad if whatever is bugging her didn't bug her any more once Dr. Narramore gave her the answer. I don't think he did give her the right answer because she don't seem to be changing at all. After she cried she went into her bedroom and blew her nose like a goose talks. Honk. Honk. I can make fun of her about this because I blow my nose the same way. That's why I don't blow my nose in public. It's so loud, but that don't stop mama none.

There's some stuff you just don't bring up to mama. She gets her feelings hurt real easy. She does try to cook right and feels bad when something don't come out like she wants it to. She cooks real good most of the time though.

Well mama ain't anywhere close to being happy, and it seems like she's never gonna to be happy again. She walks in a daze or she yells at me or Thomas for something or other that we did wrong. I suppose all mamas are like this, but I never been in nobody's house just to find out—you know, like a spider on the wall. When I do go for real to someone's house, they are like the Cleaver family on TV: all sweetness and love. I think they do that to put on a show. It don't seem natural to me. I think they are just playacting. Mama and daddy playact when we have company over, and we have company over a lot. You know, like missionaries or people from the church. Mama makes a lot of food when the company is over. Before the people come over to our house, mama tells us kids that we have to cut back on our food so that there is more than enough for our guests.

[If Dad wasn't having affairs, I'm sure he had a wandering eye. There is also the possibility that he wanted nothing to do with having sex with my mother. Reasons? I have no idea.]

Chapter 20: It's Elementary, My Dear

1967

If it wasn't for Kamm, I wouldn't have any fun or friends. We're real close now.

The first time she came over to my table to eat lunch with me, I said, "Are you sure you wanna eat with me?"

She looked at me kinda funny and said in a matter-of-fact sort of way, "Why not?"

Then I said, "'Cause no one wants to eat lunch with me and you might get teased if you do."

Pretty as you please she sat down, and we never talked about that again. Unless she's sick or something, she always eats lunch with me now.

No one but Kamm, at least for now, really knows me. Last semester I switched a class with lunch so we could hang out together after eating. I finally have a real friend! I feel real lonely when she's not at school.

Mama and daddy give me lunch money when mama is going someplace and doesn't have time to make our lunches. I usually spend it on candy and popcorn. I do the same thing with the money I earn. Kamm does the same thing with her money. There's a nice lady who pops and sells the corn right outside of the lunchroom/auditorium. Sometimes the popcorn smells so good I just wanna die. Another lady is in another booth and sells the candy. I started eating Jolly Rogers sour apple sticks and Big Hunk candy bars. If you slam the apple sticks or Big Hunks down on a table or something hard, like cement, it will break into tiny pieces, and you can eat them in class when the teacher isn't looking. I also chew gum in class when the teacher's back is turned. I've been doing the gum thing since elementary school and I've never been caught.

I finally get to go to G.A.A. (Girls' Athletic Association.) Kamm's going too. Two teachers have to come to the games when we ride in the bus. Usually it's dark outside, but since we have to play outside during soccer or field hockey season, they make sure that we play during the time of year when it's still light outside.

Our team is the bare minimum. What I mean is, we don't have a defensive team or stand-in if someone gets kicked out of the game or gets hurt. The bus ride feels lonely even though Kamm and I always sit together and talk about our school day. The teachers all look like they don't want to be with us and just sit in their seats like lumps on a log. I don't know about my teammates, but it makes me feel like our team won't win even before we play.

This time we're going to Bazerkly (Berkeley) High to play soccer. I must say that I'm good at soccer. I can run down the field and carry the ball faster than anyone else. But this time I'm afraid to play because there are several big, rough girls on the other team that are mean looking.

I was leading my team down the field when one of the big, rough-looking girls from the other team said, "Let's get the little one."

I was super scared after they said that because I knew they meant me. Well, I was so nervous that I ran faster than usual, but there was no one for me to pass the ball to. My team didn't catch up with me, so I had to take the shot. But I missed the goal. I suck at making goals, but I had no option but to kick the ball toward the net. I missed, so the big girls had little to worry about. I could tell that my teacher was pissed, but she should have told the team to run faster and told me to pass the ball rather than try to shoot. In other words, stall till the team caught up. Well, maybe I could have figured out the no-shooting part by myself, but I really wanted to make the goal and show off to the teachers.

Ms. Dovzak comes along sometimes. I try not to look at her, but something inside me just can't help it. All I can do is think of her. Our team is bad, and we never win any games no matter what sport we play. I don't think the teachers work with us enough or put us though our paces.

Actually I'm sure of that.

Kamm told me one time that my mama called her mom on the phone. That's what she calls her mama: Mom. And she calls her daddy, Dad. I like that. It sounds more grown-up and, when I say it, I *feel* more grown-up too.

I asked Kamm what my mama said on the phone and she answered, "She's spying on you."

I started wondering how mama even got Kamm's phone number. When I heard that mama called Kamm's mom, I just knew for days that Kamm wouldn't be my friend no more. This made me sad and angry. I'm pretty sure mama has done this with all my friends along the way. She tries to break us up. I would begin to make a friend, and all of a sudden they would stop being my friend. I always thought it was something I did that made them stop liking me. I would wonder about why that was. I don't know. It always made me feel worse about myself when that happened.

Kamm asked me why I was sad and I told her. She said, "No matter what your mother does, it won't change our friendship."

I was so happy I could bust. Kamm is one friend that I would get to *keep* as a friend.

Did I tell you that Kamm is adopted? Well, she is. She now says she feels just fine with that and is glad that she has the nice parents she has. I can't imagine what that would be like. To be adopted *or* have nice parents. She doesn't ever get into trouble or get punished. I wonder what that would feel like too. She also gets to hang around her friends after school. Her parents give her all kinds of freedoms.

I'm writing music now. Well half way. Kamm and I do it together. I think I'm a little better than her, but I'm not gonna say anything about that because it would hurt her feelings. Sometimes we go into the practice rooms and just make up music. There are five practice rooms side by side with upright pianos in each of them. I play the oboe or the piano. She plays piano too. But she plays the bassoon best because she takes private lessons on it. Sometimes we turn the lights out, and only the light from the little eight-by-ten-inch window comes into the room. She and me like to do music in the dark because there's no distractions. It feels better. It feels like having a secret.

Kamm figured out that you can faint by breathing real fast and then holding your breath. I like it because you get tingly all over your body. I still pass out in real life but not nearly as often as I used to. The doctors have run more tests on me but still can't figure out why I pass out.

Kamm don't pass out regular but fakes it in class so she can cut a class. She's teaching me all kinds of ways to cut class too. It's so easy! I can't believe it! Like, one way is to say that you need to look something up in the library. The teacher gives you a little blue slip of paper and lets you go with a smile. It's called a hall pass. Once you get a few excuse slips that let you walk around the school when everyone else is in class, you can be out of class. The slips that the teacher writes in pencil are the best because you can erase the date and time, and off you go. We use these over and over again. It doesn't take a big brain to figure that out. I was just too afraid to do it before, but I do it all the time now.

I meet up with Kamm to sit and talk about stuff. I just know I'm gonna to get caught, then get into trouble at school and home, but I don't care. I feel free when I'm able to cut classes. What's one more punishment to me, anyway? I can't breathe without being grounded now.

Oh, sorry. I said that before. I repeat stuff because my mind repeats it over, over, and over again in a circle that won't stop. I'm just trying to make sense of the world. I think I really am going crazy. No kidding! I tell Kamm that, but she says that I'm not. I just have to trust her, I guess.

One day I decided to call mama, mom. like Kamm calls her mom. I was shivering in my boots. As usual, when I came home from school, mama (I mean mom) told me what to do right off the bat. I usually say I'll do whatever it is, but this time I said, "O.K., mom." She looked at me totally shocked but didn't say a word. Now *that* surprised me! I expected that sometime that night I would be called on the carpet for it, but all mom did was tell daddy that I was now calling her mom.

I heard them talking, so I went into the room where they were and I piped in, saying, "And daddy?"

"Yes?" he said.

"I'm going to start calling you dad."

He said with a grin on his face, "Oh you are, are you?"

I calmly and grown-up-like said, "Yes" and walked away.

I heard him laughing from the kitchen. I guess because daddy (I mean dad) laughed, mom didn't look so unhappy with me.

As adults say, "It's all part of growing up."

I have to wear a huge full-mouth retainer every night for about two years. Each week I turn a little wheel in the middle that makes the retainer spread apart so that my bite will get bigger. When I go to the dentist, he puts a little putty here or there on the retainer or drills little parts to help straighten my teeth. Mom and dad gave me a choice of braces or retainers. I'm already the laughing stock of my school, so I for sure wasn't going to wear braces. Retainers cost a lot less too.

At the dentist's I walked into the room with the receptionist and sat in a chair, waiting for the doctor. Oh yeah! I never told you, I don't think, but we are not allowed to have comic books at home. Mostly because they cost money and dad says they're a waste of time. When I go to the dentist, I read comic books all I want the whole time I'm in the examining room, unless the doctor is doing something on the inside of my mouth. Go figger. Sometimes he has to fill a cavity and tells mom it's to be expected when someone wears a retainer. He drilled and drilled on my teeth, left the room, and finally came back with this gray rubber stretchy thing over a wire frame that is about three inches square. He put this thing over my mouth, then started making noises with a tool—rubber squeaky noises when he pushed the rubber into my teeth. I still don't know how you can squeeze rubber into a tooth hole and come out with a hard, shiny silver filling.

What was I talking about? Oh yeah, my retainer. Well I went in, and lo and behold, the dentist had two new retainers for me. One is for the top of my mouth and the other is for ... you get it.

I only bring this up because when I eat lunch at school, I get food under the retainer. So I decided to sneak my retainers into my lunch bag just before I start eating. A couple of times I forgot to put my retainers back into my mouth. Yep, you guessed it. I threw them into the garbage can by mistake. I'd called my mom, and she'd come to the school with my little brother, Thomas, and we'd look through all the garbage in the white elephant (dumpster). It was disgusting. Especially the milk that was already going bad in the sun.

Boy, am I lucky. Every single time, we found the bag with my retainers in it. But mom also found out that I don't eat my apples or bananas. I love apples and bananas, but mom puts overripe ones in my lunch bags. I *hate* overripe fruit. I did find out that I wasn't the only one to throw fruit away though.

The janitor, while he helped us look for the retainer, said, "These kids throw away all kinds of food. I go through the trash and find perfectly good apples, oranges, and bananas and take them home and wash them up. Nothing wrong with them. I don't understand why they throw perfectly good fruit away."

You're not helping, I say in my head.

I wanted to lie and tell them that the apple the janitor was holding (which had been mine) had come from some other kid's bag. But for some reason I didn't get into trouble over throwing my fruit away. Guess mom is giving up the war on me.

I know Kamm's mom is real nice. Kamm says she's nice like that all of the time. I'm not supposed to go to Kamm's house, but a couple of times I snuck over there for lunch. Mom don't know, and Kamm's mom's not gonna to tell her anything. Her mom made real good tuna fish sandwiches that were real thick, and boy oh boy, the piece of cake she brought in for us to eat was *huge* like in the movies or TV. There was lots of frosting on it too. I couldn't believe it! I asked Kamm if she always got that much to eat. She looked at me kind of puzzled and said, "Sure."

I have to tell you something. It's a secret, so don't you *dare* tell anyone else. Kamm asked me one day, "Have you ever tried pot?"

I said, "No."

She asked, "Would you like to?" I was kinda scared to say no because it's real important to keep Kamm as a friend. But I've heard that if you try pot, you'll get addicted to it and then take harder drugs. I'd do just about anything for her. But I was afraid also because I didn't wanna get into trouble and I didn't want *her* to get into trouble either. But it's not like I didn't want to try it really. She said we could smoke some at her house. She lights incense to make the smell in the room cover the odor of the pot. She says her mom and dad never know that she is smoking it.

So I snuck over to her house for lunch and we sat and talked while we smoked, handing the pot joint back and forth. I knew I was getting high because I was happy inside and out.

I liked that.

I have these blue sunglasses that I found. The lenses are blue, I mean. I wear them to and from Kamm's house and feel real groovy in them.

Mom asked me one day, "Why are you wearing sunglasses inside?"

I just said, "'Cause."

And she said, "I'll bet you been smoking *that* marajewonna with *that* Kamm."

I couldn't believe she'd guessed that. I nearly busted up when she said "marajewonna" though. I guess she heard about pot and now thinks everyone is smoking it. That's mom for you. On the other hand, she can almost always tell when I'm up to something. I don't know how she does it, but she knows. Well, it used to be that way, but now I hide a ton of things from her and she never figures them out.

I don't know what it is, but mom don't like Kamm *at all!* She hardly knows her too. It turns out I was safe that time because she never figured out that I had actually been smoking pot and was high.

Kamm and I talk on the phone all the time. When I hear a click, I tell Kamm that someone is listening in. This really, really bugs me. I'm pretty sure it's mom trying to find out what Kamm and I talk about so that she can try to split us up. What Kamm and I talk about is our business! Not anyone else's. Besides my diary, I don't have any secrets to keep to myself. Kamm is the only one I trust with my secrets. I think mom reads my diary, but I'm not for sure. To be safe I started writing backwards like Leonardo da Vinci did. Kamm is the one who told me that I could do that. At first it took forever and a day to write that way, but now I'm pretty good at it. Also Kamm and I have some code words so mom or anybody else won't be able to understand what we write or say. If someone is listening in on the phone, we just talk gibberish.

I feel like a prisoner with an extended fence! There is no freedom. I thought about that saying, "If mama ain't happy, nobody's happy." That's true. While the family puzzles about my dimpled chin and where I got it from, I just wonder if they know what I think of myself. If *I'm* not happy, it makes more sense. You'll see what I mean.

I'm actually a very powerful person though because if my parents knew I was cutting classes, they would take some sort of action. Of course. What would *you* do if I was *your* child? See what I mean? You are moved to a thought, and that thought takes the form of an action or inaction. If a parent decided to do nothing, that is still an action. And if they change their mind, that is an action too. Funny how both of those words, *action* and *inaction,* seem so different but are the same. If I say "action," you know what I mean. If I say "inaction," you know what I mean. Both of those words are a form of action, though, when you get right down to it. I'm a prisoner because of mom's action, or not one because of inaction. Either way, my parents control me, but from those two things I can decide what to do and how to react. The power is back in my hands. I also understand that depending on what I choose to do, there are consequences. Either creates a prison for me in my life.

O.K., I can sound smart sometimes. I'm a smart aleck.

Kamm and I talk about stuff like this all the time. The parts I don't say to Kamm, though, are in my diary. And that's what I'm gonna tell to you. Some of it, I think, is embarrassing to say out loud.

So here goes. Hope you listen good because I'm only going to say it once. (Now I sound like my parents.) This stuff is not even in my diary: I worry about stuff all the time, like having good grades, Kamm, mom, dad, Celya, and Thomas. Mostly I worry about me going insane.

This next part that I'm gonna tell you is the part that's hardest to talk about. You gotta promise me that you won't tell *anyone*. Promise? O.K. then.

Me and Kamm skipped class and sat down in front of the school to talk. The place where they have classes and administration are up some stairs, so we were sorta hidden down where they couldn't see us. The P.E. classes, gym, and playing fields are all down where Kamm and I were sitting. There are no windows so no one could see us there.

One time Kamm pretended to faint when she was with the school counselor, and he touched her breasts when he thought she was passed out. *That's gross!* Makes me feel real bad for Kamm, but she says she don't mind none.

She said, "The counselor thinks you and I are lesbians because we are so close and hang out together all the time."

I know from the library books what *lesbian* means. It's a bunch of ladies that live together on an island. But I played dumb and said, "What's a lesbian?"

She said, "When two girls like each other too much."

Hmm. That's about what I read. Sorta. Not really. Most of what

I read about was an island where just women lived. Hmm. As I sat next to Kamm thinking about this, I felt like I was turning red. I sure hope I wasn't. I don't want Kamm to think that I'm thinking that I'm a lesbian. But I'm beginning to think that I am. Kamm and me are just friends though.

So I said, "I don't feel lesbian. I don't think I am one." But I lied. I don't know much, but I know I don't like boys, men, and other girls except for Mona that one year. I know that this is not normal. I have never lied to Kamm before.

"I don't think I am either," she said.

Deep down inside I wonder if I am because of how I've had feelings for some of my teachers while I've been growing up. It feels so sinful and dirty when I like someone a lot. I don't know why I feel that way because no one ever talks about being a lesbian in church. I don't mean being in the church building. I mean no one who is a Christian ever talks about stuff like this. I think Ruth and Naomi in the Bible were lesbian. I *love* that story.

I think I do love women, but it's not sexual. I just don't know what goes on inside me. I know it feels good to love someone that doesn't hurt you. But on the other hand, I hurt inside. Maybe that's what they mean by the word *longing*. I do know that I don't want much to do with boys. Maybe that's because that Randy hurt me so bad.

Once I was walking home and a boy threw a firecracker that went off as I stepped over it. It scared me to death. Now that's not funny. Another time (and this happened twice) one boy in a car reached out and hit me on the butt when I was riding home on my bike.

Another time I was walking and my legs hurt bad. Some boys in a car stopped just in front of me and asked me if I wanted a ride. (I'm not supposed to get a ride home or to school with anyone, including people that mom and dad know, even people from church. I don't understand that.) Anyway, this time I was in so much pain that it didn't matter to me what mom told me not to do. Besides, I thought it might be fun to be with some nice boys for a change. When I walked to the car, they pulled forward.

I stopped in my tracks. One of the boys leaned out the window and said sweetly, "Oh, come on. We really do wanna give you a ride home." I went to get into the car, and the driver pulled a little ways away from me. The boys did this two times. Soon all the boys in the car were laughing and they burned rubber pulling away from me.

I cried. Now it's back to the boys picking on me. So now you know some of the reasons I don't like no boys. They are just clean plumb mean!

I don't like most girls either. The popular girls are always making fun of me behind, or for that matter in front of, my back. They snicker when I walk by or say things like "Just look at her!" My friend Kristina from kindergarten hangs out with the popular girls, but she don't ever say anything bad when she walks near me or when I walk by her.

The other girls laugh at me and point at me so everyone can see and hear. I was having a bad day today, so I started crying when they made fun of me. Actually I almost cry regularly when they do this to me, but I try really hard not to. I looked at Kristina, and she looked like she felt sorry for me and guilty that she hung out with those other girls. But she just turned her back to me. I don't think I saw her hanging out with those girls ever again. I know she is a good person.

The other girls are super mean. I'm the only one they pick on. It hurts, and it hurts real bad. I wish I just could hide away from those girls. Now other girls are starting to say things behind my back. Boys too. Guess they wanna be cool. I guess. I guess I'm ugly and not like anybody else in school, or they wouldn't pick on me. I just don't know what is really wrong with me that they can see in me. Does that make sense? For some reason I'm a bit off. Off from the regular people. I feel ugly inside and outside. I look in the mirror all the time to try to see what they see, but I can't see what it is.

I still wear hand-me-downs or my other clothes over and over again. Only time I get something new is if I make it. Well, that's not all the way true.

Most of the time some of the girls tease me about my clothes, shoes, and whatever else they feel like teasing me about. I wish I were dead. I wish they were dead too! All I want is for someone to love me special.

Dad says to me, "You're good for nothing" and mom says, "You're nothing but trouble." I know that they are right. Seems I get worse and worse. I like Ms. Dovzak, (she's one of the P.E. teachers) in a special way (that's what I call it) and I know that it's wrong, but I hurt so much inside because I like her so much. I just can't help it. I write notes to her all the time and sneak them onto her desk. I hope that she will love me too, but I can't tell if she does.

One thing that's embarrassing is how we have to shower after gym class. I have to wear foot braces *and* a back brace now. I can't understand why the girls don't make fun of me when I undress. Maybe it's because they have to hurry and get showered and dressed for the next class, so they don't have enough time to pick on me. I'm the most ugly, dumb person at school, so I'm sure that's why they pick on me. When everyone is dressed and heading to the next class, they make fun of me then. I get so mad. And I get mad at myself if I cry. That's so childish! But it does hurt real bad.

Just today the student body committee voted on us girls being able to wear pants instead of dresses to school. It came out that we *can* wear pants. When I got home I told mom about it, and she said that I'm not going to wear pants at school. "No daughter of mine is going to dress that way, so don't ever ask again. Do I make myself clear?" she said.

So there's just one more thing that the girls can tease me about. I know I keep saying that over and over again. Sorry.

Mom don't care if I stick out like a sore thumb. I can't do what the normal kids do and I can't even go on field trips. Even if she says, "O.K.," I end up not going because she uses that as punishment, so I can't go to nothing extra except G.A.A. (Girls' Athletic Association). But if I get into trouble, I can't go to the games. Mom uses anything she can to punish me. She don't care that I look like a weirdo at school. *She* don't have to go there and be made fun of. I don't even know if she knows that I'm still bullied at school. I stopped telling her about that when I first went to junior high school. She's powerless to stop it and I'm powerless to stop it. So why talk about it except to you? You are powerless too. Just thought I'd let you know.

Kamm figured out how I can wear pants at school. I carry my gym clothes in a bag, so one day out of the week I carry pants, then put them on in the gym locker room.

Just after vacation, I did a diving forward roll over five girls in gym class. It was a perfect dive except I forgot to do something important. I was supposed to tuck my head down, but instead I dove head first right into the floor. What does that make it? Three times that I have hit my head hard? That's not even counting the times I hit my head passing out. Once again the teachers made a big deal of it even though I told them I was fine. I don't like special attention like that because it gives the mean girls ammo.

Mom lets Thomas have it a lot and smacks him around almost as much as I get hit and punished. I feel bad for him but can't do nothing to help him. It would be like when Celya tried to help me when I was a little girl. No way, Jose. Dad often says, "Jeannine, he's just a boy. Let him be." This means he don't want mom to hit or punish Thomas and to let him be a boy like other boys doing boy things. That don't stop her too much. Hey I'm a tomboy and ... well. You get my drift.

Dad walks around looking upset and worried all the time now. Used to be that mom and dad fought on payday, which is Friday, but now it seems like they fight all the time. I just hide in my bedroom. Once dad comes home, all hell breaks loose and mom gets at him about spending money and what he should and shouldn't do to save it. It's still the same, but now dad don't act happy when we go shopping. He gets irritated. Mom even gets mad when he sometimes (far and few between) spends money on her. She'll yell, "Billy, we were going to use that money for blah blah blah." I can't believe she criticizes him for wanting to show her love.

Usually he just walks away looking hurt.

Don't get me started on what love means to mom. She says, "If you did such and such, you would show me that you love me." She says this if she wants me to feel guilty. I feel guilty about most everything now even if she's not around. She throws love back in my face. "If you *really* want to show me that you love me, you would *be* such and such," she says. "You just wasted hard-earned money and my time by doing what you just did."

Now, sometimes she says just the opposite and says that she knows that I love her because I vacuumed or, let's say, washed and waxed the car for her. Stuff like that. It ain't true that I'm showing love most of the time because to me those are just chores to keep her off my back *and* it keeps me from getting bored.

I can't figure it out one way or another what makes mom feel that she is loved or happy. Sometimes I do stuff for her just so she won't bug me and to have something more to do. I do something for her so that she'll shut up. *Just shut up!*

Mom don't punish dad, but she sure lets him have it when he comes home from work. It's as if she takes all day figgering out what to yell at him about. She fusses at him all the time now no matter what he does. I think that's why he frowns a bunch. Nothing is good enough for mom.

It don't seem like no one is trying to make anyone laugh or is happy except for Thomas. He's always telling one joke or another to get us to laugh. He's pretty smart, because it works. What can I say? He's learnt from the best. Oh. I think I *did* say that before. It bears repeating though. Sorry.

I think mom won't be happy till all us kids leave the house. She says that, anyway. "When you all leave, there will be peace and quiet around here ... *finally!*" Maybe that's true because I upset her even if I breathe. I mean, honestly, how long can a person hold their breath? She even told me to stop smiling the way I smile. I don't know what she's talking about, so mostly I don't smile anymore.

Did I tell you about the time that mom tried to get out of our

VW Bug when it was still moving? We were on the way back from church. She opened her door to get out and dad had to slow down. This happened over and over again until he used the palm of his hand to knock her head hard up against the window so she'd stop. It worked. I hadn't ever seen dad hit mom, but I guess he had to this time to knock some sense into her. It *was* real scary to see her do that. Like a crazy woman.

Well, alls I know is that nobody is happy in our house no more. My sister is like dad—off in her own little world. Before she went away to college, she was either reading or practicing her viola or piano. She practiced piano real hard so she could win the Pamela Knight Award . A girl named Pamela was in the music program and was killed. I don't know much more than that, other than everyone wants to win that award and you have to be the best in music in the senior class. Our piano is in the living room just a couple of yards from our bedrooms, and at five in the morning Cel would be practicing the piano.

It's like being in hell in our house. Not that I've even visited hell. I'll let you know after I get there.

So it's darn tootin' true. *Nobody* is happy in our house. Not even close to that.

Chapter 21: Deeper Meanings and Tangled Thoughts

1968

I'm finally able to take art. Some of the kids are so talented! What I do is so different from what the other kids do. I don't think I'm good at it at all. I'm sure not good at sculpture. I like art a lot, but I don't think I will ever be as good as the talented kids in class. I enjoy it, but it's not as easy for me as music.

Something that's really cool is the ceiling of the art classroom. You know how some ceilings have panels of plastic with lights behind them? Well, someone took the plastic out of the art room ceiling and put up full-size figures of people from a crime scene. They look just like shadows. One is a dead body with a gun set off to the side. Other figures are all laying down in different positions. It's a real trip!

Mr. Benezra is my teacher. He's out of sight. He keeps looking at the piece I'm working on and telling me that I'm doing a good job and have real talent. "Real," meaning that "you are not talented at all but I don't want you to feel bad about yourself." I will have to think about that some more. I think he's wrong because my art is so different than anyone else's in the class, and what I'm doing sucks.

Oh yeah, I forgot. Mom's always made me and Cel take summer school classes. She most wanted Cel and me to learn shorthand and typing. Luckily, when I started high school they didn't teach shorthand no more. I'm taking typing instead of short-hand. (I type really fast now except for the numbers.) There is only time for two classes in summer school, so I'm in typing and art.

I'm no damn good at making pottery or jewelry either. I'd like to know where all this talent is hiding. My art is not so good. How do I know that it's not? Because what I do in my mind does not look like what I do outside my mind. It's so confusing. I wanted to go into drama, but mom still forbids it.

I always check out a bunch of books from the library and walk with them to and from school. They are sure heavy. I wish I was really smart. Anyways, the books are heavy and my arms ache walking the two and a half miles to school and back. Mom and dad won't let me ride my bike to school now because lots of bikes get stolen. On this I agree. Anyway, if I can't be smart, I'm going to pretend that I am so the other students will *think* I am and leave me alone. It's fun acting like a different person than I really am. I've been able to change my voice and mimic famous people since I was a little kid. I have fun doing that with Kamm. She can't do that. Anyways, trying to look smart is heavy. Just joking.

Mostly I have trouble in history and math. I can't remember names and numbers. Don't ask me why. Oh yeah, I forget: I was dropped on my head as a child. I love the sick joke that says, "The doctor slapped your mama in the face instead of you be-cause you was so ugly when you were born." I think that's funny. Maybe that's what really happened to me when I was born. Not really, though I wish someone would slap mom in the face all the time so she could feel what it feels like. But mom doesn't hit me so much anymore.

I can tell you that bruises are nothing compared with a broken bone. I was excused from class (a real excuse this time) and told to go to the library because I'm not allowed to read certain books assigned to us because they are sinful. So on the way to the li-brary I seen this boy come tearing around the corner lickety-split a few times. I don't know why he had to run, but he always looked a little scared. Well, this one time I was walking and he accidentally hit me full force. He almost fell, but unlike his, my feet went clean plumb out from underneath me. Pow! I landed on my tailbone on the cement. It was hard to get back on my feet. The boy was long gone, so I couldn't ask him to help me. It hurt a lot. So much so that it was real hard to sit down through classes.

My family took a little vacation after that happened. We went to the snow, taking a brand-new aluminum toboggan with us. My tailbone still hurt, but I was not going to miss riding that toboggan. (Do you know what a toboggan is? Look it up! Just kidding. A toboggan looks like a candy cane.) The one thing you don't want to do when you are riding a toboggan is sit on the little slats that divide you from the person in front or behind you. If you land on it, you can hurt your tailbone. Well, dad pulled the toboggan up the hill and sat at the front, Thomas sat down behind him, then my sister in front of me. Lo and behold, when we got to the bottom of the slope, we couldn't turn the toboggan enough, so we hit a tree dead on. The front of the toboggan was crumpled like aluminum foil. I landed on my tailbone when I hit the slat. I got up to go to the car, and my tailbone (which that idiot at school broke) really hurt bad.

Mom thought it was broke and wanted to take me to the doctor, but I said no because doctors cost money and we can't afford it. I didn't tell her that, but it's the truth. The rest of the family would have to do without because of a stupid doctor visit. But can you believe it? About a couple of weeks after the toboggan ride, that same fool guy came sliding around the corner and knocked me down again. Well, if my tailbone wasn't broke by then, it sure felt like it. It definitely felt worse than a bruise.

I have a lot of music and sports awards. The one award that I most want to win is the Pamela Knight Award. That's the one my sister really wanted and deserved but didn't get. I have been working hard (if you can call it that) for two years in music. When the school orchestra performs, I always get the solo on oboe.

Oh, I forgot. This is real important! I got a brand-new guitar. Mom and dad said I could pick one out once Mr. Boyd (my guitar teacher) said that I was ready for one. I still played Granma Burrough's guitar and it didn't stay in tune no more. There are two electric guitars I had my eyes on. One is an olive-green Fender Rhodes and the other is like a Trini Lopez Sunburst Gibson. It was a hard choice. I thought about which one to pick for a couple of weeks. Just knowing I could be playing one or the other excited me to no end.

I chose the Gibson. So, to make a long story short—too late!— I was asked to perform on that guitar with the regular choir and the super choir, and I was as nervous as a dog because I had to play in front of the schoolkids and I didn't want to mess up. Lord knows it would have been one more thing for them to ... do I really have to say that again?

Oh, by the way, I performed a piece I wrote on the piano too.

Mr. Bee asked me to sing a song for the Contra Costa School District get-together. All the teachers and principals were going to be there. I knew one of the songs well enough because I sang it quietly to myself when the orchestra rehearsed it. That's probably why Mr. Bee asked me to sing it in front of all those teachers and principals. I had a long blue dress that fit the period piece, and in the drama wardrobe I found the perfect hat. Finally I was "on." When I do any kind of performance, it's the quiet that makes me nervous. It's as if everyone has taken a breath together and is waiting on me for them to let it out.

The orchestra gave their introduction, then I began to sing. I think I sounded O.K., but I was absolutely dumbfounded when the crowd gave me a standing ovation. Mr. Bee was smiling ear to ear. I don't think I ever seen him smile like that before. I bowed and was going to leave the stage while the clapping continued. Mr. Bee stopped me and told me to sing it again.

"Again!? The same song?" I asked.

He nodded with that smile on his face and raised his baton so that I would have no doubt that it was indeed the only song the orchestra knew. So I sang again with more feeling than I did the first time. Once again, to my embarrassment. I got a standing ovation. It seemed to go on forever!

Wow! Can you imagine how that felt?

As it turns out, me and Kamm are in the running for the Pamela Knight Award. How hard is that? My best friend is running for the same thing at the same time. I wanted her to win, but I wanted me to win more than her. We turned up to the awards show and both of us were as nervous as all get out.

The Pamela Knight Award was the last to be given out. Finally ... *finally!* The host announced the award by first telling the crowd about its meaning. I expected him to say, "The envelope please," but of course he just had an old piece of paper. He went on and on about the award and the achievements we all had to do in order just to be nominated for it. I looked at Kamm and she looked at me. Mona Lisa had nothing on us as we held our breath.

Then it came. It happened: "And the winner of the prestigious Pamela Knight Award is ..."

Well, it was me.

The crowd stood in ovation as I walked to the podium to receive the award. Forget the award. I just wanted to walk up there without tripping and falling. I knew that the actual award was a plaque that stayed behind a glass panel in the school. But there my name would be. I won the award for my sister, and I could say to the naysayers, "In your eye! Take this, suckas!"

My sister Cecilia couldn't be at the award presentation because she's in college, but I honored her more than they could ever have honored me by winning that award.

∞∞∞

Oh the tangled web we weave when first we practice to deceive.
Sir Walter Scott
Marmion, Cannto VI Stanza 17
1808

When you feel unloved and beaten down, if you have any

spark of hope inside you, you start to reach out. At least that's what I do. I want the peace that comes with acceptance.

I most want to be held. Physically held.

After a while, my trying to get good attention went into a partial lie. If I can't talk about my home life—and we are forbidden to talk outside the home about what goes on behind closed doors —I embellish my feelings. If and when I do this, I do get extra attention. I cry too, though not to get the kind of attention I want. Sometimes with Kamm I seek out a little bit of my family's "what it's like" truth. Just the little bit that I let out takes a bit of pressure off of my shoulders.

I learned that word *embellish* in English class, and it hits the thing right on the head. The word means that I take what is true and say it in such a way as to make the person I'm talking to feel even badder for me. It's not nice to do and I *know* it's not nice for someone else, but I so want ... well, you know.

If

If you can keep your head when all about you
Are losing theirs and blaming it on you,
If you can trust yourself when all men doubt you,
But make allowance for their doubting too;
If you can wait and not be tired by waiting,
Or being lied about, don't deal in lies,
Or being hated, don't give way to hating,
And yet don't look too good, nor talk too wise:

If you can dream—and not make dreams your master;
If you can think—and not make thoughts your aim;
If you can meet with Triumph and Disaster
And treat those two impostors just the same;
If you can bear to hear the truth you've spoken
Twisted by knaves to make a trap for fools,
Or watch the things you gave your life to, broken,
And stoop and build 'em up with worn-out tools:

If you can make one heap of all your winnings
And risk it on one turn of pitch-and-toss,
And lose, and start again at your beginnings
And never breathe a word about your loss;
If you can force your heart and nerve and sinew
To serve your turn long after they are gone,
And so hold on when there is nothing in you
Except the Will which says to them: "Hold on!"

If you can talk with crowds and keep your virtue,
Or walk with Kings—nor lose the common touch,
If neither foes nor loving friends can hurt you,
If all men count with you, but none too much;
If you can fill the unforgiving minute
With sixty seconds' worth of distance run,
Yours is the Earth and everything that's in it,
And—which is more—you'll be a Man, my son!
Rudyard Kipling
1892

People act funny after I hand a note to them. I feel desperate inside. If someone would only understand me. Hear me. I could know who I am and figure out why I act the way I do. I don't understand, though, what makes me feel like someone else would understand me. But I keep reaching out. Maybe there is someone somewhere that can help me fix what is wrong inside of me.

What is it that makes the other kids pick on me? People seem to be pulling further and further away from me. So whatever is wrong with me is probably getting worse. Yeah, Kamm and I are friends, but that's mainly because of the music. I wonder if she would still be my friend without the music. I'm guessing no. I feel like a hideous monster.

My sister is in college now. I sure miss her. It hurts like an ache in my stomach that won't go away. It's like being hungry for no good reason. My shoulders feel heavy too. I miss her so much.

I write to her a lot. She writes back but really can't afford the stamps.

She's majoring in music. She says that when they have their big dorm competition show, she's going to try to get mom and dad to let me visit her. I sorta know that they will let me go because Celya is asking and I'm not. My grades are up, so they can't say I can't go because of my grades. I try to be good so that they won't punish me for any little thing and not let me go.

Mr. Crusen, Larry, who is real handsome and young and who used to be our youth director in church, volunteered to take me to Cel's school. Is that heavy? He actually has to go to the area for some other reason, and his whole family is coming too. Seeing Cecilia is far out. but what is really out of sight is that I won't have family around me and I will get to know a little bit about college from her and at least meet the friends that she talks about in her letters to me.

The drive down isn't so bad. It's hotter than the dickens, but I'll put up with anything just to get out from under mom and dad. Mostly mom. Dad is much more lenient.

Kamm's a good friend, but I feel trapped and depressed with each passing day. I just don't get it. I don't know how to live life so that everyone is happy with me. I mess up all the time. It works out that people like it when I kiss up to them. but that isn't the real me. It's just something I learnt to do at home to try to get my way.

I don't know who I am, and no one seems to be able to help me figure it out. Adults just don't talk much to kids. Or maybe they just don't want to talk to me. It's all screwed up in my head. All twisted around, up and down. All I know is that Kamm is helping me to keep my head on "when those around me are losing theirs," or something like that. It seems that when I have one thought, another thought pops up that is exactly the opposite of the first thought, then another thought comes up that makes the other two thoughts wrong. ALL WRONG!

That's it! *I'm* all wrong.

Then there are these other voices in my head that tell me to do this or do that and almost shout at me. Am I going crazy? Probably. I DON'T KNOW! Maybe they will have to take me to Napa, the state mental hospital for crazy people. I feel crazy inside of my head. If Kamm really knew what was going on in my head, she wouldn't like me either. I'm pretty sure of that.

Wanna hear something strange? There is this girl in school that looks as sad as I feel. She's in my P.E. class. I went into the bathroom and she was there.

I said, "You look so sad. Why?"

Then she said, "Because my mother broke my spirit."

I just said quiet like, "Oh." I really don't know what she means and she didn't seem to want to talk any more about it. She just hung her head and cried. I felt sad for her. I think (if I actually knew what it meant) that I would know if my spirit was broken.

I think mom is right though. She will ask me what's wrong and sometimes I say, "I'm depressed," but most of the time I say, "I'm bored." When I tell her that I'm depressed she says stuff like (in a huffy way), "Well I don't know what *YOU* have to be depressed about."

Sometimes there is a pretty girl that I sort of follow around between classes. I want her to like me, but I'm pretty sure she don't. Someone please like me. I want to be normal like the rest of the kids, but I don't know how. Well, most kids seem normal, but what do I know? *No, really!* I just don't get any of this stuff. I wish that, *poof*, I'd be gone. You know those families on TV are not real, but it seems from the little I've seen that most families are pretty close to what you see on TV. I wish I lived in a happy family.

My "friend" Marilyn from junior high hasn't been in school for a long time. That happens sometimes when a family moves. I didn't tell you much about her. She is a big girl, weight-wise, with short curly blonde hair and big ol' thick glasses and dresses that make her look like a dork. She's kinda off normal a bit looks-wise. She is real nice though. I think I told you that her father is one of the coaches at De Anza where I go to school? I know that the girls pick on Marilyn too. I still don't want to be her friend.

No, it's not like what you're thinking. I just get picked on so much that I don't need one more thing or person in my life so that I get picked on more. Does that make any sense?

I asked mom why Marilyn wasn't in school no more and she said, "Because she had a nervous breakdown." I'm not sure exactly what that means, but I do wonder if Marilyn had to go to Napa State Institution. I've never been there, but mom says it's a really bad place to "end up in."

Maybe I will end up there. Mom keeps saying I will. That's why I don't talk too much about how I feel deep down inside even to Kamm. I feel so alone. I'm pretty sure that no one will ever love me in a special way. Now that Cel's gone, I feel lonelier. I wonder why Marilyn had a breakdown in what my mom says "is a very nice home." She means the people, not the house itself. We don't have one of those though (a very nice home). I think mom thinks we do though.

Maybe Marilyn had a breakdown because she was picked on like me, though I don't think she's been picked on as much as me for as long as me. Maybe I'm crazy and I just don't know it. I think that maybe most crazy people don't know they are crazy. At least I think that might be true. Crazy is as crazy does. Who's crazy, I ask you?

One thing I know for sure: I love music and it takes me to many places. Sad, happy, full of joy, sorrow, love, and hope. It's my life. I wish we were rich so I could go to Juilliard. I just know I would love it there instead of boring old college. I could actually learn something that matters to me.

I'm sending away for college catalogs to see what one I can go to. I want to go to Platt College, an art school, but no way no how can we afford *that*. So I'm stuck with a couple of choices. I want to go to UC Berkeley, but mom was definite about my not going there due to the "bad influences and the children you would hang out with. I know you."

Yep! A place where I could finally breathe. Mom and dad are stuck on Christian colleges. There are three choices. One is called Pensacola University in Florida. Mom says, "Oh that would be too far away from us." Another one is called Biola University near Los Angeles. And finally the absolutely positively worst choice is the Christian school in San Francisco. No how no way for that school because I would have to live at home. Oh, come on now. Twist my arm.

Except for summer, it's always freezing in our house. Mom is trying to cut the electric bill in half. Dad put in what he calls forced-air heating, and I don't think it's near as good as what we had. That new heating system is pretty groovy in the summertime though because it blows cool basement air up through the vents into our house and cools the house down.

I swear (not really) that Thomas is growing a whole head taller each year now. I never thought of him as growing or growing up. I don't know why. But one thing I *do* remember if I don't remember anything else is what dad said: "You shouldn't pick on him like you do. Someday he's going to be a lot taller than you and the tables will be turned. He will be able to clean your clock." This means Thomas will fight me and win easily. I don't believe that will ever happen, but I must say it makes me a little nervous sometimes when I'm mean to Thomas. You know I don't want to be mean to him—it's just that he's the only person shorter than me that I can pick on.

Everyone tells me what to do, when to do it, and how to do it. He's just a punching bag to me. All my anger goes toward him. Most of the time he doesn't deserve it, but I can't seem to help myself.

I do and don't want to have children when I get married. I don't mostly because I don't want to treat them as bad as I've been treated, and with my anger I'm sure I will be as hard on them as mom and dad have been on me. I do love children though, and they cozy up to me too.

I still have *terrible* nightmares, and I still try not to fall asleep, but of course I can't keep my eyes open all night long. This seems harder to do when I go to bed hungry and have been told to "think about it." If I do something wrong, that's the punishment. So I don't get all the sleep I need. One time I was in history class in the back row (finally I get to sit there instead of under the teacher's nose). Anyway, I was so tired that I said to myself, *I'm just going to rest my head on my arm.* Before you knew it, I was off in la-la land. I sorta heard the bell ring, but it only rang in my dream and it wasn't loud enough to wake me up.

I was snoozing and drooling when I heard my name being called off in the distance a few times, but I couldn't seem to wake up. Finally I felt a hand gently rocking me. It was the nice boy who is always kissing his girlfriend in the hall during breaks. He shook me again, and finally I was able to wake up. The teacher and the kids still there were smiling at me. I was sure I would get into trouble with the teacher, but she didn't say one little thing about it. Now that was outa sight.

I never tell Kamm this, but she really is saving my life and keeping me alive. Because of her, I have someone to talk to and have fun with. She don't care what I'm like. She gave me this really far-out cloth purse that looks like an Indian-made bag. That kinda pattern. Ziggy zaggy. I love that purse. One, because Kamm gave it to me, and two, because it's groovy and with it.

Kamm came up with the idea that I could shove my pants and blouse in the purse and change into them once I'm at school so that I can look like the other kids. So I do this even though I know I'm not supposed to. But it's important to me to not stand out like a sore thumb like I do in my dresses. It was a good idea until mom came to pick me up from school after I had passed out. I forgot to change my clothes before she showed up. What an idiot I am. She said something like, "Even though I told you not to wear pants at school, you went behind my back and did it anyway." I just slouched down in the car seat and didn't answer her.

I could care less anymore what she does to me or says to me. From that time on she let me wear pants. "If you can't beat 'em, then join 'em," she said.

Kamm is teaching me a lot of stuff that I never knew. She doesn't make a big deal of it either. She really is a good friend, and I'm glad that she is my best friend and I'm hers. I would die for her if anything happened. She is so brave to hang out with me. I don't know if … Well, I *know* I'm not brave enough to do that for someone else. Just look at Marilyn. When she really needed a friend, I wasn't there for her. This is especially bad because I know how it feels to be picked on and have no friends.

Mom got me a job to earn some extra money. I iron this lady's stuff and make ten cents for each thing I iron. My legs and back hurt something awful when I have to do the ironing, but mom don't seem to care if that's how I feel. I want the money, so I do the ironing. I'm pretty good at it too. I iron in the garage so I don't have to listen to mom and dad carry on. They seem to fight nonstop. It's cold in the garage, but it's nice and peaceful.

That part I like about this whole thing. Being alone at home.

Chapter 22: It Smells Like Burning Rope

1969

Drugs are all you hear about now. On the TV, on the radio, and at school. They talk about how horrible drugs are and that parents can find out if you use them by following a few simple clues. These clues are mostly about pot.

<u>Clue Number One</u>: You can find out if your child is smoking marijuana because the smoke smells like burning rope.

I don't know about you, but I don't think very many parents have ever smelled burning rope. I wonder if they try to burn rope to see what it smells like once they know it's a clue.

Someone forgot to tell *me* that you can also smell pot on someone's clothing.

<u>Clue Number Two</u>: You can tell if your child is smoking dope if their eyes are dilated and glassy.

The Clue Room forgot to mention that darkness dilates eyes.

Now we know why some hippies wear sunglasses. It's not because it's too light outside or in. I think I will start wearing sunglasses just to freak mom and dad out. I love doing stuff like this to them. It throws them off course. And make me feel so happy.

<u>Clue Number Three</u>: Your child's grades will drop.

Well, what the freak!? My grades go up and down all over the place. So that means I'm on drugs? Probably uppers and downers?

<u>Clue Number Four</u>: Your child starts associating with the "wrong" crowd.

Guess I'm safe there since I don't hang with any crowd.

<u>Clue Number Five</u>: You find rolling papers or gator clips in your child's bedroom.

And maybe I just want to smoke cigarettes. Oh yeah, those are a drug too.

<u>Clue Number Six</u>: You find what looks to be oregano in a baggy in your child's pocket or room.

I personally would add parsley flakes and marjoram leaves to the list, but I guess someone smokes pot in the Clue Room and didn't want to give all the clues away.

<u>My</u> <u>Clue Number Seven</u>: If your child starts singing the pot theme song, "Frank Sinatra's Do Be, Do Be, Do," your child is probably smoking pot.

Anyways, I think being bored is another clue. I'm bored all the time. Look, I've lived in the same house for all my life, and there's nothing new to do around here. When I come into the house, mom sometimes ask how I feel, and I say, "I'm bored," and she says, "Well, there is *plenty* to do around here so that you won't feel bored anymore."

She just doesn't get it! Being home is like being in a prison. You can't go out with your friends to do fun stuff—parties, dances, football games, and stuff. Obviously, mom was never young.

That's not true. Actually, she was young when she had Cel. Maybe that was her fun, but how the heck do you get pregnant if you can't date? What do I know about pregnant other than if you date boys, that's what you can get? Hmm.

No it's not worth it. Dating boys, I mean. Do I lie?

So, with almost all the fun things that kids do that you can't do, what else is there to do but take drugs and smoke pot? Well, I don't take any hard drugs. And I don't believe that when you smoke pot you can get addicted to hard drugs. Good grief. How much trouble could I ever get into?

Well, let's see.

I already took medicine cabinet pills (none of which really

worked), and I smoked pot. Twice! Well, my life looks like icing slowly dripping down a cake, or like my fav Salvador Dali's melting clocks art. I love that one. He has clocks all over the place that look like they are melting over walls and stuff. Well, you get what I mean.

It's the lazy days of summer without any of the fun. I need fun to breathe. Kamm tries to think up ways I can do this, but let's face it: there's only so much you can do for fun in a prison.

Today I took a bunch of aspirin. I mean seven to be ex-act. (I love playing with words.) Well, that backfired on me real good, as mom would say.

In P.E. (physical education for you slow learners), we had to do the 350-yard walk/run test. I was up against Kamm *again*. I never ever win any races. I try. I really do. Anyway Kamm was pulling away from me. Now, it wouldn't be so embarrassing if Kamm wasn't pigeon-toed. Poor thing. I never ever mentioned it to her even though we talk about my shoes, braces, and stuff.

Anyway again, I ran as hard and as fast as I could, but I just slowed down more and more. She won. I came in dragging, huffing, and puffing, and I fell (on purpose) on the grass. My teacher (Ms. Dovzak) rushed over to me and *told* me to get up and walk around.

Yeah, right. I was about to puke my guts out and knew full well that it was because of the aspirin I took. You'd think that the aspirin would have made me run faster because it's kind of an upper.

Anyway, I told her I didn't want to.

She said, "Get up!" and pulled me off the ground. All the girls had worried looks on their faces, but I didn't know why. Then Ms. Dovzak shocked me. She leaned me up against the front of her body, slipped an arm under mine, put the palm of her hand over my heart, and began walking me around.

Was I embarrassed?

You have no idea. There are a few of the popular girls in that class. And I was feeling some funny feelings that felt good, which made me even more embarrassed. I'm sure any of the girls could see that. But they just kept watching me and looking worried.

No, *horrified* is a better word.

Finally, the teacher stopped walking me around, and I asked why she done that. She said, "Because you were as white as a sheet and your heart was pumping out of control."

And I thought, *So?* But finally she let me lie down.

What were all those strange feelings I felt just being touched by Ms. Dovzak? I like and hate those funny feelings. I don't tell Kamm about them because they somehow feel sinful. For the rest of the day I couldn't stop thinking about the whole thing, and I felt more embarrassed and sinful the longer the day got. Kamm could see that something was wrong with me, but I said I was just down.

But I'm not down at all right now. I'm happy as can be. Someone actually touched me in a good way. So that's how it feels. Wow!

When I got home the yelling at me started all over again.

I, "should do this," which I haven't done.

I "shouldn't do that," which I had done.

I "better get it together or you know what?"

This started all over in the morning with, "You better do this." "You better do that when you get home from school today." "... *that* Kamm blah blah blah."

One morning I took Dramamine as soon as I got to school. I felt trippy and sick at the same time. When I walked into the cafeteria at lunch, the kids looked at me like I'm ugly or something. As usual. Kamm had to go to the doctor, so she wasn't there. Mom had to go someplace, so she gave me money to buy lunch. While I was carefully walking to my usual table with a tray full of food, a popular guy tripped me. Luckily I didn't fall down. The kids watched me and laughed.

Those feelings of aloneness came back to me again.

After I finished eating, I decided to hide out in the gym locker room. And I wrote a note to Ms. Dovzak about wanting to die.

While I was hiding, I changed into my P.E. clothes because P.E.

was my next class anyway, and I didn't want to have to change in front of the popular girls. Then I went into the caged equipment room. They lock up the gym stuff there at night so no one can play with the equipment or steal it. I figured it was a safe place and that no one would find me there. I hoisted myself up onto a high bench.

I was "feeling sorry for myself." *What a strange saying that is. Sad is a better word than sorry*, I thought. I hopped down and closed the door to the room almost completely. That was better. I was feeling sad for myself. And I started crying because I was so down and feeling that old feeling of how awful I am.

One more time I was struggling with wondering, *Should I or shouldn't I kill myself?* Then I saw her. *Oh no!* I thought. *Here comes Ms. Dovzak. What's she doing here? She should be in her office like she usually is. She can't possibly want anything in here. She's looking all over the place. Maybe she will pass right by. I hope and don't hope she will find me.*

Ms. Dovzak means so much to me. Guess you could say I have a crush on her, which sounds silly and wrong all at once.

The door opened and she walked into the room. *Now what do I do?* I wondered. I was wiping my eyes just as she came in.

She said, "Oh." I guess she was a little surprised that anyone would be in the caged area. "What's the matter?" she asked.

I didn't say anything, but I started to cry again. She came near me and said, "Open your legs."

I shook my head. Then she took my knees in her hands as she faced me and pushed my legs apart so she could step in close to me. *What are those funny feelings I feel?* I thought. *No one ever stands that close to me ever except mom when she's yelling at me sometimes.*

Ms. Dovzak said she understood that I feel sad most of the time.

I said, "No you don't!"

"I see you walking and know that you are sad. Are things bad at home?" she asked.

I nodded. Then it all spilled out of me. "It's like a prison," I said. "I don't get to do anything that the other girls do, so the girls make fun of me at school. I don't get to go to, like, the movies, dances, football games, or anything. I have to wear those corrective shoes, the braces, and the back brace. The only friend I have is Kamm. No one else wants to be my friend because I'm weird."

She said, "That's really rough, and I can see why you are depressed. I just want you to know that I *do* care about you and what happens to you. You can come to my house anytime when you feel especially down. I live just up the hill from you."

I said, "My mom would never let me come to see you. She don't let me go anyplace by myself."

"By yourself? Why not?" she asked.

"Because she never lets me go anywhere outside the house. She just doesn't without any reason other than she don't want me to get hurt."

"No? Not even to Kamm's house?"

I said, "Well, I've snuck over to Kamm's house a couple of times at lunch."

"Good for you!" Ms. Dovzak said. "You need to do that more often. It does sound like you are kept pretty tight to your mother's apron strings. Sometimes you don't come to G.A.A."

"Yeah, I can only come when my regular grades are up or if I don't get into trouble. Then I'm grounded."

"So they even take that away from you," she said. "I wondered why you didn't show up sometimes. So that's the reason. Don't they know that the team counts on you to be there regularly?"

"My mom don't care. My parents don't care about anything when it comes to me. So what's the point?"

She said, "Of living? I understand why you feel that way. I do understand why getting good grades is important. Do you study?"

"That's all I ever do when I get home from school. That, practice music, and chores. I have a lot of chores to do."

"Yes. No one likes to do chores, do they?"

I shook my head.

"Well, I'm sure they think all this is for your own good, but I don't agree with them." Then she looked at me real close. "You're not telling me everything are you?" she said. It was more a statement than a question.

I said, "No, because I would get into trouble at home. I mean I would really get it."

She looked surprised. "How would they ever know?" she asked.

"Mom knows everything I do. I don't know how she finds out stuff, but she does and we are not supposed to tell anyone what goes on in the house. About the family, I mean."

She said, "Well, at some point, maybe once you graduate, you will be able to talk to someone like me. You will be eighteen then and an adult. Then you can do whatever you want."

"You don't understand. It won't make any difference to mom or dad," I told her. "That's why I want to go away to college. Then I wouldn't have to be around them."

"Or follow their damn rules." I was shocked again. Teachers don't swear. I kinda liked it, but I must have turned red because she asked, "Why are you embarrassed?"

"You said that word, and we are not supposed to swear."

"What? *Damn?*"

"Yes. We can't read certain books at school if there is swearing in them."

"Oh, I see. Just one more thing isn't it?"

I nodded again.

She said, "Well, know that I'm here for you. I had no idea that you have been *so* depressed. Some parents." She shook her head. Then she said, "I have to prepare for my next class. Why don't you come in after school and we can talk some more."

"I can't. I have to go straight home after school."

"Oh, I see why now." She walked away shaking her head some more. She then turned around and said, "I don't want you to do anything silly. Do you know what I mean?"

I knew. She meant suicide. "I won't," I told her. "For at least now."

"Do you promise?" she asked.

I nodded my head, and she left. I thought, *Now I've done it.* Well, I never promised a certain time or day that I wouldn't "do something silly." I just promised for a little while. And boy, if my parents hear about this … well, you know. I've said way too much. To Ms. Dovzak and you. Way too much. This is diary stuff that you keep to yourself.

No, I shouldn't have said anything.

Then the big, out-of-sight, far-out, groovy thing happened the day after that. Kamm brought me the Dramamine that I'd asked for, then she said, "Would you like to take some acid? I got some from a neighbor up the hill."

I thought about it, and we talked about it, and she finally said that it was on a baby aspirin and I probably should take only half the dose. She told me that she had already taken the other half and had an out-of-sight trip.

She was sad because I was down. She told me that most people who take it have good trips. She said she knew taking it would bring me up. So I let her give me half a pill. I thought maybe it would help, but I was too afraid to take it and possibly have a bad trip thing. But it was either that or kill myself. Maybe both.

I just don't care anymore.

I put the pill into my purse, thinking, *Whatever happens, I don't care. I don't care about anything anymore.* I'm probably going to hell for those evil feelings and thoughts, anyway. Not to mention how I feel about Ms. Dovzak and how evil those feelings are. I have no plan to take the acid any time soon, but I do feel powerful and in control with that tiny pill in my purse. I have a secret, and mom can't take that away from me. She figures out almost all my secrets now, like I told Ms. Dovzak she does.

Nothing changes at home. Chores are first and mom is yelling at me. Once most of my chores are done, I have to practice oboe and guitar. I don't mind doing this. After that is a crummy, dry dinner. Mom cooks fish a lot. I hate fish and steak, but mostly liver. She puts too much pepper on meat when she's not paying attention, which is most of the time. Then she overcooks stuff or burns it. We have to eat it that way because we don't throw food out. She *does* make some good stuff, though, when we have the stuff to make it with.

It's so cold in the bedroom, and I mean cold. I don't have too much homework, so I'm going to scrunch down by the heater and read. I always do dishes right after we eat, so that's something I never have to take care of later.

I hope mom don't catch me reading. Sometimes she doesn't say much except, "Oh, I just wanted to know where you were." Like I could go anywhere. Sometimes, though, she sees me reading and gives me "something better to do." It's never something "better."

When I do homework, it's hard. I'm not that bright, so it's harder for me than some kids. Sometimes the words blur together, and sometimes I fall asleep at the desk or it takes forever to write a paper because I have to look up every other word. Also my stomach hurts like mad because I'm hungry.

I've made everything worse by talking to Ms. Dovzak. She's going to tell someone, then I'm going to be in trouble. Damn it, George! There's only one way out of this: the Dramamine that Kamm brought to school for me. She thinks I'm taking it to try to get high, but that's not it. It's the something silly that I'm planning for tomorrow. I just can't go on any more. It's useless to try. Nothing's going to change. Nothing!

And now I've really embarrassed myself in front of Ms. Dovzak. I can't believe I said all that stuff. It just came rushing out of me. I needed someone to know. Just one someone.

A few days have passed since I talked to Ms. Dovzak. So I'm in the clear. I kept my promise. When I got to school this morning, I told Kamm that I took the Dramamine just so she could keep an eye on me before I croaked. I'm not telling her that's what I'm planning. She would try to stop me. I just told her that I took the pills, and we agreed that I would go to the P.E. locker room if things got weird.

I ended up feeling sick to my stomach. I felt tight and loose all at the same time. I'm not so sure now if I want to die. I felt yucky.

Everything was kinda greenish. I was afraid I was going to pass out. That would be melodramatic, wouldn't it?

I just want to go to sleep and not wake up. I decided I would go lie down on a bench in the locker room. I felt terrible. That did make me feel a little better, except for how my back hurt. Oh well. You can't have it all. I was just wondering what would happen if someone found me. I had decided that I wouldn't care when guess who came in the locker room.

Not again. Ms. Dovzak. I said to myself, *What did I expect?*

She came over to me as I struggled to sit up. No, not because of the Dramamine. I normally have trouble sitting up. She gave me a hand. "Did you go and do something silly, Cynthia?" she asked.

I lied. "No."

She said, "You are as white as a sheet. Come with me. I want you to go to the nurse."

"No, no! I can't!" I cried.

"You look horrible. You must be coming down with something."

"I'm not. Just leave me alone. I don't want no help. I'm fine."

But Ms. Dovzak wouldn't take no for an answer. "You are not fine. At least I want you to lay down in the staff bathroom. There's a bed there."

I resentfully said "O.K."

Once I laid down, she put a blanket over me and said, "Now, what did you take?"

"Nothing," I lied.

"Cynthia, I know you took something. What did you take?"

I told her.

"How many did you take?"

I lied again. "About seven." In fact, I took more like fifteen. I didn't want to have to go the hospital and have my stomach pumped. Like I told you, I heard that is awful.

She said, "Well, O.K. I think you will be all right. But you just lay there. We will have to talk later when you feel better."

I said, "O.K." Then she went into the office on the other side of the door. She sure didn't look too happy. She even looked pissed off.

Someone was in the shower, and I wondered who it was. *I wonder if they will come out naked*, I thought. *What am I talking about? What difference does it make? I'll just close my eyes or, better yet, hide under the cover. There! She, whoever she is, can't see me. I don't want anyone else to know I'm here anyways.*

After a minute or so I peeked out. It was some teacher. And she wasn't paying no never mind to me. Good!

When school was finally over, Kamm came and got me. I got up and didn't feel funny at all—or at least not as sick and funny feeling as I did at first. I told Kamm what happened, and she thought I did a real cool thing. She didn't know that I was trying to kill myself. I just hoped the two-and-a-half-mile walk home would clear my head. I sure didn't want mom to know what happened!

I will never fit in. Who am I kidding? The popular girls are right. I'm just a dork and nothing's going to ever change. Me, I mean. I'm never going to change. Most of the time I don't even know what I do that makes people not want to be around me.

Then, one day when I was walking to school, I decided that I just couldn't take it anymore. So I popped Kamm's pill into my mouth. *Who cares anyway?* I thought. Acid scares me, like I told you. But I didn't care no more.

So I took it. But I didn't feel a thing. All my happy feelings left and I felt nothing but loathing for myself. I *hate* myself. I decided that I must have gotten the side of the pill that didn't have any acid on it. I figured that Kamm must have had a full dose and didn't even know it. I wanted to have a good trip. I can't stand being in this body any more. I need a vacation.

When I got to school, I met up with Kamm and told her, "I took it."

"The acid you mean?"

"Yeah. I took it on the way to school. I don't feel nothing though. Are you sure my side of the pill had acid on it?"

Kamm smiled. "Yes, I'm sure. I sure hope you have a good trip."

"Yeah, right. If it works."

Kamm said, "Oh yeah. It works. Something is going to happen to you. It just hasn't happened yet. You'll see."

I started feeling more funny right then. "Kamm, I'm scared. I just want to stop being myself for a little while. I don't want to have a bad trip."

"Oh, I don't think it's going to do that. You will be yourself and will see a lot of funny things."

A little while later, whatever I looked at began to change. I didn't see no funny things at all. I saw horrible things. I went to signal Kamm outside her class. She went up to Mr. Benezra and got a hall pass.

I was tripping bad. Kamm was worried, so she went off to that man counselor and asked if I could go to the nurse's office and lay on the bed there. She said she told him about the acid. I didn't think that was a very good idea, but she said she had to tell him so that she could sit with me for the whole day. I heard that sometimes a trip will last eight hours, then sometimes you start tripping again.

"Kamm, I can't take that if I start tripping again," I told her. "If that does happen, go get Ms. Dovzak. She'll know what to do."

Kamm said, "I will have to get the counselor too. He told me to tell him if anything bad happened."

I didn't like him being part of all this, but Kamm likes him even if he did feel her up. "I don't want him to be here if something happens," I said. "Promise me that you'll get Ms. Dovzak."

"I promise."

After eight hours, school was over, but my trip wasn't. I started going right into a flashback. Then it started all over again. Those ugly faces. Like demons all around me. I couldn't fight it again. I was too tired and too tired to care.

"Go get Ms. Dovzak," I told Kamm. She rushed out of the room, then the counselor came in. After only a few minutes, Ms. Dovzak was standing beside him.

"We are going to have to call your parents," the counselor said.

Kamm was real upset. She said to him, "You promised not to tell. You promised!"

People say they promise something, but it never turns out that way. They up and leave you in a mess.

I guess the counselor went to call mom. Ms. Dovzak walked beside me with her arm around my shoulder. It didn't matter. She's a traitor too. She wasn't supposed to be in on all this going-home business. She was supposed to get me out of this and make it so the counselor wouldn't call my parents. She didn't say a thing to me while we walked. She must hate me. I'm so stupid for trying the acid. I should have known better. I should have gone to the back of the school and just laid there on the ground.

Mom pulled up in our light-green VW. She looked worried, but there was a tinge of anger there. Right on the edge. She talked with the counselor and Ms. Dovzak. I tried to send Ms. Dovzak mental messages. *Please please please don't tell her what we talked about. Please!* But I wasn't saying anything. I felt like I wasn't part of any of it.

Finally, mom got into the car and I did too. Mom said, "They are going to meet your father and me at home."

Once we got to the house, I walked right into the front room like I was told to do. Ms. Dovzak and the counselor came in together. We just sat there waiting for dad. Mom asked a few questions. I bitterly answered with a lot of hatred behind my words.

"Is this the first time you did anything like this?" mom asked.

"No," was all I said.

"What else have you taken?" she asked.

It doesn't matter, I thought. I felt cornered and embarrassed, but I eventually answered, "Just medicine cabinet stuff."

"From here?" she asked. "We only have Dristan and aspirin. Is that what you took?" Mom takes Dristan for her sinus headaches.

I said, "Sometimes." I was so angry, I couldn't keep it out of my voice. Mom looked so loving, but she's not that way most of the time. She was making me out to look like a liar to Ms. Dovzak. I told Ms. Dovzak the truth about home, but mom was making it like I hadn't. I hated this. I wanted to go away somewhere and never be found.

"Where did you get the other drugs from? As if I didn't already know. Was it *that* Kamm?" mom asked.

I said nothing. *So what!* I thought. I was just floating around in my head.

The counselor said, "We can hold her back. Not let her graduate."

My heart sank.

Mom said, "Oh, no. She's worked very hard and must graduate."

The counselor said, "Well, she needs to get help. We can let her graduate if she goes to a therapist."

Just then, dad finally walked in the door. Boy, that was quick. He looked all worried too. Mom told him what had just been said then turned to me. "Go to your room and lie down now." She said this softly, as if she was ashamed of me.

I left and did lie down in bed. I could hear their muffled voices, but then I started seeing the most beautiful crystal palace with crystal walls. Everything was clear crystal and I heard this wonderful music. *Maybe this is what heaven will be like,* I thought. It was so beautiful and peaceful.

Then I fell asleep.

That weekend mom explained to me what was decided. The counselor said I have to go to a therapist as long as I can. Mom found one that can take me on the weekend. I have to go to see that person at least five times. That's all the insurance will pay for.

So that weekend, mom, dad, and me popped into the car and headed to San Francisco. I asked why we were going there, and mom told me that there were some Christian people that were willing to work with me. We parked at a curb in front of a building. The place was really weird. It was dirty and cold looking. It was dusk, and the city was strangely quiet. We went up some steps. The place looked creepy and run-down inside.

"We want you to stay here so you can get some help," dad said.

"No way. I'm not staying *here!*" I almost yelled.

Dad looked angry. I never talk back to him.

A man came out to get us.

"Cynthia, we need to get you some help, and this is the only Christian place we could find," mom said.

We went inside, up a flight of stairs, and into a cluttered office. This counselor/preacher type sat across from us with his legs crossed. Mom told him what had gone on.

The counselor/preacher man jumped in and said, "We can't *make* her come here. She has to come under her own free will or it won't work."

Points to the professor, I thought. "Well, I'm not staying here. I don't have a drug problem," I said. Mom was acting like I was taking hard drugs all the time or something. They were sure making a big deal out of all this. That's normal for them. I just said, "It's no big deal."

We left.

Mom gave me a speech later, when we were home. "Your father doesn't want to do this and says you will grow out of all this. But the counselor wants you to go to a psychiatrist. Regardless of what your father says or what you think, even though it's going to cause a hardship on the family, you are going. Do I make myself perfectly clear?"

"Yes."

When I got to school on Monday, I told Kamm everything that happened.

"What a bummer," she said.

"Yeah, I know. I don't want to tell the psychiatrist one thing that I'm thinking about. But I don't know if it will make a difference because they can read minds, you know."

Kamm nodded seriously. "You don't have to tell him anything. Just sit there. He can't make you talk if you don't want to."

So that's what I decided to do. I realized that I didn't need to tell this person nothing. But deep down I thought that it wouldn't make any difference what I said or didn't say.

When I found myself in the psychiatrist's office, he was smoking like mad and said he didn't think that what I did was all that serious.

I said, "You better not tell my mom that. She's got it all worked out in her head that I'm an addict."

He chuckled. "It doesn't seem like you are."

I just shut up at that point. I looked all over the room and figured out what he must be like in real regular life. I was trying to distract myself so he couldn't read what I was thinking. He asked what I was thinking and I told him.

He said, "Well, this isn't my office. I just rent it on the weekends. But there are two other psychiatrists who work here during the week. Can you tell me what you think they are like by looking at everything around you?"

"Sure." And I did.

He said, "You are remarkably accurate. How did you learn to do that."

"I didn't. I just figured it out. It's kinda obvious, don't you think?"

He said, "I don't think I could do it. And I'm certain most other people couldn't either."

Big deal. So I figured out what some other idiot psychiatrists were like. Big deal! It didn't mean nothing.

The doctor was smoking one cigarette after the other. I watched him do that as he asked questions. I just gave him little answers like, "Yes. No. Sometimes. I don't know." Stuff like that. He wasn't going to get anything out of me.

I ended up seeing him for five weeks in a row. The last session he asked to talk to mom alone. Cool. I could dig it. I decided that maybe he would find out what a nutcase *she* is. Now that I could handle.

After talking to mom, he called me back into the office and asked, "Do you want to know what I told your mother?"

I was in shock! He was actually treating me like I matter. I said softly, "Yes."

"I told her that I don't think you have a drug problem, but that you are depressed and basically acting like any other teenager acts." He smiled, and I was so relieved. He got nothing outa me. Nothing!

So now Mom's been ranting and raving about *that* Kamm and wants me to stop hanging around with her.

"You can't make me," I tell her. "She's my one and only friend."

But that don't stop her from calling Kamm "*that* Kamm." I don't care. I'm going to do what I want when I want. It just doesn't matter anymore. Everyone made a mountain out of a molehill. They don't even know about my wanting to kill myself. They would take me to Napa if they knew that.

Kamm has been acting funny around me, and I finally found out why. She feels bad because she told on me about the drugs and thinks I will fink on her about giving me the LSD. I just keep telling her that there isn't anything that could make anyone drag anything out of me about her.

"Do your mom and dad know anything about the acid and that you got it from me?" she asked.

"No," I answered. "But mom tried to guess." Then I thought about the other people who know about the acid. "Your counselor is not going to tell on you, right? Because of what he did to you?"

"No," Kamm said. "I don't bring that up because he didn't know I was awake when he touched me. But I think that's why he's keeping his promise to me not to tell anyone about all this. And he better not. I will tell everyone what he did to me."

I asked, "So we're safe, right?"

From that time on, we were just like before. Laughing and carrying on. You know, something in me changed though. Not toward Kamm. This is something deep inside of me. It hurts, but I have no words for it. It's like a deep pit. Deeper than the one I usually feel.

It's like depression with hunger all mixed up in it.

∞ ∞ ∞

The family is running late as usual, so I run into the side door of the Richmond Auditorium. Graduation ceremonies will begin in just a few minutes. I feel so proud because first of all, Grandma and Grandpa Rasmussen are going to be here. Secondly, I've done all I set out to do as a senior. I conducted the orchestra, played solos all over the place, got into super choir, and won the Pamela Knight award.

I'm heading to the stage to warm up with the orchestra, and before I get there a teacher says, "Are you Cynthia Burrough?"

"Yes?"

"You have to sit in seat four. You're one of four honor students."

I'm confused and say, "But I'm supposed to be with the orchestra." Then I rush up the stage stairs. I guess Mr. Bee heard everything because he told me that I could slip out of my seat to receive my diploma, then return to my seat in the orchestra.

The orchestra plays "Pomp and Circumstance" forever. I hate "Pomp and Circumstance" anyway, but with a graduating class of three hundred and sixty five students, there was no choice in the matter. I still don't see why it's a big deal to graduate fourth in my class. I just wanted to graduate, and that's all that matters to me.

It means I can leave home once college starts.

I can finally breathe for the first time in my life.

Chapter 23: No One Wants to Be 'It' All the Time

Count For Me
COUNT FOR ME!
I CAN'T
AH ... COME ON COUNT!
I'D BE EMBARRASSED. NO ONE JUST COUNTS.
OH.

HEY! WOULD YOU LIKE TO PLAY A GAME?
O.K.! WHAT?
HIDE AND SEEK; YOU'RE "IT"!

I *could* count
just as well as anyone.

Did you ever play "hide and seek"
and as soon as you reached one hundred
someone would call
"aullie-aullie-auction
free-free-
free"?
It's kind of like they never wanted to be found
or they never wanted to lose
and you'd be "it"
for a long time.

LOVE FOR ME!
I CAN'T
AH ... COME ON, LOVE!
I'D BE EMBARRASSED, NO ONE JUST LOVES.
OH.

HEY! WOULD YOU LIKE TO PLAY A GAME?
O.K.! WHAT?
HIDE AND SEEK, YOU'RE IT!
I *could* love
just as well as anyone.

But ...
No one likes to be "it"
all the time.
It's no fun.
Cynthia R. Burrough
SELAH
University of Biola, 1970

I have taken you back to key moments in my young life. I want you to know that this is not a book written from the place of ego. I'm not much different from the other walking wounded who are around you. The details of my life have been for your edification in hopes that it will help you better understand yourself and those around you.

There are many who have suffered and are suffering far more than I can imagine. My heart and soul go out to those people.

No, my story is not special, nor by any stretch is it the worst of the worst.

My story does have its share of mental illness or something very close to that, if that is possible. Perhaps the characters waver between illness and healthiness and occasionally slip over into complete sickness. It is not and shall never be that person's fault for good or evil.

Therapy was not readily available when I was growing up. Plus, there certainly was a stigma and plenty of misinformation regarding mental illness at the time.

Everyone makes choices as adults, but the mentally ill brain has a short in its neuropathway or, via personal circumstances, has been rewired. There is *still* a stigma around mental illness. I know this and wish to put some minds at ease. Mental illness is not a death sentence, and healing can happen. I believe that most people have a degree of emotional illness—areas in their lives that require special attention.

In my case, some of the scars still exist. I shall never be completely sound even if the mental health community suggests otherwise. Even if they preach from the hilltops that total recovery is possible or that "one can thrive." In some cases this may be true, but it is not so for me.

Even with all the self-help books lining shelves in almost every depository, some souls still suffer from mental illness or at the very least emotional unhealthiness. Some people in the medical field believe that post-traumatic stress disorder can be healed. Perhaps for some it can, and to that I say a hearty "amen." In my case, PTSD rears its ugly head, surprising me from time to time. And it is still active. It's just under the surface.

I continue through life with a personality disorder. I have difficulty with individuals in positions of perceived authority. I also struggle because of a bipolar 2 syndrome disorder that falls on the manic-depressive side, though for the most part this is controlled with medication. As I often tell my medication-wielding psychiatrist, "At least for this week I'm not running down the street naked."

A while back my sister and I were walking toward a high school theater to listen to a concert. A small group of teenagers were walking behind us giggling and talking. I immediately thought they were talking about me, as egocentric as this was. So I went into that semi-paralyzing mental place of shame, self-degradation, and anger. Later I shared with my sister what had happened. I said, "I thought I was over that!"

People will walk up to me and begin speaking, and you could peel me off the ceiling. I avoid people at almost any cost, and

I'm always terrified when I meet new people or go into a group environment. I have been in only one loving relationship, and it started over the internet. It was safe for me, and I gradually let that person get to know me. Very gradually.

Life has been and still is a challenge. I do best when I work alone. I absolutely do not play well with others because I have trust issues, many buttons, and boundary difficulties. I do have close friends, but far fewer than a handful. I've lost friendships and don't have a clue why. A lost "friend" is not normally forthcoming when I've somehow injured them.

I've been fortunate enough that throughout my life I've been able to work alone. In a work environment, my stress level skyrockets. My self-critic is relentless, and I wonder if I'm going to be criticized or let go. Just going to work can be a major victory, and at any given time I will lose it and shock the hell out of those around me because normally, they say, I'm "such a sweet person."

It has been and still is a mystery when someone suggests, "Just be yourself." I don't have a clue what that means. If it means being comfortable in my own skin, I'm still evolving. I don't believe that learning ever stops if I'm willing to do the work. I welcome hard lessons because if I learn them well, I will have improved and, in a certain way, grown toward wellness. This sometimes requires a laissez-faire attitude and "going where angels fear to tread." It also requires at times a degree of bravery if I dare to choose a completely well-functioning life. It certainly is not for the weak.

And so we begin.

As I grew up, I never understood why I was singled out and made to be "it" many times. Sometimes it was good, but mostly it was bad attention that I received.

There was a great deal of ignorance in my immediate family. Grandma Rasmussen was probably the most educated and probably the least understood by anyone. Perhaps this played a part in my love for her. She was so very different from anyone else I knew. She actually read books and the newspaper and knew how to communicate her opinion. She wasn't always bad-mouthing other people in the family. At least not to my knowledge. If she complained about someone, it seemed it was for good reason.

And she was my champion. When Randy picked on me, she indignantly said to my mother, "If she was *my* child, I would march right up to that school and make sure something was done about it!" And I had no doubt whatsoever that she would have been the proverbial squeaky wheel when it came to me and my welfare.

When I was sad, she would sing "When You're Smiling" to me. I used to cry at the drop of a hat. Curiously, even as adults, my sister, brother, and I cry easily.

I would never say that Grandma was a good mother because my mother was greatly damaged by her mother's inattentiveness. And Mom's father abandoned her. I know that Mom was emotionally, physically, and sexually abused. For all intents and purposes, she loved her mother but was bitter about many things her mother did—things that ultimately added up to abandonment on different levels. I will go no further because the stories are hers to tell or not.

I will never know or understand the great physical abuse that both Mom and Dad dealt out to me as a child. There is no doubt that, as my sister says, "You got it the worst."

My sister was a hard act to follow because she was a quiet soul and rarely got into trouble. What is most definite was the damage she suffered by having to watch the beatings that my brother and I got.

Mom didn't graduate high school, and when she was an older adult she struggled academically before she finally got a GED. My father never graduated high school, having left a year before graduation. He was mechanically gifted, and most of his training was on the job. He was no dummy, since he taught himself trigonometry. Mom was the go-getter, while Dad sat passively on the sidelines.

Mom is somewhat socially adept. However, thanks to her crazy disposition, it is rare for her to hold onto friends. Aunt

Carol was her best friend during her earlier years. Aunt Carol said that Mom was a "real pistol." That implies a host of characteristics that Mom exemplifies. Mom is also a Gemini and displays that dual personality to the hilt if one believes in astrology. She does have a dual personality. One minute she can be loving and kind, then switch quickly, jabbing a knife into a back and saying, "Well, that's just the way I am. People can take it or leave it."

I think that Mom loved us but couldn't cut the cord as healthy parents do. As an adult I would cut it, and she would sew it back together repeatedly. She didn't understand that as I grew, I gradually needed—no, longed—to grow and mature on my own terms.

In my story, Dad is somewhat missing. This was true on the psychological level as well. He truly was not very present. I never asked him what he thought about when he was like this. Maybe it was his way of coping with life or surviving with Mom. He was pretty even but had a horrible temper. It was "duck and cover" if Dad lost it. We'd say, "Everyone look out, because here it comes." And his temper could lead to potentially dangerous situations for Mom and us kids, as I've shared. He did, in his own way, apologize to me when I was an adult, saying, "I think we were a little hard on you."

Don't sigh.

Mom has never apologized or come anywhere near that. It is sad that they both had to live with the pain and guilt of their own actions, if that is even possible. Perhaps it is possible subconsciously, but I'm not a therapist. Dad was at heart a very sweet man, and Mom is a loving mother if you are around her on a good day. I think that perhaps she has struggled with depression and anger issues for the better part of her life. I also feel that I was, in part, her scapegoat.

And I really do think she was ill prepared for an overactive child. But who isn't? A few years later they might have prescribed Ritalin for me. I was so excited by life. I most certainly didn't like frilly things and was more like most boys in behavior.

I thought I was in my best clothes when I wore a cowboy hat, boots, and six shooters. I guess now it was in part an homage to the Burrough family.

My sister has said that I was just being a child and that my punishments in my earlier years were way over the top. The punishments took various turns until I went to college and was left alone. Can you believe that I was actually homesick after I left home?

Grandpa Burrough was, from all observance, an alcoholic. I believe that his lack of morals progressed as his drinking progressed. In his perverse way, I think he loved me, if you can call it that.

That given, as the story goes, on the rare occasions that we children were allowed to stay at Grandma and Grandpa Burrough's house, Grandpa watched as other men molested me. I believe the molestation started when I was about three or four and continued until I was well into grade school. It stopped when I became too old for Grandpa to control. I've wondered if this was because my much younger cousin became "available." I never asked. He did take me out of bed and carry me to God knows where. I thought everything was pretty much okay because he was there watching over me.

Why did he do it? I don't know other than to feed his appetite for alcohol and voyeurism. After all, money did change hands after the sexual events. I also think that Grandma was regularly drugged so that she wouldn't catch Grandpa in the act. I feel she did to some extent know what was going on.

I had the repetitive bad dream about someone coming to get me because the living nightmares were just that: Grandpa came to get me out of bed. Also, on some occasions my parents yanked me out of bed. I was helpless and didn't even know I needed help, but somewhere inside I was very frightened. I believe that my fear of the dark was due to the episodes that took place under the cover of darkness.

I still have great difficulty being around strangers, and unfortunately my anger has reared its ugly head when I've been alone with some men. When I was on a date and it became sexual, I immediately developed a grinding migraine. These were instantaneous, and I never knew how relevant they were.

It has taken years of therapy to get to the root of my depression and disabilities. There was a turning point when my therapist said, "Cyndi. Children don't have the capacity to have the kind of nightmares you have described."

You see, I thought that the molestation was just an *imagined* nightmare, not something based on reality. I had many symptoms as a child, but my parents didn't see them because psychiatrists in those days didn't educate the public about sexual abuse symptoms.

I do not feel sorry for myself anymore. It's just part of my story. On the other hand, I can't help but wonder how my life would have turned out without the physical, psychological, emotional, and sexual abuse. What would I have done with my music skills? What would I have done with my art skills?

Even though I have held several jobs, I usually left them after a short period of time. I believe the longest that I worked in one place was about four years. All other jobs averaged one to two years.

There has been much healing and many changes, but I still wonder why I am as I am. Others have gone through so much more and *seem* to be whole, functioning members of society. But that's merely a supposition on my part.

I am sometimes amazed by how well children are treated by their parents and appalled at the abuses I've seen other parents dish out. Mostly I look at a child's eyes when this happens, and there is usually a sadness that cannot lie. I look into the eyes of children no matter what. Their eyes tell stories that their mouths can't begin to verbalize. I know that at least part of my spirit was broken. Perhaps this is what I see in a child's eyes. Maybe it's the feeling of hopelessness. All I know is that I recognize it, and it tears my heart out.

Chapter 24: As Is the Tree

Grandma Rasmussen was a key player in my childhood. She always treated me lovingly and gently, as did my Aunt Carol. I believe that Grandma was instrumental in helping me get though a tough period in my childhood.

She also believed in my artistic and musical talents. So clearly, her encouragement led to my musical activities in junior high and high school, where I excelled with honors and awards. But even with that, my self-esteem was all but gone and is something I need to work on to this day.

As a very young child I would sit on the seat of our swing set in the backyard and talk to myself for hours. Being an extremely active child, this was completely out of character for me. It was a coping device, and now I understand I was depressed even at that age. I would soothe myself by going over the abuses and evaluating whether I did or didn't deserve them. Of course, I had no idea that any abuse is undeserved. I desperately needed a fighter on my side. But no one stepped forward, so I knew it was up to me.

Another coping device that comes into play in my life is dissociation. I may not like this, but it's still there. In grade school the teachers called it daydreaming.

Abuse can take many forms: verbal, physical, emotional, and psychological. My hope for any child suffering from abuse is that they have a loving and caring adult in their life who will acknowledge their pain and stand up for them. Advocate for them. Even a stranger who sees the signs of abuse should step forward for a child or adult in need. I believe that the teacher who called me to her classroom did the best she could, but she didn't have the skills or patience to draw out deeper truths from me. She saw the bruises on my body but could pull nothing from me because I thought that she would hurt me too.

A certain amount of trust has to be present with a child or an adult in order for them to acknowledge and share scary information regarding abuse—especially if the abuser says that the incidents must stay behind closed doors. One needs to look out for the welfare of the child. And foster care is not always the best solution because the abuse can continue even in a new environment.

I can tell you the battles I fought during the writing of this book and what I did to pull myself out of depression. Distraction, medication, and sleep help me a great deal. Also being thankful for the littlest things helps pull me out of myself. Just being helpful helps. It helps others and me at the same time.

I am not a therapist. God forbid. Some professionals may think that, for the most part, depression is due to circumstances outside the individual, such as failed relationships, eviction, money difficulties, and the like. While these certainly may augment depression, my depression is twofold: physical and emotional. I use medication, which wasn't available to me until my late forties. Prior to that, only a few of my coping skills were in place. I just didn't know how to deal with depression. I felt isolated and alone. I didn't know that so many other people struggle with it. I just wanted to stop hurting and thought about ending my life.

I eventually used alcohol to deaden the pain. Medication is a wonderful tool, but it doesn't take care of all the causes of depression. I have to get into the solution, be honest with myself, and do away with the "yeah buts." My life depends on it.

I heard once that "a rut is a coffin with the ends kicked out." I prefer to say that depression is a casket with the ends kicked out. I had (and still have) to claw my way out of the coffin sometimes.

I moved from therapist to therapist, and very little help was offered in this arena. Talk therapy is important, and I don't mean to downplay its usefulness. I had to tell my story to one other person in this world, but knowing that there may be deeper reasons for the depression was key. Also—and I cannot stress this enough—a therapist must build trust and be themself. It wasn't until therapists shared part of their emotional story that I began to progress. This may go against the dos and don'ts of the profession, but for me it instilled trust.

I didn't know how to navigate life in the present, so therapy helped as much as possible in this area. I knew what a only few emotions were, so with continued effort, I was able to have words and a voice regarding my feelings.

If you choose to be in therapy, I can only emphasize the importance of being as open as possible and extremely truthful with the therapist and yourself. Without these two things, therapy is of very little use. Bottom line is that some therapists haven't a clue as to what to do with a truly depressed person. It's a hit-and-miss thing. For instance, I found that some coping devices, such as affirmations, backfired on me. The negative part of my thinking set out to disprove the affirmations, making the positive statement null, void, and painful.

I've decided to share some ideas that have helped me. Some were almost unbearably far away until I got the hang of how to crawl out of the pit of depression. I will also include things that impacted me and kept me going in high school and as a young adult.

I used to look for solutions outside myself. I thought others knew much more than I did, so I leaned on them. I don't know if this was a good thing or not, but it helped me gain some footing. I must say that I learned that willingness is my toolbox. "I'm not going to be depressed at least for this one second more!" became my mantra. I needed to stop the downward spiral as soon as I was aware that it was in play.

I must ask myself, What is setting me off this time? What are my buttons and crossed boundaries? I've had to look at the possibility that if I become angry, a button had been pushed or a boundary crossed, and I needed to check out why I'd reacted a certain way. I've said to myself, *What part of this is the truth and what is false?* I can't help but think that buttons are from past pain and healthy boundaries are established for the present. If someone criticizes me and I become hurt and angry, I need to say to myself, *There must be something in their criticism that smacks of the truth for me, or it would roll off my back.* I don't want to turn their words into depression. Instead, I want to get rid of the button. I've had to ask myself, *Is this their stuff or mine?*

Comparisons are a sticky wicket too. Sometimes I've said, "My pain is and was worse than yours. Look at what I've gone through." Why did I think this? Well, I wanted to be special. But someone else's pain is just as valid as my pain. Pain is pain. I had to try out empathy for a change. I had to learn to treat others as I want to be treated, with an open mind that listens to their story.

These are the tools that help me bob to the surface when I'm depressed or frustrated. If all or some of these help you, wonderful! If not, don't give up. You can create your own tools that will help you survive one second, minute, day, or days more.

Remember, though, to never get too tired, too hungry, or too stressed. When I have been able to be observant, I can note almost right off the bat that addressing my fatigue, hunger, or stress may be the first of many solutions. Or, at the very least, recognizing that I'm tired, hungry, or stressed can be a hint that I'm beginning my downward spiral.

I might also add that when my hygiene is less than appropriate, that is certainly a warning signal for me.

Isolation is a biggie too. This particular one is still very difficult for me. It requires that I step out of my comfort zone and leave self-criticism at the door. I am terrorized by the fact that I need to do whatever is possible to release this book to the public. I don't know about you, but fear keeps me stuck. I have both reasons and excuses for not following through. I will need to walk past my fear and set about making the release of this book happen.

Baby steps are okay.

I have had to avoid acting out mentally as an adult. My mother may have been at her wits' end because I was an overactive child. Ann Logsdon (who worked primarily in the area of disabilities) created this definition of acting out: Behavior that is "physically aggressive, destructive to property, verbally aggressive, or otherwise more severe than simple misbehavior. Acting-out behavior is disruptive in any setting ..."

My acting out was internal rather than external. Depression is anger turned inward. So I had to figure out what I was getting from being depressed. What was the payoff? In part, for me, it was seeking out the attention of someone I saw as special—a person who seemed to care about me. I thought that I wanted sympathy. I didn't know the difference between it and love.

Therapy required me to look at what I thought were embarrassing parts of my personality. I chose a person important to me to lean on. I thought that the person I admired had magical, understanding powers and knew how to find all my solutions. Also wallowing around in my depression just felt familiar and good. It's like a fluffy cloud that I wrap myself in.

Even though I was creative and talented, I needed to go to a place of anonymity. That is, I needed to create just to create. I needed to quiet the critic inside me. Usually this happened in group settings where no one knew of my talents, such as it was at the alcoholic and drug addiction recovery program in Sylmar, California, known as Oasis.

In various classes we were called on to express our thoughts via drawing. The women would ooh and ah over my drawings until finally I felt accepted for myself. Then I told them that I was an artist. I wanted to be liked for myself and not my talent. Nor did I want others to fall into the envy trap of thinking that I was better than they. I didn't make myself talented; I just came into this world that way.

Admiration and envy are two different things. The first is, "This is what I see in you," and the second is, "I see this in you and want it for myself. It's just not fair!"

It may sound silly to those of you glued to your beds, but I decided that sleep would get me past a few hours of wanting to kill myself. It worked, and at times it still does when I am overwhelmed, stressed, and down. I go to sleep for a nap that lasts hours. I still have vivid dreams but few nightmares. There were years when I feared going to sleep due to the nightmares. Luckily, and with much work in therapy, that changed.

By the way. If you don't have a lot of money, there are clinics, resource centers, and community health resources that you might find, as well as therapists who work on a sliding scale or even for free. There are shelters and support groups that you can go to if you are being abused. My second therapist delayed any cost to me until many factors came into play and I could pay her back. Guess I was in pretty bad shape when I first came to her.

Let's get real. I *WAS* in bad shape.

In these past few years, the weight of depression has been more manageable. One thing that helps is looking at and talking to nature. Believe it or not, this can be hypnotic for me. Many moments pass when I am outside myself.

And music. Ah, music. That soothes my soul too.

> Consider the lilies of the field, how they grow; they toil not, neither do they spin ... even Solomon in all his glory was not arrayed like one of these.
> St. Mathew 6 verses 28 and 29
> The Holy Bible
> King James Version

Having an attitude of gratitude helps me now when I remember to shift my thinking. "What in the world do I have to be grateful for?" I will ask.

I start with the tiniest of things. "Do I have shoes? Do I have a bed to sleep on? Can I breathe? Do I have some food?"

I take nothing for granted.

Now, this is a very silly-sounding thing to do, but it's difficult: when at all possible, I try not to think.

Primarily and normally, my thoughts cause me a great deal of trouble. This is because I am inundated with negative thoughts at a volume that becomes unbearable. I've said that I took over the abuse where my parents left off. Changing those negative thoughts is like trying to climb Mt. Everest with petroleum on my hands and knees. It's nearly impossible, so I have other tools to help me. Such as meditation.

At first in therapy, it was suggested that I read many self-help books. While these books helped me (at the very least) establish a language and gave me temporary assistance, I used the information against myself. "Look!" I'd say out loud. "You can't even do these things that are suggested." So I eighty-sixed self-help books and articles.

Oh, please, please do not let this happen to you. Read the books and articles. Some of them can be quite helpful. Remember that my tools are mine and may not necessarily work for you.

Instead of reading the books, I started watching shows whose host or guest had gone through a lot worse than I. These people gave me hope and a belief that if they could get where they were, so could I someday. I needed all the encouragement I could get, and a few times they shared their own tools.

I also needed to know how to avoid manipulation. It took me way too long to figure out when I was being manipulated for someone else's gratification or when I was trying to manipulate others. I'm still learning about this. Now I try to avoid manipulation even if I have to rely on anger to do it. For example, I was unaware that my second therapist did a great deal of manipulation. I thought that what I was asked to do outside our sessions was okay because I was special and she was such a wonderful, caring person. How could I doubt that she wasn't looking out for my best interests?

I now minimize the time I spend with negative, unsupportive people. I had a student/friend who repeatedly said, "Life is hard." Yes, it can be, but hearing that phrase over and over again was not good for my well-being. If I say, "Life is hard," guess what? My life will be hard. I will bring that little phrase to fruition.

The flip side is true also. In public or with a friend, I constantly say, "Sorry, excuse me." Well, I might as well say, "Excuse me for breathing. I'm not equal to you. Just thought I'd share that with you." When someone says, "You're okay" in response, I've come to see that they are right. I AM okay!

Sometimes I have what I call a "how dare you" attitude when I am down. I get angry and start mentally yelling at someone in my past or present. However, I cannot yell externally. I've chosen not to. Anger seems to turn depression inside out for me. The "how dare you" attitude also raises my self-confidence and personal position of power. I see how I value myself enough to say, "In your face, so-and-so or such-and-such."

I think that a lack of self-confidence has been a key factor in my depression. "I'm not good enough, strong enough, bright enough, etc." As Oprah Winfrey quotes Maya Angelou, "If they (I) knew better, they (I) would do better."

I don't excuse my parents, but I do try to understand abuse. I could have come out as an abuser myself. But I broke the chain.

There is also stubborn willfulness. "Don't you dare tell me I can or cannot do this. Who do you think you are?" I love this kind of anger when I can remember to pull it out of my toolbox. It's got to be one of my favorites, and it works extremely well for me, if only for a little while. Again, this is internal dialogue. Terry Cole-Whittaker voices this in the title of one of her books, *What You Think of Me Is None of My Business.*

Also, take judgment out of the picture. "Why don't you do this?" or "Why didn't you do that?" Meddling in someone's else life is a no-win for me and for them.

Forget the "inner child" B.S. if it no longer is helpful to you. One year I went into a store after Halloween and purchased a Wolfman T-shirt. I felt a bit embarrassed about wearing it at first. It wasn't Halloween anymore, so I told people I was wearing my "inner beast" T-shirt. After a few chuckles here and there, I realized that I was onto something. The last thing I needed was an unruly and self-pitying child in my mind. What I needed was to connect with an inner beast—a position of power. From then on I wore the shirt with pride, and this year I purchased a number of inner beast shirts.

Hey, it works for me, people!

Along with this idea is to not take "no" or "I can't help you" for an answer. There is always someone or something who will help me out. For example, I've been forced to look for new places to live. Once my landlady said that she was selling my place. This is nothing new to me because I have moved probably about twelve times for a variety of reasons. Finding a place that would work for me on a limited budget was not an easy task. As I searched, my ugly, bad-mouthing demon of depression nearly overtook me. But I was able finally to get into action. This would not have been possible in my past. But with discipline, I've learned to take on the littlest tasks when I'm depressed that invariably lead to larger tasks. How little?

Bending down to a piece of paper that has been on the floor for weeks and picking it up.

Making just one call today.

This is not to say that my depression went away, but I felt a sense of accomplishment, and with each day I found a new task to do. Sometimes getting into action is quite helpful. Eventually my depression lifted if only a notch or two. It is, however, hard to get into action and resolve to stay there.

The action also helps me take control and begin to face external elements that previously caused me to feel helpless. I had to acknowledge my successes no matter how small I thought they were. I was taking my power back.

I also liberally use "this or something better" as another tool that Terry Cole-Whittaker came up with. When I have a need or want, I go to this place when things seem hopeless. I take a big, relaxing breath and say to myself, *This is what I want. And if that's not big enough, I want something better than what I can think of.* Sometimes I don't know what "better" looks like, but I have patience—enough patience to find out what it does looks like.

Time constraints don't work well when I'm panicking, so when this happens I do the exercise again. I breathe. I let people know what I'm looking for, and nine times out of ten they help out. People like to help me. Right now I desperately need a better car. I don't know how this is going to play out, but I've no doubt that I will get a much better vehicle. I just believe this will happen. When people logically say, "You can't" or "You won't," I say to myself, *I can! I will!*

Fear keeps me stuck. I need to face my fears and realize that I'm not helpless. I'm in control. I then feel that I'm not so much at the mercy of people, places, and things. I've taken my power back. I'm just as important as you. I push on. When I was looking for a new place to live, I made more calls and came up with creative solutions to find something affordable.

A very wonderful thing to do, even with depression, is to go out of my way to compliment and acknowledge other people. This has made a huge difference to me. I reach out to people to show love and compassion.

Listen to people. Really listen. You'll be amazed at how well this works. Complete strangers sometimes open up to me and start sharing from their souls. I try to treat others the way I would like to be treated. I try not to fall into the trap of "Why don't others treat ME that way?" I do not expect payback. If I find that I want something in return, that's when my ego rears its ugly head. That is a no-win way to look at it.

Humor is also very important. When I was trying to get out of my shell, I found myself on a bus engaging others in small talk. One day I sat down next to an blind older man. We started talking about the entertainment industry, which led us to the topic of movies we enjoyed. The whole bus got involved silently by nodding and smiling. I said, "One movie I really enjoyed was *Dirty Old Men*." The fellow next to me looked stunned until I said, embarrassed, "I mean *Grumpy Old Men*." Everyone on the bus laughed, including me.

Now here is where I need to say that any number of my tools can seem to fail, and I end up sitting on the pity pot. The old "woe is me, poor me" thing. If I go into this mode, I give myself only so long to sit there. Then I try to move on. There are so many patient souls who have helped me along the way. I must at all cost take my focus off myself and put it on others. I can catch myself doing all the talking in a conversation. Then I think, *Am I the only one in this conversation? That's rude of me.* This is not to say that when I first began to use this tool I meant every word I said or listened with ease. Hey, it's hard for me to sit still in any circumstance, let alone listen to someone for a long length of time.

That, my dear, is why I am not a therapist.

A very important tool that I started using only a few years ago is making amends. I asked for forgiveness from people I'd hurt, but I never went directly to the person. I knew my limitations. For instance, I once "borrowed" a professionally made tape and did not return it. When I faced this, I gave all the tapes I liked to a secondhand store. It felt so good to get out from under what I'd done. Others may disagree with this approach, but I don't think confrontation is my best move.

I also have to de-stress when I'm depressed. I've been careful to make amends when I'm not depressed. One thing that was and is difficult is practicing forgiveness for my error or screwed-up thinking and making emotional amends when necessary. I need to own my part. Clean up my side of the street. I need to make an attempt to shift my patterns. So I try to make amends in the present. Please be aware that abusive people will try to make you wrong when you offer amends. Walk away. They are not worthy of you even if you don't believe that in real time. Leave.

I also ask what my part is in being depressed. Is it because of my past or is it caused by something that is going on now? What do I need to do to get out from under it? Medication does not take away depression entirely. At least for me. My contribution to my depression is believing that I'm not strong enough, good enough, smart enough, and so on. There have been times when I couldn't see how I could possibly get out of a situation, but the bottom line is that it is I and I alone who will recognize what is happening in the now, and only I who can turn it around.

I also need to steer clear of "coulda, shoulda woulda." I try not to think, *If only I had done …* For example, at one point when I was unemployed, I was depressed and did not pay bills on time. So I had late-payment fees for the following month, when I knew

I still would not have the money. This was a problem. But I had to get real and know what part I may have played in creating that problem.

I can tell you that living in my car and having diarrhea (somewhat caused by stress) was no fun, yet I had created that too. I had refused to give my landlady the full rent all at once. So she evicted me. I thought that she shouldn't need all my rent all at once because *I* needed the other half and she had plenty of money. I wanted a financial cushion. I wanted to feel secure in knowing that I had enough money for alcohol too. Toss into the mix a broken car that I was unable to move for the weekly street cleaning. This earned me a number of parking tickets, which exacerbated the situation.

Was I depressed while this was going on? You better believe it. I asked a friend for a loan. He said no. I was angry because I knew he had lots of money and I, after all, was "good for it." I never entertained the idea that it was his right to say no. There are so many other details involved in this story. But all said, I helped create a situation that caused my homelessness, starting with depression, stress, and "stinkin' thinkin'." My depression became worse and worse, and I ended up in a hospital for a seventy-two hour suicide watch.

I had to acknowledge that there really are some things outside my control.

But when I was down, the last thing I wanted to look at was how I'd been passive or aggressive. I wanted people to say, "Poor little thing. Nothing ever seems to work out right for her." It was an old pattern, and this was part of my payback. It was partly why I was depressed. Luckily, homelessness lasted only a brief time. A friend found me in my car and hustled around trying to find digs for me and my pets.

I lived out of my neighbor's garage for a time because I had rented it to store my stuff in. Once I was out of the picture, she stole the journals I was keeping in her garage and started reading them to anybody who would listen. It was very hard to forgive her. I wanted to know why she would do such a thing. But, as in a lot of cases, I might never know the why of it. She accused me of stealing from her and said she was paying me back. But I never stole from her. Those journals were to be the core of a book I wanted to write. (Just a side note: In retrospect, I'm glad those old journals were taken. Otherwise, I never would have written the kind of book that you are reading now.)

It's most difficult to forgive myself and not let my inner critic run around in circles like mad, condemning me for so-called heinous actions. The internal blame game is still a demon on my back. But one day I had had enough of that particular demon and yelled, "ENOUGH!" It worked! I use this little tool when I remember to, which is not often.

Boy, has that demon had a heck of a good time while I've been writing this book.

Depression for me is like slipping into a soft chair that continues to sink down as I sit in it. There just doesn't seem any way out. You may have sat in a real chair like that and found it almost impossible to get out. Someone may even have needed to help you stand up.

One of the most painful things one of my therapists said was, "You have a dark, empty hole in you, and it will never be filled." If you don't know how depressing this realization was, then you probably don't have a hole of your own. And thank the gods for that. My hole was there because I'd lacked loving parenting as I grew. Now, because I'm an adult, it will never be filled. Never.

That was one of only two times I actually sobbed in therapy.

But not all has been death and gloom in my life. There are high points too, such as the births of my sister's and brother's children. Walking alone with a child is one of the most precious moments I've had. Listening to them, asking questions, and seeing the world anew from their point of view was a gift. Playing in my band was another high point. This list goes on and on. During those times when I wasn't depressed, I would say to myself, *See what I would have missed out on if I had killed myself?*

I have to stop my stinkin' thinkin'. Depressed or not, my thoughts focus too much on negative things. Not too long ago I was babysitting a little girl, and she said to me, "You shouldn't talk like that about yourself." In another instance, one of my proofreaders said, "Cyndi, don't tell people about your mistakes." We were in a social setting, and she was not referring to the book. In either case, I had no idea what I had said to bring on those comments. I guess those kinds of thoughts and words are just that automatic for me.

Changing the way I think and speak requires me to stay in the moment. I have to ask myself, *What's going on now? How am I acting, speaking and thinking in the present?* I must try to find the positive in myself and situations. Life can be difficult due to circumstances outside myself, but if I focus on the negative I can easily slip into depression. I feel that in ALL situations there are positive ways of thinking about things. For instance, I once again have to find a new place to live as soon as possible. With my current credit rating, this will be a challenge. To turn this from a negative, I keep telling myself that there is a person somewhere who will rent to me even with my low income and current credit score. Will it be easy to find a place? No! But I refuse to cave in to thinking that I will end up homeless. I know that this will never happen to me again.

With that, I do need to ask myself, *What is the worst thing that could happen to me?* This is when my spiritual beliefs kick in. I believe in reincarnation. And I do not want to come back to Earth and have to do this all again. So the next logical thought is, *How do I get into the solution?* I can give myself a pep talk and say, "I really don't know if that will happen."

A therapist is invaluable at this point. I have only my answers to these questions. You will have to find yours.

I finally learned how to act as if. Once again, this came from Terry Cole-Whittaker. If I'm depressed, I do this: I act as if what I want is already happening. For example, right now I'm boxing up my things so that I can move at a moment's notice. I'm acting as if I have already found a new place to live. I'm clear about what I want. I have expectancy without expectation. And as long as I stay in my current place, at least I'm more organized.

But I find myself in a situation that is abusive. I know this. I've tried everything to protect myself and have tried to outwit the person involved. Many have asked, as have I, "Why is this person doing these things to you?"

I have a few ideas but have never come up with a solid answer. There are two words that seem the same but are very different: *excuses* and *reasons.* I make excuses when I want to weasel out of something I've done that was less than perfect. I've had my reasons for staying in the house I'm living in now. People have told me to look for a different place to live, but I love my place and thought I would be able to live here for a very long time. Plus, I just don't want to move yet again. So I resist their suggestions and hold onto the hope that the troublesome neighbor will move instead.

I also ask myself, *Is this life lesson for me or for them? What can I learn and do differently in this situation? How can I change? Is there anything I can learn spiritually from this situation?* These questions do not pardon the abuser. But they lift the false blame I might place on myself. I must accept the fact that I've done nothing wrong. There is no excuse for abuse.

Given all of the above, I continued to fine-tune this book and found myself writing notes particularly regarding this chapter. I asked myself what else should I be sure to include to help others work through depression and abuse. One note I jotted down was, "Take your power back and leave, leave, leave. When someone is causing physical, emotional, and/or psychological pain, reach out for help and leave." A few days later I looked at my note again. Wham! I thought, *Boy, this is the pot calling the kettle black. I need to leave even though it will mean that I have to give up the beautiful place I'm in.*

If you decide to leave an abusive place and person, make a plan. Stay as safe as you possibly can. If you have items that are important to you, such as photos, give them to a friend to hold for you. If you can't do that, there are lockers you can rent. Make a list of what is important to you and slowly and gradually tick things off your list.

If I had the power to change things, I would not have my life be any different than it has been. This statement may shock you. You may wonder why I feel this way, given all that has happened to me. The answer is clear to me. My dear reader, if my life had been different, I wouldn't be able to understand someone who has been abused and help them out. So, I must continue on to find out if my life turns around and offers me peace at last. I have to stick around to find the answer to that.

There is always hope. I would not be the person I am today had I not survived many circumstances.

I'm in a lifeless, dark prison. It's winter. This is all that I know. All seems hopeless.

The door slowly opens. My eyes sting as I see the light. Slowly I step out onto the soft, dark dirt. I bend down and touch the ground. It is all that I see because of the blinding light. I grab a handful of dirt and bring to my face. It smells musky and somehow pleasant. I look up. There is no beauty to be found other than the light, cleansing air, and brilliant blue sky.

I'm finally free.

That seems to be enough. That's all there is save one old fruit tree that looks dead. Although this is better than the dark that I've known for years, it is ugly. I have no idea what this tree is capable of.

Eventually buds begin to appear. Then these buds turn into leaves, followed by the glory of beautiful blossoms that are stunning to behold. Finally, nodules aplenty begin to show. They are green, so I think more leaves will sprout. But eventually they expand and grow, turning into sweet, beautiful fruit.

Staying in the present helps you realize the future. I recognize that I am beautiful like the tree, with many lovely qualities: always changing and growing.

And now because of my past, I find myself recognizing beauty.

Acknowledgement

The author would like to give a special thank-you to all those who have been supportive in the writing of this book. She would like to give a heartfelt thanks especially to Kristy Phillips (editor), who gave enormous amounts of time and suggestions while editing this book. Also she would like to thank Dean Sangalis, Brenda B. Morgan, PhD, Frieda M. Barna, Caroline Stone, Keris Eure, and Diane Fishman for their contributions to this manuscript.

Made in the USA
Monee, IL
22 June 2023

36047608R00152